Praise for Sean McManus and the Irish National Caucus

'This is a hugely important book. It is probably the most significant memoir in the historiography of Irish-American nationalism since *Recollections of an Irish Rebel* (1929) by John Devoy.'
Washington Irish Committee

'No one has done more than Father McManus to keep the US Congress on track regarding justice and peace in Ireland. Indeed, I believe historians will record that no one since John Devoy (1842–1928) has done more to organize American pressure for justice in Ireland.'
Congressman Ben Gilman (R-NY). Chairman, House International Relations Committee

'Fr Sean McManus has spent a lifetime leading the fight to achieve a peaceful solution to the conflict in Northern Ireland. That so many Americans and, particularly those in American government leadership roles, joined in the effort to achieve a peaceful resolution of the conflict is a credit to his courageous and inspiring leadership.'
Bill Flynn, Chairman Emeritus, Mutual of America; Chairman, National Committee on American Foreign Policy

'Fr McManus, from his Capitol Hill office, has been a prominent and influential figure in the quest for progress and peace with justice in Northern Ireland, blending knowledge of his native land with experience drawn from his years of dealing with the intricacies of the political system in his adopted one. His has been a unique role. Long may it continue.'
Ray O'Hanlon. Editor, *The Irish Echo*. New York

'Fr Sean McManus is a man to be reckoned with when it comes to advocating causes. His espousal of the MacBride Principles back in the 1980s caused fits for the British government . . . McManus has also been a constant watchdog in Washington on Irish affairs and has been hugely successful in setting the Irish-American agenda over the past 30 years.'
Niall O'Dowd. Editor, *Irish Voice*. New York

'The master . . . in publicity terms, is Father Sean McManus, a burly, plausible charmer whose Irish National Caucus has taken center stage . . . the good Father has made himself expert in congressional lobbying techniques . . . I spent a long and, to be perfectly frank, rather enjoyable afternoon with Father McManus in his Capitol Hill office . . . and it became clear that he hadn't been raised as a clerical apologist for nothing.'
Christopher Hitchens. Public Intellectual. Author of *God is Not Great* and *The Missionary Position: Mother Teresa in Theory and Practice*

'As a writer, singer and performer of Irish ballads, I know the value of voice, words and thoughts that expose injustice. Over the last 40 years Fr McManus has been the powerful voice that has kept the US Congress involved in the struggle for justice and peace in Ireland.'
Derek Warfield. (Young) Wolfe Tones

'I am a Protestant (which normally I would not mention). However, I had to turn to a Catholic priest, Father Sean McManus, to seek justice for the murder of my son, Raymond Jr . Father Mc Manus helped me get a powerful Congressional hearing into young Raymond's murder and expose state collusion in his murder.'
Raymond McCord Sr., Belfast

'Ireland's had Red Knights in times gone by but for the past two generations it has had a White Knight on Capitol Hill, Fr Sean McManus. He has fought the good fight for peace and equality at the very heart of the US administration, enduring barbs and brickbats from the elites but earning the reward money can't buy: the heart-felt gratitude of Northern nationalists. He has been a beacon for seekers after justice from all backgrounds, and his *Memoirs* is a must-read.'
Máirtín Ó Muilleoir, CEO Belfast Media Group

'Thank-you [Fr McManus] for your gracious invitation to become a "Congressional Friend" of the Irish National Caucus. The warm welcome that I have received from the Irish people on my visits there has gladdened my heart and made me always hopeful that people throughout Ireland will live in a climate of peace and nonviolence.'
Senator Hillary Rodham Clinton (D-NY) 2003 (appointed US Secretary of State by President Obama in 2009)

'It is my sincere hope, and prayer, that peace and unity will soon come to Ireland . . . I commend the Irish National Caucus for its unceasing effort to make this dream a reality.'
Senator Strom Thurmond (R-SC) 1982

'As Chairman of the Ad Hoc committee for Irish Affairs, I . . . commend the Irish National Caucus for your steadfast advocacy on behalf of human rights . . . Fr McManus is "The Apostle of Human Rights for Northern Ireland".'
Rep. Mario Biaggi (D-NY) 1980

'I wish to commend the Irish National Caucus for its peaceful work toward that end [peace and unity].'
Rep. Geraldine A. Ferraro (D-NY) 1982 (in 1984, former Vice-President and presidential candidate Walter Mondale chose her to be his running mate)

'I support the Irish National Caucus because it represents a compelling voice for fair employment, legal justice, and lasting peace in Northern Ireland.'
Rep. Joseph P. Kennedy II (D-MA) 1988

'I support the Irish National Caucus in its important work for justice and peace in Northern Ireland and would be proud to be associated with this worthy organization.'
Rep. Peter T. King (R-NY) 1994

'I have found that the principles of the Caucus, i.e. working in a nonviolent manner toward peace, justice, freedom and fair employment in Ireland, are inherently consistent with my own beliefs.'
Rep. John M. McHugh (R-NY) 1994 (appointed United States Secretary of the Army by President Obama in 2009)

MY AMERICAN STRUGGLE FOR JUSTICE IN NORTHERN IRELAND

Fr Sean McManus, born in Kinawley, County Fermanagh, is a brother of Frank McManus, former MP, and Patrick McManus, an IRA member killed in an explosion in 1958. In 1971, McManus, a Redemptorist priest then based in Scotland, was arrested in Northern Ireland during an anti-internment demonstration. His superiors sent him to the United States in 1972 where he founded the Irish National Caucus in 1974, a Washington DC-based, Irish American lobby group.

www.irishnationalcaucus.org

Dedicated to the memory of my patriot brother
Patrick McManus (1929–1958)

MY AMERICAN STRUGGLE
FOR JUSTICE IN
NORTHERN IRELAND

Fʀ SEAN McMANUS

Fr Sean McManus

The Collins Press

First published in 2011 by
The Collins Press
West Link Park
Doughcloyne
Wilton
Cork

Reprinted 2011

British Library Cataloguing in Publication Data
McManus, Sean, 1944–
    My American struggle for justice in Northern Ireland.
    1. McManus, Sean, 1944– —Political and social views.
    2. McManus, Sean, 1944– —Influence. 3. Catholic
    Church—Ireland—Clergy—United States. 4. Priests—
    Political activity—United States. 5. Northern Ireland—
    Foreign public opinion, American. 6. United States—
    Relations—Northern Ireland. 7. Northern Ireland—
    Relations—United States. 8. Northern Ireland—
    History—1969-1994.
    9. Northern Ireland—History—1994–

    I. Title
    941.6'0824'092-dc22
    ISBN-13: 9781848890985

Typesetting by The Collins Press
Typeset in Bembo 10.5 pt on 12.5
Printed in Great Britain by CPI Cox & Wyman

Cover photographs
Front and spine: author photo (Belfast Media Group); Capitol Hill (iStockphoto)
Back: Hillary Rodham Clinton with author (courtesy of the author)

Contents

Acknowledgments

This book covers a lot of ground and many years, so it is impossible to thank everyone who should be thanked. In the first place, I want to thank my brothers and sisters who read the early chapters that dealt with our entire family. I also want to express my heartfelt and humble gratitude to all those good and decent Irish Americans who made my work for Irish justice possible. Without them there would have been no Irish National Caucus – and no book, either. In particular, I must thank my colleague Barbara Flaherty who made the writing of this book so much easier. She showed remarkable commitment to the project, which was immensely encouraging to me. Nothing escaped her eagle eye or her gifted mastery of the written word. Her daughter Barbara Maureen provided invaluable legal help and advice. Finally, of course, my gratitude to my publisher, The Collins Press. Any mistake or error is my own.

Introduction

The letter, dated Friday 15 April 1972, from my Religious Superior got right to the point in the very first sentence:

> 'Will you please pack up all your own belongings & leave everything ready to be sent on later without your having to return to Scotland. When this is done, I would like to see you here in Clapham [London], please, as soon as possible afterwords [*sic*], and not later than Thursday night [21 April]'.

Even if he had not said anything else, I knew the writing was on the wall (not just in his typed letter). But he continued and, after the polite, very proper British opening, he let loose:

> You will understand that we cannot any longer tolerate the harm you are doing to yourself, the Church, and the Congregation through your stupid and stubborn persistence in writing to newspapers. I do not want anyone to know your immediate destination, nor your proposed transfer from Perth [Scotland]. I once again forbid you to make any communications to the Press or Media either per se or per alium, or to call on anyone en route or before departure. You have had just enough public notice and it is time you thought about your own confreres and your apostolate. Please inform your superior, present or future, when you

leave, of my permission for you to do so, and ask them for the time being to regard it as confidential.

With sincere regards,

Yours JMJA

Charles Shepherd, CSsR[1]

There was a train strike at the time so I phoned Fr Shepherd to let him know. 'Then fly down,' he huffed and slammed down the phone. In those days it would have been most unusual for a young Redemptorist to fly from Scotland to London, so I knew I was in serious trouble.

And what was my offence? Had I mistreated people, preached heresy, denied the Real Presence of Christ in the Holy Eucharist? No, none of these. But worse still, in the eyes of some, I had broken about the only remaining taboo in Britain, especially for a young Irish priest: I had the temerity to criticise what Her Majesty's government and army were doing in the North of Ireland. Never from the pulpit, mind you, but just a few times in the press and on TV.

As I packed my bag (singular) I knew my life would never be the same again. But I also knew, come what may, I would be true to my conscience or else something would die in my soul. I would not through my silence collaborate with Britain's oppression of my country. I prayed for a steady hand and a true heart. I was worried and anxious, with no idea I was embarking on the first leg of my journey to America. But now, almost forty years later, I can smile and 'with malice toward none, with charity for all',[2] thank God that instead of silencing me, they – the Church and State – sent me to the one place on the planet where I was better able to work for justice and peace in Ireland. Charlie Shepherd from his now high place in Heaven must be echoing the famous words of Margaret Thatcher, when her Party ousted her from office in 1990, 'It's a strange old world'.

But more importantly still – and the thing that has given me the most peace of mind and spiritual consolation over all these years – is that I was able to carve out a way to reconcile my struggle for justice and peace in Ireland with my vocation as a Redemptorist priest. And what would provide me with the solid theological foundation for my work in America with the Irish National Caucus was the official teaching of the Catholic Church: 'Action on behalf of justice [is] . . . a constitutive dimension of the preaching of the Gospel' (*Justice in the World*, Synod of Bishops, Rome, 30 November 1971).[3]

This groundbreaking document could not have come at a more providential time for me. Unfortunately, it is still very little known and certainly the Bishops of Ireland, Britain and the United States[4] never seemed to stress it in regard to Northern Ireland. But for me it was 'a lamp to my feet, and a light to my path' (Psalm 119: 105). And later, when I became more familiar with the 'Social Gospel'[5] as preached and practised by the great Reverend Martin Luther King, Jr, I knew nothing was going to turn me around.

> 'Ain't gonna let nobody turn me 'roun'
> Turn me 'roun'
> Ain't gonna let nobody turn me 'roun'
> I'm gonna wait until my change comes.
> (Old Negro Spiritual)

1

Bonny Banks of Lough Erne

And for all this, nature is never spent;
There lives the dearest freshness deep down things.
'God's Grandeur', Gerard Manley Hopkins

American Catholics who were very proud of their 'historic'
parishes used to be astonished whenever I told them that
I came from a parish that had essentially existed since the sixth
century – the parish of Kinawley in Fermanagh.

I was born on 6 February 1944 in the townland of Clonliff,
which is about 3 miles from the village of Kinawley, which in
turn is about 2 miles from the Cavan border near Swanlinbar.
The historic parish of Kinawley is actually divided by the British-
imposed border. So I grew up extremely conscious that the British
government had partitioned not only my country but also my
own ancient parish. The name in Irish, 'Cill Naile', means Church
of St Naile, a famous saint who ministered in the area in the sixth
century.[1]

I was the tenth child in a family of twelve. Our parents owned
a small farm of 23 acres, on which our father, Patrick Sr, was
born (28 January 1877 – 21 January 1962). Our mother, Celia

McMullen-McManus (30 September 1903 – 28 June 1991) came from nearby Carn Mountain. When they got married, my father was forty-nine and my mother twenty-two. The back of the farm is lapped by the waters of Upper Lough Erne and the front is bounded by the Cladagh River, which empties into Lough Erne. Our home was a small thatched house. Because Clonliff Lane was entirely Catholic (nine families then) it was not provided with running water or electricity until 1960.

No memoirs of mine would make sense without full acknowledgement of my brothers and sisters, for it was my whole family that shaped me. All that is good in me, I owe, under God, to them. My faults and sins I owe to myself alone: Mary Kate (born 1927), twins Patrick and Terence (born 1929; Terence died before he was three years old), Celia (born 1931), Thomas (born 1933), Alice (born 1934), Terence (the second, born in 1937), Jim, who also became a priest (born 1938), Frank (born 1942), and finally, my two younger brothers, Myles (born 1948) and Arthur (born in 1949, died in May 1950).

My father was sixty-seven when I was born so obviously I never knew him as a young man – indeed none of us did. Yet I never felt I missed out on that account – probably because there were so many of us and because our father was always there. He would never have been absent or away from home overnight in his entire life. Because my father was himself old, I grew up revering old people and that reverence has never left me. For me, God is almost tangibly present around the very old and very young. I don't suppose any father was loved more by his children. And that is still evident fifty years later when we all get together to reminisce. A smile always breaks out when we talk about him.

My mother was a remarkably strong, independent and resilient woman – patriotic to the core with a profound trust in God. This will become very evident later in the story. In later life, she really blossomed and enjoyed her old age immensely.

There were a lot of us for a small house. Yet I don't ever remember feeling crowded and needing my own space. But of course not all of us lived in the house at the same time. You can see the closeness in age of some of the children, and the great age difference between the youngest and oldest. In that sense, as far as growing up together, we were like three different families. Mary Kate, Patrick, Celia, Thomas and Alice grew up together. Terence and Jim were the second crop. And finally Frankie, I and Myles sprouted up. There is a seventeen-year difference between Mary Kate and me, and twenty-one years between her and Myles.

Mary Kate left home for Omagh, Portadown and later England when she was nineteen (when I was only two years old). Alice went to school in the convent when she was thirteen (and I was three) and stayed in Enniskillen with our Aunt Lizzie, Daddy's sister, who had inherited a house in the town. Essentially she never lived full-time at home after that. Thomas left for England at nineteen (when I was eight) and in the same year Jim left (aged fourteen) for the Presentation Brothers in Cork, only to defect later to the Redemptorists; Terence left at seventeen (when I was ten) to work and stay in Enniskillen.

So for most of my growing up, the only permanent dwellers in Macs were my parents and Patrick and Celia, who were both adults. Frankie, Myles and I were the cubs. But we cubs also grew up with another almost-brother – our first cousin Patrick Maguire who is two years younger than I am.

Patrick with his parents, John James and Maggie, lived nearby. Maggie was my mother's older sister and they were very close. Patrick hung out with us a lot and is still like a brother to this day. In 2002 – inspired by showing the old McMullen ruins on Carn to long-lost cousins from America – Patrick crafted a moving poem (part elegy, part paean), 'The Carn Lintel', the only thing left standing:

> Tired and hungry fields, receding, as the gorse reclaims its space,
> Our ancestral tracks have vanished, footprints faded beyond trace.
> Vengeful bramble, angry briar, that for long were held at bay,
> Boldly colonise the meadow where my mother trampled hay ...
> Nettles, tall as were my uncles, stretch up from the strewn floor
> And yet, the stubborn lintel sullenly protects the door.

> Persevering through the decades, resolutely standing fast,
> Tireless, it maintains the portal; guards this entrance to our
> past.[2]

I guess I knew we were not rich but again I don't remember feeling deprived although I was conscious that Francie Reilly across the bog had a bicycle and I didn't. But then none of the McManus children ever had a bike so it was no big deal.

Country poverty, at least as I experienced it, is vastly different from city poverty. We had 23 acres of our own land to roam, not to mention the entire countryside, in perfect safety – as long as we stayed away from the river because the monster, Terry McGrath, lived there. Nobody seemed to know the origins of the story behind this bogeyman but it certainly kept us away until we were big enough. Amazingly, although we were surrounded by water, hardly anyone in our area could swim. But then, how could they? They were all scared of Terry McGrath!

Ironically, one time the river did not seem to hold fear for any of us, not even for Mother. It was during the Big Snow of 1947 from the end of February well into March when the Cladagh River was frozen over (and therefore presumably keeping Terry McGrath frozen below). I remember clearly holding Mother's hand and walking on the ice with a group of people. I can also still see in my mind's eye the little snow house that my Father and older brothers built on the back street, as we called it, which was really sort of a back yard. I was only three at the time but my recollection is vivid.

Now by American standards, the Big Snow may not have been all that big, but for Ireland it was. Newspapers at the time reported 'huge snow-drifts, some up to fifteen feet high were common in many areas'. And *The Swanlinbar News* reported 'that it had been estimated that over 1,000 sheep had been lost in the snow . . .'[3]

Out of the 23 acres of land, probably only about 15 were arable. The remainder was bog and bottomland along the edge of Lough Erne, and only good for growing bulrushes. Frankie, Myles and I used to pull the bulrushes and use them as a floatation device when we were trying to learn to swim in the shallow waters of the Lough (Terry McGrath did not inhabit Lough Erne). In fact the bulrushes were only an obstacle, a water-crutch that only delayed proper learning. Indeed, I could never really swim until at the age of sixteen I went to the Redemptorist junior seminary in Birmingham, England, in 1960. We were allowed out to go to the local public swimming pool once a week.

On the farm we grew potatoes, turnips, lettuce, carrots, cabbage and wheat – enough to keep us well fed, with chicken, hen eggs, duck eggs and bacon from our pigs that Johnny McCaffery, our neighbor out the lane, would slaughter in the backyard. Plus our diet was amply supplemented with fresh fish we caught and rabbits and hares we snared or caught with our dogs.

Not one of us was ever sick, apart from the usual stuff, except baby Arthur who had a hole in his heart – fatal in those days.

We made hay in the summer (and I never had hayfever until I came to Washington, DC) for our four to five cows, and cut turf, peat, to keep the home fires burning. Turf was our only fuel in the open hearth, and our only source of heat. The Macs were truly ahead of their time: green, all the way. No machinery of any kind. All farm work was done by shovel, spade, pitchfork and grape. Al Gore would have been proud of us.

When I was too small to spread fertiliser (a posh word for cow dung) with the grape, I spread it with my hands. Once you have done that, no job is beneath you and you come to know what holy men and women have taught from the beginning: that creation is sacred and all work has an inherent dignity.

School for all the Macs was Drumbroughas National School – one classroom, two teachers and a dry-toilet across the road. The younger children sat facing Miss McManus (no relation) and the older children sat in the opposite direction, facing Miss McHugh.

The school was about 3 miles from our house and, naturally, we walked there and back each day. In the summer we walked in our bare feet, not because we did not have shoes but because it was the custom. By the end of the summer the soles of our feet were as tough as leather.

Drumbroughas School was almost all Catholic, except for the odd Protestant. During religion class the Protestants got to go outside and there were times I wished I were a Protestant.

School never turned me on: that was the preserve of the GAA (Gaelic Athletic Association). All seven brothers were devoted to the game. Indeed, one of the family treasures is a photograph of all seven brothers togged out in football uniforms, posing proudly on the 'hill' outside the house. We had, at least in our minds, our own seven-a-side team. The photograph was taken in 1956 when all ten children were home. Mary Kate remembers Mother saying it would never happen again that all ten of us would be home at the same time. Sadly, she was right.

Patrick had played a key role in reviving the Kinawley Football Club, the Brian Borus, for which he served as Secretary. The Fermanagh GAA County Secretary, Tom Fee, would later recall: 'I remember making . . . a number of trips to the [Kinawley] parish in 1950 in an effort to have the club resurrected . . . We were fortunate enough to find the very man in Patrick McManus . . . he was the vital part . . .'[4] Patrick, however, did not play much himself but did occasionally act as referee. Thomas was a good player, although I never actually remember him playing. I do, however, clearly remember Celia cheering, 'Come on our Thomas' at a game in the old field at Carron's Gap. Thomas played on the county minors, with his buddy across the field, Patrick Murphy, Charles' eldest son. But forced emigration cut short Thomas' football career. Terence, God rest him, was a strong player, if not the most genteel. Jim left too early to play for Kinawley and there was no Under-Fourteen team then. But while he was in Cork from 1952 to 1955, he got hooked on hurling. When he came home on holidays, I remember he would strut his stuff on the hill with his camán (hurling stick) and sliotar (the ball), probably thinking he was Christy Ring[5] or one of the famous Cork players. But hurling was a 'foreign' game in Kinawley. Frankie and Myles played for the county, but I left for the Redemptorists just as I was beginning to peak: 'I coulda been a contender', as Marlon Brando famously lamented in *On the Waterfront*.

However, I did have my share of glory playing on the Under Fourteens on a joint Kinawley–Swanlinbar team in the league. We won the cup for the Under-Fouteen County Cavan League in 1956 and 1958. Frankie was the captain in 1956 and I was captain in 1958.

It was a huge thrill for us Fermanagh boys to win in Breffni Park – home pitch of the once-famed Cavan footballers. Also, I was the Kinawley captain when we won the Fermanagh Schoolboy Cup in 1959. When I left for the Redemptorists in Birmingham, England, in 1960, the only material things of value I had were the medals from those victories – and I still have them today.

While I was still under fourteen, I not only played for the Under-Fourteens, but also for the minors (Under-Eighteen) and the senior team. Which meant I was going up against big bruisers from Derrylin and elsewhere in their twenties and thirties. But I had a back-up strategy: while I played centre-left, Terence was centre-half, Frankie was centre-right and, to top it off, my brother-in-law, Celia's husband, Big Mick Ferguson, was full-back, So if 'them Derrylin boys' wanted trouble, they had come to the right place.

Our home was a devout one though we would never have been considered 'churchy'. Indeed, I never remember seeing the priest in our home until Patrick was killed. However, no night passed without Mother gathering us all around and saying the Rosary, with all the trimmings. She would recite the Litany of the Saints by heart without falter – unless one of us misbehaved and distracted her. Then she would have to stop, go back to the beginning and take another run at it. The only time my father ever 'cuffed me in the ear' was during the Rosary when he wrongly blamed me for something Frankie or Myles would do.

The spiritual world – God, the incarnation, death and resurrection of Jesus Christ, the Word and the Sacraments, Heaven and Hell – was as real to us as the land and the sky. Even more real, because we knew the material world would pass but God's word would last forever. Our theology and cosmology may have been overly simple but compared to the shallowness and emptiness of much in today's culture we had the essentials right. 'May God's holy will be done', was the constant refrain of my mother both in good times and bad – and bad times did come.

Religious vocabulary infused our culture. As a very young child, I used to think when the Gospel was read about Jesus being 'wrapped in swaddling clothes' (Luke 2:12) that it meant 'Swanlinbar clothing'. Clothing in Swad, as we called it, was much cheaper than in the North. And Hugh Cullen, a draper in Swad, had a second-hand shop in Kinawley, from which we all were clothed. So naturally enough, being a budding theologian, I reasoned that just as we depended on Swad clothing, so did Jesus because He was poor just like us.

It seems fashionable these days for writers to deplore and complain about their Catholic childhood. I recognise that *Angela's Ashes* is a classic, but I must beg to differ with Frank McCourt's much quoted line: 'Worse than the ordinary miserable childhood is the miserable Irish childhood, and worse yet is the miserable Irish Catholic childhood . . .'[6] *The New York Times* loves that sort of thing. Frank may have said it tongue in cheek, of course, but it has perniciously promoted an ugly stereotype. I must confess my experience was totally different from McCourt's. I never had one ugly incident in my childhood, which was as Irish and as Catholic as any on the planet, and which I would not change for anything in this world. I was surrounded and protected by loving parents and devoted brothers and sisters, and the greatest neighbours in the world. It won't make any headlines but it is true – and its value is more precious than rubies.

That is why I was so deeply shocked and furious to read, it seemed like every day in the 1990s, about all the clerical sexual abuse of children in Ireland and America. I used to be scared to pick up a newspaper because I knew it would smash me in the face like a fist. It has forever harmed the Catholic Church. It is a demented sickness and a criminal betrayal of the worst possible kind. But I know that, after the victims and their families, the ones most outraged are the decent Catholic priests, the vast, vast majority of whom have never harmed a child.

2

The Day Celia Was Married and Patrick Was Killed

Your joy is your sorrow unmasked.
And the self-same well from which your laughter rises
was oftentimes filled with your tears.
Khalil Gibran, *The Prophet*

But my happy and carefree childhood would soon end, on 15 July 1958: the day Celia was married and Patrick was killed. Our lives would never be the same again. But let me go back to Sunday 9 December 1956, to set the scene for Patrick's death, at the age of twenty-nine.

The family in general was not aware of Patrick's involvement in the IRA until the night before 'he went on the run'. That Sunday night there had been a parish bazaar. When the family came home (those who were still living there), Patrick sat us all down. Mother said she would stand but he insisted she sit down. He stood in the middle of the small kitchen and announced that he had something very important to tell us, which we had to keep secret – that in the morning he was leaving home as a soldier of the IRA, that we would not see him again until Ireland was free, that, if necessary, he was prepared to die for The Cause. He warned us that the police would harass us, that we could suffer reprisals and that we might be put under curfew. He stressed that the fight was against the British government, and that the family should continue to be friendly with our Protestant neighbours. He ended by explaining that nineteen-year-old Terence (the second), who had agreed in advance, would quit his job as barman in Enniskillen and work the farm. Terence's life and career was, therefore, drastically changed but no one ever heard him complain. To Terence, who died in 2000, it was something he had to do for his family and country. He, too, was an Irish patriot. (Jim, the next oldest at eighteen, was already in the Redemptorist Novitiate in Perth, Scotland.) Patrick then told us what reason to give to the police and indeed everyone as to why he had gone away: he had gone on a holiday to one of his uncles in Athlone (Mother's brother, Terence) and because war had broken out, he was afraid to return. What double irony! Patrick was fearless and never had a day's holiday in his life.

The family was shocked and stunned at Patrick's dramatic announcement, but amazingly, Mother expressed relief, as she was scared he was going to tell us he had done something bad that would disgrace the family. My father, then seventy-nine, only said one thing, 'You will not be halfway out the lane until the police know' – expressing the age-old fear of informers.

The following morning, Monday 10 December 1956, is still as clear in my mind as yesterday. Patrick was getting ready to take off. I remember him patching up his knap-sack, putting in a blanket and ponger (tin cup). He told me to go and fodder the cows and followed me out. I had two armfuls of hay and let some drop. Patrick told me to pick it up, just like our father would have directed. I noticed he was wearing big boots and walking in a different way. I later understood he was in full military mode, marching along the street (the backyard of the farm).

Back inside, Patrick would say goodbye. Mother was standing behind the back door (which opened to the inside of the kitchen) to hide her tears and sobbing. He left quickly so as not to prolong the anguish. I followed him up to the top lane, and by the chestnut tree, tearfully watched him march out Clonliff Lane for the last time, his big boots stomping on the road. I felt I would never see him again, but I did, once. In the spring of 1958, I went to a football game in Swanlinbar, at which I was not playing. On my way, I stopped at a 'safe house' in Swad to pick up a letter Patrick would leave there for our Mother. I was sitting in the room, waiting for the letter when, lo and behold, Patrick himself walked in. I couldn't believe it. I almost did not recognise him. He was looking fantastic, had put on about 14 lb (which he badly needed) and he was dressed impeccably: sports coat, shirt and tie and slacks. I had never seen Patrick so spruced up and I was struck by how handsome he was, something of which I had never been aware. Being dressed in a professional manner was obviously the disguise that worked best for this country boy on the run.

Patrick bought me a lemonade and asked all about the family. He gave me his famous 'big-brother talk'– study hard, look after my young brother Myles, then eight . . . that Frankie and I should stay away from bad company and not give our parents any trouble, etc. And, of course, I was not to tell anyone outside the family that I had seen him. Mother would have seen him a number of times, at the same safe house but our father never did see him again – something which weighed very heavily on his elderly shoulders.

Patrick was quite right when he warned us we would be harassed by the police. They raided our home often. The typical tactic was to reverse their open-backed vehicles to both the front and back doors of our little house. So when we opened the doors, we would see them sitting with their guns pointing right at us. It was meant to frighten us but it never took a flinch out of us. I remember one evening they were up in the loft, where Patrick used to sleep, going through everything. One Special Branch man made a big show of carefully examining a stamp. My lovely sister Celia, normally the least combative of the entire family, said to him in exasperation, 'What do you expect to find in that stamp – a machine gun?' Later when he went down the ladder from the loft, the same Special Branch man told us the next time we saw Patrick would 'be when they carried him in, feet first and dead'. Another

Branch man in a gabardine overcoat told Mother the best thing she could do was to turn Patrick in, for his own good. Expecting our mother to be an informer was a hilarious notion.

Other times, the Royal Ulster Constabulary (RUC) would take Frankie and me off the bus at Montiagh Cross (a couple of miles from home), handcuff us and search us. Again, if it was meant to scare us, they didn't know the Macs. We never experienced one moment of fear. Patrick's own defiance had put steel in our backbone, and there was no way we would allow ourselves to be intimidated by servants of the Crown.

Let me now talk a bit about Patrick before he went on the run.

Patrick left Drumbroughas school when he was fourteen and worked the farm with Father. Being the eldest boy in a large family, and with an elderly father, Patrick assumed a lot of responsibility. Though not well educated in the formal sense, he became a knowledgeable man, especially in Irish history. He believed strongly that his much younger brothers should have the education he himself and the older members of the family were not able to have.

Patrick grew to be about 5 foot 9 inches, with a thin, wiry frame and flaming red hair. Years later, an IRA colleague would remember he 'had a great smile', though of serious disposition. He had a healthy self-confidence and could turn his hand to many things. For example, the grandfather clock in the home had stopped for many a year. He believed that he could fix it. Without ever having seen the inside of a clock in his life, he took the inner workings apart, spread them out on the table, figured out what was wrong and restored it to perfect working order. And he went from clockmaker to boat builder. He felt a new rowing boat was needed, as the one our father had used all his life to row up and down the lough was no longer seaworthy. Patrick persuaded his father that together they could build a new and bigger boat. They worked at it for months. The maiden voyage of 'Mack's new boat' was a major event for the family and the children in Clonliff Lane.

Patrick could even turn to poetry, using it years later to pay tribute to his two IRA comrades in arms, Seán South and Feargal

O'Hanlon who were killed on New Year's Eve 1957, in an attack on Brookeborough Barracks, County Fermanagh:

> May God be with those noble hearts
> May Heaven be their home
> For they never feared the RUC
> Or B–Specials on patrol;
> In Brookeborough town they were shot down,
> In a cabin they lay cold:
> Ó h–Annluain from old Monaghan town
> And Sabhat from Garryowen

The same analytical and practical mind that led him to mend clocks and build boats led him to accurately analyse and clearly discern the root causes of oppression, division and discrimination in the North of Ireland. He took his religion from Rome and his politics from Tone. With Wolfe Tone, Patrick believed in 'breaking the connection with England, the never failing source of all our political evils'.

He became active in the anti–partition campaign of the late 1940s and early 1950s. There were rallies in the parish hall and rousing speeches from local politicians including Cahir Healy, the MP for South Fermanagh at Stormont. The family always remembered with pride how Patrick defiantly flew the tricolour from a tree. The whole parish was talking about it. But then, as expected, the RUC arrived in force to tear it down.

Patrick remained 'on the run' until the night he was killed, 15 July 1958, in a premature explosion of a bomb he was transporting. He was the Officer Commanding (OC) for South Fermanagh and in the spring of 1958 he was appointed to the Army Council.

Sean Cronin, future Chief of Staff, would later write, 'He must have escaped death or capture a score of times. And it is ironic that when death came in the end it should come in the way it did to a man so wise, so cautious, so experienced. There was iron in his soul as well as in his body and he passed it on to those who came in contact with him . . .'

And J. Bowyer Bell, in his classic history, *The Secret Army: the IRA, 1916–1970*, describes Patrick as follows: 'He was the only active IRA leader to escape arrest during the period. An intrepid guerrilla fighter, he preferred the mountains to the towns and disliked leaving his own area for meetings in strange places. Operating mostly from dugouts – a string of which he had built right across Fermanagh – he rarely slept in a house. His death was a major blow to the struggle . . .'[1]

But the family now knows that Patrick did, in fact, go to 'strange places', even openly campaigning, under the pseudonym of Tumulty, for a Sinn Féin Abstentionist Candidate, Pádraig Kelly, in County Galway in the spring of 1957. He was, in fact, safer away from his home base, where everybody would have recognised him.

Patrick was killed at around 9.45 p.m. while handing over a bomb to colleagues who were waiting on an isolated country road in the townland of Derryrealt, about 2 miles outside Swanlinbar. He had constructed the gelignite bomb himself – 'in a five-gallon gas drum with the head cut off it'. Patrick came across a field, carrying the container-bomb, stopping on the inside of the ditch below where the car was waiting. As he lifted up the container to hand it to his colleagues, the bomb went off. Patrick was killed instantly, blown to pieces. Two of his colleagues were injured. The Republican Movement would later build a fine monument on the exact spot where Patrick was killed.

To make his death even worse, Celia had been married that very day. She heard the tragic news when RTÉ announced it the following day on the radio, as she and her husband were on their honeymoon in Salthill, Galway.

The following morning after Celia's joyous wedding, the first in the family, I was woken by crying. I rushed into the kitchen and saw the local curate, Fr Gilmartin, there. I knew immediately that Patrick had been killed. It remains to this day my most vivid, traumatic moment. Jim was rushed home from the Redemptorist Major Seminary in England, and he, Terence and Michael Ferguson had to go and try to identify the 'remains', which did not really exist. No family could have been more devastated, yet no family could have been more defiantly proud. Patrick had died for Irish freedom and that, along with our deep faith, sustained us as a family and as individuals.

What the family remembers most about Patrick was his spiritual side. While never wearing his religion on his sleeve, he was deeply religious, never failing to get on his knees before he went to sleep no matter how late he came home. Patrick meditated daily through the rosary, on the incarnation, life, death and resurrection of Jesus Christ, his Most Holy Redeemer. His colleagues later in the Republican Movement all recall Patrick's devotion to prayer. One remembers: 'He'd kneel down and give out the rosary to us. I'd have to recite the rosary along with him . . . He was a religious man. He was a very great man . . . he was loyal to his country and his people . . . and the people were loyal to him.'

Another IRA colleague recounts how one night he and Patrick were pinned down by the RUC and British Army in a field just inside the border near the village of Kinawley. While the police spotlight beamed all across the field, Patrick and his colleague were hugging the ground. The colleague tried to cover his cough with his coat-collar and Patrick whispered, 'What are you doing?' The colleague explained about the cough, and then asked Patrick, 'What are you doing?'

'I'm on my third rosary,' he replied.

Patrick had made it clear that should he die, he did not want to be buried 'under the Union Jack', i.e. buried in the North. So he was buried across the border in Swanlinbar, but still part of the parish of Kinawley. Even at the funeral Mass, Fr Fox, the curate in Swanlinbar, commented on Patrick's deep faith and his devotion to Our Blessed Lady. Thousands attended his funeral and, after the Mass, the funeral cortège marched to Killaduff Cemetery, about 2 miles outside Swad. The cortège was led by a lone piper. It was the most heart-rending sound I had ever heard. To this day every time I hear the bagpipes, even see them played on TV or in the movies, I can choke up.

I distinctly remember, as the cortège passed through the village, a garda saluted Patrick's coffin. As a consequence of that gesture of respect, I always had a friendly attitude towards the gardaí – no matter what I may have thought of their political bosses.

After Patrick's death, I naturally assumed I would stop playing football for an extended mourning period as was the custom then. But Fr Fox – backed up by Fr Gilmartin – with great pastoral wisdom, convinced my mother that I should continue playing. Now, of course, one could say he also wanted to win the upcoming final in Breffni Park. Either way, it was sound advice as football helped me to cope with our devastating loss.

Shortly after Patrick's death I was playing in County Cavan on our joint Kinawley–Swanlinbar team. A fight started and a general free-for-all ensued, with spectators storming the pitch, bringing the game to a halt. Frankie and a big lump of a lad got into a punch up. As they were pulled and held apart, another fellow, a non-player, from the edge of the crowd that had invaded the pitch, shouted at Frankie: 'Your brother thought he was a tough guy and see what happened to him.' Well, that did it. Up till then, I had not been really involved in the fracas as I was more focused on winning the game. I rounded on the fellow, who was probably about nineteen or older, and charged with such fury that he took off running. I followed him to the corner of the field, where he was trapped. I let loose with the perfect upper cut (Rocky-Marciano-style against Jersey Joe Walcott) with my full body weight behind my punch, hitting him under the chin.[2] He went straight down on the flat of his back. Out for the count. Out cold.

I would hear much later that, ironically, his own family was very Republican so the poor guy probably caught hell when he got home for disrespecting the name of an Irish patriot. I often wonder what became of him, and I wish him well wherever he is. The 'big lump of a lad' is now parish priest in Derrylin and he and Frankie are good friends.

Today, in his native parish of Kinawley–Swanlinbar, the esteem in which this Irish patriot is held is demonstrated by five public honors: the monument at his grave; a monument at the spot where he was killed; a monument at the end of Clonliff Lane, close to the Derrylin-Enniskillen road; a monument just across the border in Cavan; and the Kinawley GAA stadium, named 'Patrick McManus Memorial Park'. The stadium was officially opened on Sunday 26 August 1984, and proudly attended by Patrick's mother, his six brothers and two sisters. Mary Kate, who was then in New Zealand, could not make it.

Our family has always remained very proud of Patrick, regarding him as the quintessential Irish patriot. And even fifty years later, when we are all together as a family, we can still get choked up and tearful when we talk about him.

3

The Call

An unfulfilled vocation drains the colour
From a man's entire existence.
Honoré de Balzac (1841)

On Monday 2 September 1957, at age thirteen years and seven months, I began my less than illustrious career at St Michael's School in Enniskillen, an all-Catholic school. Patrick Maguire started on the same date; Frankie had started in 1953. Myles, still only nine, continued at Drumbroughas. I would remain at that school until September 1960, when I went off to the Redemptorist Juvenate in Birmingham, England.

St Michael's was run by the priests of the Diocese of Clogher and I certainly do not owe my vocation to them because I did not like any of them, except Fr Sean Clerkin. He was the only priest who called me aside to inquire about how my parents were doing after Patrick was killed. Imagine that! The place was full of priests and yet they did not have the decency or pastoral concern to minister to a young boy deeply traumatised by his brother's death. They were more concerned about being politically correct – they did not want to be seen showing any sympathy to an 'IRA family'. If my faith had depended on those priests I would have become a crusading atheist or joined Paisley's emerging Church. But my faith was grounded on my parent's example, on the Word of God and on the tradition and doctrine of the universal Catholic Church.

I am the first to admit that I was not a model student. My entire focus, apart from football, was chasing the fair girls at the convent school and fighting the 'townies'.

People may think the big divide in Northern Ireland was between Protestants and Catholics, but to me in those days the big divide was between the townies and the country boys. The townies liked to see themselves as Teddy Boys – slicked-back hair, combed like Elvis, leather jackets and tight blue jeans. I felt a moral obligation to 'modify their thinking'. There was one period I could not walk through the town without Frankie, who was a fearsome and mighty fighter. All the Teddy Boys were scared of his deadly right hand.

There was one fellow who was the epitome of the Teddy Boy and fancied himself as something of a legend. He was older than I was (I never fought anyone younger than myself) and for some inexplicable reason, he did not seem to fully appreciate my fine Kinawley qualities. He was determined to give me the mother of all beatings and equally determined to let everyone know about it.

Anyway, I knew I was going to be back in town on a Saturday (to celebrate my birthday, 6 February which fell earlier in the week). So in 'High Noon' fashion, I made an appointment with my adversary in the Broad Meadows, then a public park by the water in Enniskillen. I had not told Frankie about it because I wanted to fight this battle on my own.

When I showed up, Mr Teddy Boy was there with a group of townies all eagerly awaiting with evident relish the impending humiliation of this poor country boy form Kinawley. Mr Teddy Boy began with a great display of bravado and showmanship, ducking this way and that, bobbing and weaving, doing the Ali shuffle even before it had been invented by Muhammad Ali – but in a mishmash of judo and heaven knows what. He would swipe at me with his right hand and then when I countered his swipe, he would duck immediately and try to grab my legs. Big mistake.

I let him try it a few more times and then finally let him grab me by the hips. Then I reached over his bent back, as his head was rammed into my stomach, and I hoisted him up and held him in that position for quite a while demanding that he give up. He refused. I then carried him – in the same locked position, backside and heels up in the air – to a barbed-wire fence, hoisted him above it and held him about a foot above the wire. 'Don't drop me,' he pleaded, 'these are the only pair of jeans I have.'

'You have only one pair [of something else] that you should be more worried about,' I retorted (that's the cleaned-up version I use for my sisters). I had, of course, no intention of dropping him. But I found it hard not to laugh. There he was being held over a barbed-wire fence – his belly facing down close to the wire – and the only thing he was worried about was his blue jeans!

I asked him if he gave up; he said yes. I asked him to promise not to bother me again and he did. So I put him down, hurting neither him nor his blue jeans. This and several other similar incidents took place before my conversion to non-violence and none of it would have been approved by Martin Luther King, Jr. But even Martin himself in his early days – during the Montgomery (Alabama) Bus Boycott (1 December 1955 – 20 December 1956) – had a gun. Bayard Rustin had to convince him to get rid of it, as it was a contradiction of Gandhi's non-violence that Martin was propounding.[1]

I continued to be a poor student at St Michael's. And continued to chase the bonnie Fermanagh lassies (and some from Tyrone and Cavan). But I was never sectarian. I dated bonnie Protestant lassies too. One of the girls would later join the Ulster Defense Regiment (UDR) and would be killed in an IRA attack on her barracks in the 1970s. I was deeply saddened to hear it.

As the summer of 1960 progressed, a 'small, still voice' kept whispering in my soul. There must be more to your life, you must commit yourself to a cause greater than yourself. I kept shutting it out. But finally it got the better of me. I was coming home one night from Aunt Maggie's. My bike got a flat tyre and somehow I didn't mind. It was a beautiful, starry night. I was walking along

Graffey Lane, going up the brae at Phil Murphy's big house, staring at the stars. Suddenly, softly, sweetly, a feeling of transcendence swept over me. And in a split second I knew I was being called to be a priest.

My next immediate realisation was, 'Sean, that means you will have give up marriage, playing football and you will not be able to join the IRA and finish the job Patrick set out to do.' It was a moment of total clarity, no drama, no thunderclaps, no gnashing of teeth. Just the profound peacefulness that comes when God makes the way clear. And, fundamentally, I have never looked back since that moment outside Phil Murphy's. I don't mean that there have not been ups and downs, nor that I have led a perfect Christian life. But I have never doubted my calling, despite my sins and failures.

In the Catholic tradition – at least up to that time – when a person had such a religious experience, it normally was seen as a call to the priesthood or the religious life. In the Protestant tradition, it is seen as 'being born again' – a deeper commitment to Christ, but not necessarily a call to Ministry. Well, of course, I had been 'born again' at baptism, with water and the Holy Spirit, confirmed in the Spirit at confirmation and nourished on the 'Bread of Life and the Cup of Eternal Salvation' in the Holy Eucharist. So to me the only next step was the priesthood. Today, however, I am sure that some Catholics have similar experiences as I had, but see it as a call to more closely follow Christ, but not a call to the priesthood or the religious life. I am sure there is a lot to be discussed and developed in this area of Catholic spirituality, but I will leave that to my big brother, Fr Jim, the spiritual guru in the family.

I realised that I would have to give up Gaelic football because I knew I would naturally follow Jim and join the London Province of Redemptorists. Plus there was that tradition: Ireland had already too many priests (little did we know how that would change), and anyway, it was heathen England that needed priests!

I never said a thing to Mother when I got home that night. I slept on it and in the morning it was still as clear as ever. So I told Mother. She nearly fell off the chair with shock. My father seemed very pleased. I think Frankie took a pain in his side from laughing. But the transition period went very smoothly.

Jim, a student at this time in Hawkstone, the Redemptorist Major Seminary in Shropshire, made all the necessary contacts for me.

On Wednesday 28 September 1960, Fr Joe Hanton, CSsR, Director of the Juvenate, the minor seminary in Birmingham, wrote to me: 'I am happy to inform you that you have been accepted as a candidate for the priesthood and . . . you will be welcome to come to Erdington [a section of Birmingham] as soon as you can make arrangements.' Thus began a whole new phase in my life.

It says something wonderful about the tradition that I was raised in that despite our absolute opposition to English rule in the North of Ireland, we never held it against the English people and never hesitated to minister to them, working for them without pay of any kind. Equally, it says something wonderful about the British Redemptorists for never holding Patrick against Jim and me. Sure, my activities later on would cause Charlie Shepherd serious heartburn, but that is a different issue from the point I'm making here.

I will never forget my voyage from Belfast to Liverpool. It was my first time leaving Ireland and my first time on a ship. Although full of religious zeal, I was nonetheless homesick. On board I was so relieved to see a Kinawley man, John Anderson. He gave me great advice: 'Don't be frightened if you think your stomach is going to come out of your body when the sea gets rough – and it always does.' Man, did it ever. I got as sick as a dog.

The following morning I arrived in Liverpool, sleep-deprived and still sick, only to be confronted by what I thought was the terrible smell of Liverpool – my first sniff of a big city. My country nose could not take it. My spirits were buoyed when Jim met me at the train and accompanied me to Birmingham. Mary Kate, who was also in England, supported me by sending me money weekly.

My first culture shock in the Juvenate was the breakfast –

fried bread and beans. Baked beans sloshed onto bread dipped in frying fat. The taste was abominable. And to make matters worse, we had to wash it down with coffee made from liquid from a bottle. Where were my porridge, my fresh egg and my fadge (soda) bread? What barbarians had I come among?

There were about forty boys in the Juvenate. I went into the senior class and for the first time in my life hit the books and studied hard. Fr James Mythen would soon amaze me by complimenting me on my Latin. In English Literature we had to study Wordsworth. My teacher, Fr Hanton, was not too good as he was just filling in and did not really know Wordsworth. But I knew who did – Master O'Shea back in St Michael's, a lay teacher whom I liked. I wrote to him, told him I needed help to prepare for an exam and he wrote me a number of pages about how Wordsworth changed English poetry, by taking it out of its baroque setting into the open countryside, etc. I aced the exam and I have never forgotten Master O'Shea who later became a priest himself. And thus began my lifelong affection for Wordsworth, who after Shakespeare, is the most worthy of all the British writers.

I was delighted to discover in my Religious Knowledge class that I was far more advanced than anyone else.

I trained myself to wake up at night to say one rosary, thereby completing the goal I had set myself of three rosaries per day – the Five Joyful Mysteries, the Five Sorrowful Mysteries, the Five Glorious Mysteries. (Pope John Paul II would later add the Five Luminous Mysteries in 2002.)

I enjoyed the Juvenate, even though the change of lifestyle was quite dramatic. I knew the one thing that could quickly get me into trouble was my tendency to settle things with my fists. I was helped by the fact that I was one of the biggest and certainly the strongest boys in the Juvenate, and nobody would mess with me, and I knew I would never hit anyone younger or smaller than me.

The other drastic change was football – no longer Gaelic but soccer. Yet I quickly got to like it while never mastering it. I played right-full-back. Later in Hawkstone, I would play in goal and really come into my own, just as Jim did.

4

Kinnoull and Hawkstone Years

Prayer without study would be empty. Study without prayer
would be blind.
Karl Barth[1]

In September 1961, I went to the Redemptorist Novitiate in St Mary's Monastery, high up on Kinnoull Hill, Perth, Scotland. I pulled up in front of the monastery in a taxi. Gave a packet of cigarettes to the driver, saying. 'I'll never use these here', and I never did.

The Novitiate, in those years, was a 'religious boot camp' – a year of unrelenting self-discipline, penance, prayer, religious training, religious lectures, long periods of total silence and manual labour.

The Novice Master (in charge of spiritual formation) was Fr Shepherd – the aforementioned Fr Shepherd, who would later pack me off to America,

The monastery had a small farm and, when needed, I had to do the milking as I was the only novice with that skill. Brother John was the farmer and I was utterly amazed to see him using gloves while making hay. My first thought was, 'What would Daddy and Charles Murphy think of a man wearing gloves to use a pitchfork?' I was also amazed to see Brother John 'ruck' the hay (build it in large cone-shaped stacks) while it was still damp. My father would have chased him out of the meadow, as you daren't ruck the hay until it was bone dry. 'It will rot,' I kept telling Brother John but, in fact, it turned out fine.

Once a year the novices were allowed a bus trip to St Andrews, not to play at the famous golf course, but to spend a day at the gusty beach. As the bus took off from the Novitiate, the Rector of Kinnoull, Fr Vincent Lucas, brother of the Provincial Fr George Lucas, sat beside me and said, 'So, Brother McManus, what part of Ireland are you from?'

'From British-occupied Ireland,' I defiantly responded. He collapsed in laughter, as he thought it was the funniest thing he had ever heard. It was my first insight into how little the average British man knows about Britain's involvement in Northern Ireland.

Despite the Spartan regime, I loved the Novitiate and experienced a deep sense of spiritual tranquility . . . no angst, no turmoil, no anguish.

But there was great sadness because my father died in January 1962. I was reading in the refectory from the pulpit-like dais (at evening meals the novices would take turns at reading aloud from some spiritual book to the entire community – the other novices, plus the priests who were giving Missions throughout Scotland). The Novice Master came over and asked me to stop, so I knew there was bad news. I had been aware that my father was failing. He asked me to come outside the refectory, and told me that my father was very ill, and that I should prepare to go home immediately.

When I arrived home in Clonliff, I found my father near death. But I took great consolation in the way his eyes brightened up when he saw me, as he clearly recognised me. The last conscious action I saw him make was when he raised up his mouth to kiss the small crucifix I held to his lips. If dying a holy death, after leading a good life, is the supreme Christian goal, then my father surely went straight home to the Father, through Christ, by the power of the Holy Spirit and into Eternal Life. I spent about a week at home and then returned to the Novitiate.

In September 1962, after two weeks of intense retreat and total silence, which I never once broke, I took my First Vows with four others. My mother and a few of my family came for the event, and then it was off to the pleasant fields of Shropshire for seven years at Hawkstone Hall, then the Redemptorist Major Seminary. (Later, Jim would develop it into a major international centre for spirituality.[2])

There were about forty students at Hawkstone. I loved all my seven years there and went after my studies with gusto, especially logic, philosophy and theology. Most of the available books, of course, stuck rigidly to the abstract, non-historical, neo-Scholastic line. Neo-Scholasticism was the philosophical theology that was taught in seminaries from 1860 until Vatican II. The *Encyclopedia of Catholicism* explains: 'Neo-Thomism in turn is a development within neo-Scholasticism, the revival of Scholastic, that is, medieval theology. Modern neo-Thomism (rarely discussed outside of Catholicism and mandated by papal documents like Pope Leo XIII's encyclical *Aeterni Patris* of 1879) sought to transcend the Enlightenment and Reformation by proposing that the thought-world of medieval Scholasticism, and particularly that of Thomas Aquinas, could hold solutions to contemporary problems.'[3]

The American theologian, Fr Thomas F. O'Meara, OP, wonderfully recreates the atmosphere of those seminary days: 'During my first week in the seminary [the Dominican seminary near Chicago] the professor introducing us to philosophy made [a] startling observation[s]: Everything a priest needed to know was found in the writings of Aristotle [384–322 BC] . . . During the first half of the twentieth century, most priests in America [and in Britain and Ireland, he could have added] received some neo-scholastic indoctrination in philosophy and theology. That simple philosophy with a black and white logic emphasized laws that had no exceptions: the laws of logic, administration of the church, abstract moral rules, and obscure rubrics for liturgy. The Church had somewhat exchanged the Gospel for Greek antiquity and its Aristotelianism held no interest for scientific America or ordinary

Catholics.'[4] Nonetheless, neo-Scholasticism taught me how to reason logically and think analytically. And I have maintained an abiding reverence for the great St Thomas Aquinas, whom we now know should not have been pigeon-holed the way some neo-Thomists tried to do: 'Many sought through Vatican power a monopolistic and dictatorial control over Catholic thinking, and, in the name of Thomism, warred against modern philosophy, science, and politics as well as ecumenism, vernacular liturgy and modern art. This monopoly of thought ended when Vatican II (1962–1965) affirmed modern biblical, patristic, systematic, and pastoral theologies, many of which were rooted in Aquinas' historical openness and positive depiction of God and humans.'[5]

In time, I would come to realise that the best way to understand the change brought about by the Second Vatican Council was to see it in terms of a paradigm shift: a shift from classicism to historical consciousness – from a classicist to a historical conscious Weltanschauung (world view).

Classicism views reality in terms of the immutable, the never changing. It uses the deductive method of reasoning: from the universal to the particular. This is best illustrated by the following syllogism, which was taught in Scholastic logic to every student for the priesthood, up to the mid 1960s:

> All human beings are rational.
> Seamus is a human being.
> Ergo (therefore) Seamus is rational.

Classicism uses the *deductive method* of reasoning. It seeks conclusions that are always true, in all situations: if it was true in 1962, it is true in 2062. Historical consciousness uses the *inductive method* of reasoning: from the particular to the universal. The conclusions it reaches (from the ground up, so to speak) will be based on changing circumstances and history. It does not seek absolute, dogmatic certitude but settles for moral, practical certitude. Vatican II would attempt to explain the faith, not just hand down authoritarian decrees, as in the style of Vatican I (8

December 1969 – 20 October 1870) – the foundational style of teaching as opposed to the apologetic.

My greatest regret is that the Scripture classes were so poor. Most of the teachers were inadequate. In fact, Jim was the only really good teacher, and that is not a matter of standing up for my big brother. Every student would agree with me. Jim had been ordained on 12 January 1964. Most of the family, many of our relatives and neighborus from home came to Hawkstone for his ordination. It was a most special day in the life of our family. After ordination, Jim went to Rome for further study for four years. He taught Moral Theology for my last year in Hawkstone.

Despite the poor quality of the teachers, Jim excepted, it was still a great time to be embarking on theological training. Vatican II started on 11 October 1962 and soon seminarians would no longer have to be taught in Latin or read the Divine Office in Latin, the Mass could be said in English, the 'new theology' would emerge, etc. It was really an exciting time – the ecclesiastical version of the Sixties! But no long hair, no dope and no sex.

Eucharistic theology became my particular interest, and I have kept up my study of this subject over the years. While I have always been prepared to question Church teaching on a variety of subjects, I've always been very careful on Eucharistic Doctrine which is, in a uniquely special way, the ultimate responsibility of the Magisterium. Get the Eucharist wrong, and you get the Church wrong – and vice versa. The age-old maxim nails it: 'The Eucharist makes the Church and the Church make the Eucharist.'

But I also came to believe that every good Catholic needs a good dose of Protestantism. So I developed a great interest in Martin Luther and his 'Justification by Faith alone'. I soon came to believe that Rome and he were just talking at cross-purposes and that, as in all fights, as the rhetoric heated up, the positions unnecessarily hardened when a resolution was possible. Fr Shepherd (yes, the same, now the Rector at Hawkstone, and the teacher of Church history) cautioned me about my enthusiasm for the heretic Luther. It was, therefore, a very happy and emotional day for me when, over thirty years later, I attended the National

Cathedral (Episcopal) in Washington in 1999, to celebrate the signing of The Joint Declaration on Justification by the Vatican and the World Lutheran Federation. Yet, for me, the occasion was tinged with sadness as I reflected how easy it is for leaders to change, leaving their followers hung out to dry: 'Oops, it was all a misunderstanding, now let's move on.'

I was also very disappointed that the historic Joint Declaration did not receive proper attention. For goodness' sake, here was the edge issue, the leading cause of the Reformation being essentially agreed on by the Pope and the Lutherans, yet Northern Ireland, of all places, does not give it due attention. What's wrong with that picture?

Fr Shepherd even taught the notorious Syllabus of Errors, issued by Pope Pius IX in conjunction with his encyclical *Quanta Cura* (How Much Concern) (1864) as if they were revealed truth, instead of being, in part, the paranoid fears of an emotionally unbalanced pope. Among other things, they condemned freedom of conscience, freedom of religion, freedom of speech and the separation of Church and State. And here Scottish theologian, Fr Fergus Kerr, OP, is not far off the mark when he says, 'The history of twentieth-century Catholic theology is the history of the attempted elimination of theological modernism, by censorship, sackings and excommunication . . .'[6]

However, I have other issues with Pope Pius IX. On 12 January 1870 at the urgings of the British government and sycophantic Irish Bishops, Pius IX excommunicated the Fenians, not only in Ireland but also in America: 'the American or Irish society called Fenian', as the decree of condemnation put it.[7] Had Pope Pius IX condemned the Fenians because he believed in the philosophy of non-violence, that would have been a different matter. But that Pope did not believe in non-violence. He had his own papal armed force, and he had earlier appealed to Irishmen to come and fight for his Papal States. Hundreds of Irishmen – including Fenians – answered his call. So it was OK for Irishmen to fight for the Papal States, but it was a sin for them to fight for Ireland. Years later in Washington, I would write to the Papal Nuncio objecting to the proposed canonisation of this anti-Fenian, anti-Semitic and anti-freedom pope.

But my reading in Hawkstone was not just Scholastic. I set out to read all the great Irish writers, starting with Edna O'Brien. I read James Joyce's *Ulysses* three times in Hawkstone. These books were still on the forbidden index but a travelling library (a van) would come regularly to the end of the Hawkstone road, and I would go out there to meet it each week. No matter how hard I tried, I could not make head or tail of *Finnegans Wake*. William Trevor became one of my favourite Irish writers.

Life at Hawkstone was not just all spiritual and intellectual for me. We played soccer three times a week and had some fine players. After Jim left, I took his place in goal and was in my element. I could soar like an eagle and catch the ball knowing none of the other players could touch it with their hands (except the other goalie at the far end of the pitch), and that no big bruiser from Derrylin would be spoiling my catch. In this way, the Gaelic footballer was in heaven playing goalie in soccer. It spoiled you rotten. However, diving on the ball at the players' feet was a skill that had to be mastered. When I first saw Jim do it in Hawkstone, I was amazed and wondered how he could do it without getting his skull split open. But I soon got the hang of it.

In the latter years, we were allowed to play 'outside' (non-seminarians) teams.

I remember once a local team came to play us at Hawkstone. I could tell immediately that they had a condescending attitude to 'us monks', that they thought we were a crowd of sissies . . . and that they had an anti-Catholic attitude (my Northern Ireland background gave me an unerring nose for that).

They were several years older than we were and they clearly thought they were masters of the game.

In the first minutes of the game, the ball came into me and I charged out to get it. One of their forwards blatantly jumped into me with both knees. When I cleared the ball, I turned to him and for the first time in years I reverted to type – to the Kinawley footballer – and told him: '*do not come back like that again*'. He sniggered and replied, 'Every time, mate.'

The ball soon came back in at chest level. At this level, the goalie has a great advantage from the point of physical contact (although the invading forward has the opportunity to take a low ball away from you). I saw our friend charge me and as I grabbed the ball firmly to my chest I swung my left shoulder hard to meet him. I knocked him a couple of feet off the ground, landing him flat on his back. His fellow-forward roared at me, 'You're supposed to be a preacher.' I replied, 'And I have given him a sermon he'll remember for the rest of the game.' And he did too. He never came near me for the rest of the game.

Well, we went on to beat them in a ridiculous fashion, 7–nil. They were the worst team I had ever seen in my life – absolutely hopeless. All hat and no cattle. Now to be fair, they were probably up late drinking beer the night before and rejoicing how they would thrash 'the monks'. None of our team smoked or drank, we were young and fit and we sent them 'homeward, tae think again.'[8] One thing is certain; none of them was ever recruited by Manchester United.

The students did not drink alcohol, except for a glass of very ordinary wine with meals on special and rare feast days. Ironically, I was a Pioneer (had taken the pledge not to drink) until I arrived in Hawkstone. When the newly professed novices arrived from the Novitiate at Hawkstone, the tradition was to give them a glass of sherry. I was told that my religious vows superseded all other pledges and that I could break my pledge. I would later come to see that as 'religious imperialism' and always regretted breaking my Pioneer Pledge. (In 1988 I redeemed my pledge and stopped drinking completely.)

But while in Hawkstone, I became a winemaker, and a moonshiner – a maker of poteen!

There was an elderly couple that lived on the Hawkstone property in an old gatehouse to the former Victorian mansion that Hawkstone was. My mother used to stay there when she came to visit Jim and me. One day the man of the house served Mother and me a glass of white wine. It was delicious. I had never tasted anything like it. 'What is that, Harry?' I enquired. 'It's rhubarb wine,' he replied, 'and if you like it, wait till you taste my elderberry wine.' I asked him where he had got it. 'Made it myself,' he said proudly.

I was instantly hooked. Not on the wine, but on vinification, the process of making wine. I picked Harry's brain and he was only too pleased to enlighten me. I went back to the monastery and immediately went to see the Rector, then Fr Nolan, who was originally from Dublin. (He was a wonderful man and I had huge respect for him. Years later, he would pass on to me, through a trusted courier, Jim, an IRA belt that was used in the GPO in 1916. It is a brown leather belt with a heavy brass buckle, which is inscribed with Óglaigh na h-Éireann, 'soldiers of Ireland'. The other end of the belt, also brass, that inserts into the buckle has a harp embossed on it.) In retrospect, I now see that my visit to Fr Nolan was my first lobbying job. I proposed to him that he give me permission to start making home-made wine to be used on Feast Days . . . that there was a long tradition of monasteries doing so, that we had an very fine, classically built wine cellar. In fact, the wine cellar was so good that even Winston Churchill wanted to buy Hawkstone for that reason alone, but could not afford the taxes. (After the Second World War, a lot of the great mansions were bought by religious or educational institutions because individuals could no longer afford them.)

Fr Nolan, in his great voice and with a trademark slap of his hands, said it was a splendid idea and told me to go right ahead. Thus my life as an oenologist (wine 'expert') began. At that stage I had no idea of trying to make poteen and so had not mentioned it to Fr Nolan. Anyway, there was no way he could give me permission to do something that was, ahem, well, not quite legal.

I began as I always begin: by studying the subject. I got dozens of books from my friendly travelling library at the end of Hawkstone lane, and boned up on the quite surprisingly popular English tradition of brewing home-made wine.

I scoured the countryside looking for the right containers. In an antique shop in Shrewsbury, I ferreted out three amazing five-gallon pottery vats, like something out of Sinbad the Sailor. The vats, wide at the bottom, tapered into narrow necks – perfect for my mission. I fermented (the science of which is called zymology) rhubarb and elderberries, separately, in my prized vats and after the allotted time, I drained the contents, put in isinglass to bring all the impurities to the top, and tied the opening off tightly with a heavy cloth.

At the appropriate time, I bottled the wine, put it safely away in one large cubicle in the wine cellar, built a little door and put it all under lock and key. I would occasionally check the door to make sure none of my brothers–in–Christ had been tempted. None of them was. In due time, the wine was served to great acclaim.

Now the great philosophers teach us that knowledge should always be progressing and advancing. So in that grand tradition, I says to meself: I wonder how poteen is made. Wouldn't it be a worthy project to make it, purely for the science of it, you understand?

So I wrote to Frankie and asked him to find out the recipe and to mail it to me. There was no tradition in Clonliff of making poteen. If you wanted it you had to go to the law-breakers across the river in Knockninny–Derrylin.

Frankie duly wrote back to me with the recipe, warning me to drink only the most 'infinitesimal amount' (the actual words, I still remember). In fact, I drank only two teaspoonfuls.

Then began my second scouring of the countryside. How to find a 'still' (the pot or container used for distilling poteen), without calling it that? Again, my Guardian Angel led me to a shop in Shrewsbury that had the perfect container: a five-gallon copper pot with an airtight lid. (One needs a copper pot to avoid the danger of poisoning. Even though the big bruisers in Derrylin used tar-barrels.)

Then I would need to solder a copper pipe or tube, with a small opening, into the still. That was no bother. But how to make the copper pipe into a 'worm'– the coiled pipe, in which the vapour would be cooled and condensed, under cold running water? That stumped me. Now, bear in mind there was no Internet in those days, and I could not go around asking people for help in making a still. Only one other person knew about my secret project. Finally I turned to a man I admired and trusted – Eddie Corish. He had been a Brother in the Irish Province and as an older man decided to become a Redemptorist priest in the London Province.

Eddie was a man for all seasons, deeply spiritual but with a very practical mechanical bent. 'How can I, Eddie, twist this copper pipe into a coil without closing the air flow?' 'Very simple,' responded the intrepid Eddie. 'Fill it with sand and twist it around a metal bar, horizontal to the ground, then shake the sand out.' 'You are a genius, Eddie,' says I.

My first attempts did not work out too well. I started with the normal Irish method, fermenting potatoes. But I soon discovered it was much easier and far better to distil the rhubarb wine. It was a real thrill to see the first bubble of distilled liquid shyly emanate from the end of the worm, linger a moment, then gently plop into the container below. To add to the thrill, I ran my still in an unused room next to the room of the Professor of Moral Theology (not Jim) who was totally unaware. Unlike the big bruisers from Derrylin who used a turf fire in the bogs to do their distilling, I used a little gas stove. I sent a bottle of the poteen to Terence in London and he told me it was the best he had ever tasted.

I kept four bottles of poteen in my room – and never touched it – waiting for Christmas. After Christmas dinner, I invited a select few whom I knew I could trust, and who regarded themselves as guys who could hold their drink, to a classroom at the back of the building. I produced a bottle, and quoting my older brother Frankie, cautioned them to only consume the 'most infinitesimal amount'. I demonstrated its potency by first putting some in a teaspoon and setting it alight. I poured each person less than half a shot. Some sipped it straight, some drank it with orange juice. I demonstrated my caution by only sipping two teaspoonfuls. Then they claimed I had exaggerated the strength of the poteen and called for a refill. I remonstrated with them again, but George said,

'Enough of the Irish baloney [or some such word that implied the Irish like to exaggerate], Sean, give us more poteen.' So I relented.

Now, the classroom that was doing double duty as a monastic shebeen was about three lengths of a football field – up a long corridor, past the individual rooms of the revellers – from the students' common room. We knew we had to be there before too long as that was the only night, Christmas night, that the Rector would visit our common room – which was very large, with a stage, billiard ball table, TV, etc. The Rector now was Fr Shepherd (yes, *that* Fr Shepherd). On the way up the corridor, I lost five of the lads who 'could hold their drink'. They went down like logs and I had to carry them to their beds.

I went into the common room and Fr Shepherd was sitting in a large circle talking to the students. I took my place, wondering what had happened to Pat. He had not fallen down, so where was he? I didn't have to wait long. Pat was seen as an ascetic, who spent long hours in prayer. He had Bedouin blood in him. In a short time, the bold Pat burst into the common room, still dressed in his habit but with a white bath towel wrapped around his head, Bedouin-style, and without further ado exploded into a Bedouin dance for about ten minutes. I was sure our game was up, that Charlie Shepherd would be on to us, but there he was doubled over, convulsed in laughter, like everyone else, at the extraordinary spectacle.

When I was leaving Hawkstone, I destroyed the still and refused to pass on my esoteric skills as a moonshiner. I was scared if it was done wrongly it could poison someone. Thus ended my career as a poteen-maker, a bootlegger. I was about to say that I had never touched the stuff again, but I did.

In 1977, the American Ancient Order of Hibernians (AOH) was holding its convention in Killarney. I was travelling down from Fermanagh to it and stopped overnight in the home of a high-up Republican and teetotaller. I had a terrible awful cold, with my chest totally congested. I worried how I could make the convention. To my amazement, this teetotaller who was regularly raided and harassed by the Special Branch, produced a bottle of the illegal substance. Made me a very large hot toddy, told me to drink it all down, and in the morning I would be as right as rain. And, honest to goodness, when I woke up the following morning, it was if my cold had been a dream. It was gone completely, no congestion, no cough, and I felt terrific! No wonder poteen was the universal cure for farm animals in those days in my part of County Fermanagh.

The Sam Browne belt that Fr Nolan had passed on to me was not the only Hawkstone connection with IRA history. There was a much closer link – a living, breathing one: the students' Confessor, the saintly Fr Liam Pilkington (1894–1977). 'Pilkie', as we affectionately called him, had been the Commandant of the Third Western Division, IRA, who took the Republican side in the Civil War. In 1924 he joined the Redemptorists in the English Province. In his seventies, he became the Confessor for the students. We would line up at his door, and when my turn would come he would say, 'Come on in, Brother McManus and I'll clean your skillet (absolve your sins).'

He never talked about his IRA years (1913–1924) except to Jim and me. When he used to talk to me, after a while his hands would shake, as is common with many old soldiers, and he would end the conversation. He knew Liam Mellows, who swore him into the Irish Republican Brotherhood (IRB), Michael Collins, Éamon de Valera, etc.

I think he was a bit prudish. He said he was appalled by Collins' bad language, 'The foulest mouth of any man he ever knew.' And he never politically forgave de Valera. On one occasion Dev went to Cape Town, South Africa, where Pilkie was stationed at the time. Dev went to the monastery to see him, but Pilkie refused to meet him. He always believed that they did not need to sign the Treaty (that lead to the partition of Ireland), that they could have kept fighting because they were at their very strongest. Yet he mentioned that, years later as a priest when he was some place in England, walking around 'acres and acres of munitions' he thought to himself, 'we must have been mad to think we could beat them'.

He showed me a prayer book (which I wished I had got) that was given to him when he was a political prisoner by the Catholic chaplain, an English priest. Pilkie had told him that when Ireland was free he was going to become a priest. The Chaplain jokingly inscribed it: 'May you achieve the goal you desire, instead of the gaol [deliberate old English spelling] you deserve.' Pilkie still got a great kick out of that and would smile with delight.

Sometimes in Hawkstone, Pilkie used to preside at the 'preaching academy' – weekly, a student had to preach a memorised sermon from an approved source, in front of all the other students, while an older, experienced priest would sit in to evaluate the performance. Well, one day it was my turn to 'preach'. I had memorised a sermon and had entitled it 'The Last Day by Father James Joyce'. (In fact, it was my own editing of Joyce's famous 'sermon' by the Retreat Master in *A Portrait of the Artist as Young Man* – hardly an 'approved' source, as Joyce was still on the Index, the list of books banned by the Church.) My thinking was that these English blokes would not recognise Joyce's 'sermon'. But, ah man, didn't Pilkie come in to preside over my sermon? There was nothing, however, I could do but plough ahead as I had nothing else prepared. So I gave the sermon, announcing that the author was Fr James Joyce:

> The last day had come. The doomsday was at hand . . . And lo, the supreme judge is coming! No longer the lowly Lamb of God, no longer the meek Jesus of Nazareth, no longer the Man of Sorrows, no longer the Good Shepherd, He is seen now coming upon the clouds, in great power and majesty, attended by nine choirs of angels, angels and archangels, principalities, powers and virtues, thrones and dominations, cherubim and seraphim, God Omnipotent, God Everlasting. He speaks: and His voice is heard even at the farthest limits of space, even in the bottomless abyss. Supreme Judge, from His sentence there will be and can be no appeal . . .

On the way back, I walked down the corridor with Pilkie and

he told me it was the best sermon on The Last Day he had ever heard in his life. He then asked me about the 'priest' who had written it (he clearly had not connected 'Fr Joyce' with *the* James Joyce). I certainly was not going to tell a lie to my Confessor, so I levelled with him. I thought he was going to have a heart attack. 'That blackguard,' he hissed. 'He was as bad as Yeats, who couldn't believe in Jesus Christ but did believe in fairies.' And with that he turned on his heel and strode off in righteous exasperation, his military step more pronounced than usual.

I was ordained on 1 September 1968. That was another very special day for our family, most of whom came to the Ordination with relatives and neighbors from Kinawley.

Our class stayed on in Hawkstone until the following summer, finishing our studies. Then it was off to Bishop's Stortford in Hertfordshire, southeast England, for our Second Novitiate – a six-month period for writing sermons for the parish missions. Even this quiet town had an IRA connection. In 1953, Cathal Goulding and Seán Mac Stíofáin, each of whom would later become Chief of Staff of the IRA, were arrested there with a van-load of weapons stolen from 'the officers training corps armoury of Felsted School in Essex'.[9]

Our class then went to different areas. I first went to Birmingham, back to Erdington Abbey, and then to the Redemptorist House in Liverpool, as part of a Parish Missions team. I preached missions and school retreats in a number of places in England and Scotland, thinking this was what I would be doing for the rest of my life. I had no idea what lay ahead.

5

The Troubles Come Back to Haunt

But just as I thought I was out, they pull me back in.[1]

Meanwhile, I had been keeping an eye on the developing political situation in Northern Ireland. Civil rights marches had begun in 1968 only to be met, inevitably and predictably, by the brute forces of the deeply sectarian and anti-Catholic State that the British government had violently and undemocratically created in 1920.

This artificial State had a two-fold purpose: to ensure a continuation of Britain's foothold on the island of Ireland, and to place the Unionists/Loyalist/Protestants in a permanent position of supremacy. Protestant supremacy would be guaranteed by discrimination, repressive legislation and a deeply sectarian and bigoted police force, the RUC and their auxiliaries, the B Specials.

The 'credit' for this masterstroke goes to Winston Churchill who in July 1920 posed the question, 'What if the Protestants in the six counties were given weapons and ... charged with maintaining law and order and policing the country?' The British government then proceeded to set up the new police force and recruited the Ulster Volunteer Force (a fascist Protestant militia that had threatened armed rebellion against the Crown) wholesale into it.[2]

The peaceful, non-violent marches were beaten off the streets by Protestant mobs, incited by the demagoguery of Protestant politicians and clergymen, and facilitated by the RUC and the B Specials. Think Bull Connors and his racist police 'keeping uppity blacks in their place' in Birmingham, Alabama, 1963, and you've essentially got the picture. In 1969, Bombay Street, a Catholic street in Belfast, was burned out by mobs, while the police looked on and the B Specials participated in the burning.

From the outset, my brother Frank was in the thick of the civil rights struggle, becoming chairman of the Fermanagh Civil Rights Association. On 18 June 1970, he was elected, as Unity Candidate, MP for Fermanagh and South Tyrone. For the next four years he was hardly out of the news, and never out of danger. On 18 January 1971, he was jailed for six months for leading a proscribed civil rights march. In May 1971 there was a national census in Britain and Northern Ireland, and the Catholic community, including a number of priests and teachers, refused to comply with the census in order to protest against the corruption of the judicial process and the systematic violation of human and civil rights.

Meanwhile, I was tormented by all of this. I was safe in Liverpool and feeling guilty. Women and children were putting their lives on the line while I was safe and secure preaching from nice, cosy pulpits all across England – the country responsible for the injustices in Northern Ireland. But what could I do? Hadn't I abandoned all patriotic duty when I became a Redemptorist? Wasn't there the cardinal Redemptorist rule, that a young priest did not rock the boat – on anything?

Some may find it hard to understand why it was so difficult for a young priest to speak out in those days. As I look back now, I even find it hard to believe it myself. But the ecclesiastical, religious climate then was almost cult-like in its control on individuals and in the blind obedience it demanded. 'Blind obedience' was seen as following the will of God. But what if God was not blind to injustice?(God 'is a God of justice', Isaiah 30:6 and 'hates injustice', Isaiah 61:8).

What if God demands of all his followers, especially priests, to work for justice? ('This is what Yahweh asks of you: only this, to do justice, to love tenderly, and to walk humbly with your God.' Micah 6:8.)

How could the Catholic Church wash its hands of 'the Irish problem'? What if silence in the face of injustice is complicity with that very injustice? I knew I could not live in denial. After much prayer and the most serious reflection I had ever done since my decision to become a priest, I decided not to comply with the census. I released the following statement (which, on reading now, does not seem that much of a big deal but it was for me at that time):

I have refused to cooperate with the census. I have refused to fill in the form sent to me. I have done so as a means of protest against the general injustices perpetrated by the Unionist Government in the North of Ireland. More specifically, it is a protest against the Northern Ireland judiciary who blatantly apply a double standard in the administration of justice: one of ridiculous leniency for the Unionists; and one of vigorous severity for the non-Unionists. The latter is exemplified not only in the well known cases of my brother, Frank McManus, M.P. and of Frank Gogarty, Vice Chairman of the Civil Rights Association, but also in numerous recent but less publicized convictions.

I want this carefully considered gesture of mine to be an expression of solidarity with those priests and teachers and others in the North of Ireland who have taken similar action. The fact that I live in Britain and received a somewhat different census than the one issued in the North of Ireland does not negate or diminish the intelligibility of my protest, because – to state the painfully obvious – Britain and the North of Ireland are not unconnected. Moreover, the above mentioned people in the North of Ireland are not opposed to the census in itself; they are, like me, simply using it as a means of protest.

I want to make it perfectly clear that I am not opposed to the census. I neither resent nor do I object to any single question asked in the census form which I received. I find it perfectly reasonable. In fact, I consider it a social necessity, and I truly regret that I am forced to refuse my cooperation.

Furthermore, because I am a priest, I find it embarrassing that I should have to make such a public protest ... but then a Christian conscience or sense of justice is not always a comfortable commodity.

I was the only priest in Britain – indeed, the only person in Britain, period – to make such a protest. The papers gave it small coverage. But poor Charlie Shepherd reacted as if I had called for the abolition of both the Papacy and the Monarchy. He telephoned me in utter panic and told me to pack my bag and go immediately to Kinnoull. I did.

On 18 May, Frankie was released from prison, saying defiantly that it didn't do him 'a damn bit of harm' – in the sense that it had not intimidated him in the slightest, as the authorities had hoped.

Frankie then set his wedding to the fair Carmel Doherty of Lisnaskea, County Fermanagh, for 11 August 1971, and asked me to perform the ceremony, as Jim had a few years earlier performed Terence's wedding.

Two days before the planned wedding, on 9 August 1971, the British government reintroduced their favourite weapon for keeping uppity Catholics in their place: internment, imprisonment without charge or trial.

Frankie was sure he would be interned, but he was determined to get married first. I drove him over the border to a safe house in Swanlinbar the night before. He came back the following day for his wedding in Lisnaskea. The British did not arrest him – perhaps they thought it would be stretching it a bit, even for them, to intern a Member of Parliament. Frank left for London on his honeymoon, and to attend parliament to condemn the introduction of internment.

On 13 August, a large march was quickly organised in

Enniskillen to protest against internment. Naturally, Terence, Jim, Myles and my brother-in-law, Michael Ferguson, attended. And I attended.

The RUC and British Army were clearly out for blood. They bullied and harassed the peaceful crowd and inevitably the young men were not going to take it. A riot broke out. Tear gas was fired into the crowd. I did my best to calm things down, even pulling a brick from the hand of a very agitated young man from Kinawley, whom I knew very well. Then I spotted a group of RUC men flaying into another young guy. I went over and said, 'Come on now, there is no need for that' and non-violently interposed my body between the young man and his police attackers, as I had read the civil right activists in the American Deep South had been taught to do. An eyewitness to my arrest, Martin O'Brien, who would later become a reporter and producer for the BBC, recounted in the *Fermanagh Herald*: 'Then Fr Sean McManus CSsR who had been trying to restrain the crowd was arrested'.[3] (Later in court the policeman who arrested me alleged I had broken his hold on a person he was arresting. That was not the case. Furthermore, had I wanted to use physical force, it is not his 'hold' I would have broken!) I was immediately arrested, which I did not resist, and frogmarched to a police van. I was unceremoniously dumped into the van, landing on a young lad crying on the floor.

Immediately, another young man whom I could not properly see, as the inside of the van was dark, gave me a black beret and asked me if I would keep it because if it was found on him the police would use it as 'proof' that he was in the IRA. I put the beret in my pocket.

The next thing, my young brother Myles was tossed in on top of me. Eventually the van took off for the nearby Enniskillen Barracks. It was somehow obstructed and had to stop and the two policemen jumped out of the front. Suddenly the back door of the police van was swung open with a mighty heave. Big brother Terence, always the rescuer of his younger brothers, commanded: 'Out yous get.'

With that, several young lads bounded like hares out of the

van. I grabbed Myles and stopped him from jumping out, in case it would only make matters worse for him. It is an action I have often questioned. Could he have got away, free and clear? Overall, I doubt it. It is almost certain the police knew who he was and that is why they had arrested him. Even if they did not know him, they would have quickly found out because of the informers and agents they had interspersed throughout the crowd. Then they would probably have put out a warrant for Myles' arrest for escaping from police custody, thereby increasing the seriousness of the charge. Myles then might have been tempted to slip across the border, and in no time would have been on 'the most wanted list', not because he was a member of the IRA but because he was a brother of the local MP, Frank, whom they took glee in harassing.

And of course, had Terence been caught freeing the prisoners, he would have been in serious trouble. Eventually, the police van made it to the barracks. When I walked into the holding room there were dozens of young men lined up before a policeman sitting at a make-shift desk in the middle of the room, taking down statements. Now I was glad I had been arrested as I could see someone had to stand up for these worried young lads. In a very loud, commanding voice (well trained by years of elocution in Hawkstone) I said, 'Do not tell them anything until you are first advised of your rights.' That seemed to steady the young men and they all looked relieved, as the room fell silent. Then a short, mean-looking British soldier, in full infantry regalia (I think), got in my face and pulled me over to the corner of the room. He was the very embodiment of Synge's 'loosed khaki cutthroat'.[4] Sticking his finger in my face, and glaring up at me, he spat, 'You have no rights and that's what's killing you.' I told him that though he had no idea he was doing it, he had just summed up British rule in Ireland – we had no rights and it was killing us. He gasped and stared at me helplessly.

I then said, 'Now you come with me,' and motioned to him to follow me back to the policeman behind the desk. I said to him, 'This soldier tells me we have no rights, is that right? Do you agree with him?' The RUC man had the decency to lower his head and not say a word. It was very clear who was in charge – the British Army, not the police. I had been told once before by another Englishman that I had no rights. In my last year in Hawkstone, while I was ordained, I went to see the Prefect of Students, Barty Meehan, to ask if we could stay up to watch an Irish film on TV (I think it was *The Informer* or *Shake Hands with the Devil*). Barty said no. I pressed the case and said we should have the right to watch it. 'As a Redemptorist, you have no rights. You gave them all up when you took your vows.'

I was beginning to get fed up with Englishmen telling me I had no rights.

At 2.00 a.m. the police tossed me out on the street, not caring that my home was 8 miles away. I would later learn from my study of the Black Freedom Struggle in the US that it was a favorite tactic of the racist police – dump the blacks on the street late at night and tip off the Ku Klux Klan. But before I left the barracks, I got – or so I thought – the assurance from the Enniskillen RUC Chief Inspector, H. J. Currie, who had been previously stationed in Kinawley, that neither Myles nor any of the other young lads arrested would be mistreated. Nonetheless, after I left, the police would point their guns through the spyhole in the door of Myles' cell, and say, 'Shall we shoot him now, or later?' They would keep switching the lights on and off, go into the cell and give him a good whacking. That went on throughout the night. Remember, this was only at the start of the Troubles. Can you imagine what the police did when the Catholic community really rose up in rebellion, and when they captured actual members of the IRA, which Myles was not? The following morning, Myles was brought to court, fined and released.

Meanwhile, while the rioting was still going on and while Myles and I were still at the barracks, Frankie got a telephone call in London from the wife of a local Catholic politician: 'Come home, Frank, the town's in flames and ALL your family has been arrested.' Hell of a way to begin a honeymoon.

One of my in-laws, an elderly lady, on learning that her priest-relative had been arrested by the hated RUC, flew into a righteous rage and declared that the arm of the arresting officer (a Constable Frederick Scott) would 'rot from the shoulder down' and to back up her prediction she quoted Scripture: 'Touch not my anointed . . .' (1 Chronicles 16:22). Who says Catholics don't know their Bible? I hope Constable Scott did not lose his arm. I often wonder what happened to him and I wish him well.

The British soldiers and the RUC did not scare me, but Charlie Shepherd did. What would he do now that I had been arrested in a riot situation? He would certainly have no precedence to go on as I was almost certainly the only Redemptorist from the English Province to have been arrested.

I returned to Kinnoull and waited to hear from the police. I was summoned to appear in the Enniskillen Magistrates Court on 6 September 1971, charged with 'obstructing a Constable in the due execution of his duty'. When the Resident Magistrate, Mr John W. Adams, asked me how I pleaded, I responded: 'I do not recognise the authority of the court.' Fighting words and a characteristic tactic of the IRA.

The Magistrate imposed a fine of £20 to be paid in fifteen days and, 'in default of payment to be imprisoned in the Prison of Belfast for the period of three months unless the said sum be sooner paid.' I also refused to pay the fine.

I had not told my brother Frankie, who sat with me, that I was going to refuse to recognise the Court. I did not want to implicate him so that he could truthfully tell the media that he was not involved in my decision. I was also concerned that there was some parliamentary rule in the House of Commons which the British could use to expel Frankie for being complicit in such 'treasonable' language.

I had, however, given an advance copy of my statement to Sinn Féin's office in Dublin for release the moment the hearing was over.

My statement got wide coverage. *The Irish Times* not only wrote a report on the court hearing but also printed my lengthy statement, word for word, which, given the history of that paper, amazed me. My statement was as follows:

[I] refused to recognize the Court because it has no legitimate authority. But that is only the 'tip of the iceberg'. I do not, I never have and I never will, recognize the colonial State of British Occupied Ireland. This State exists because of a morally and politically criminal action. It was illegally imposed by force, and it is illegally sustained by force, against the will of the Irish people. Therefore, its institutions, its laws, and its legal and political expressions are invalid.

The creation and maintenance of this State blatantly violates God's laws and the natural law, because its fundamental principle is 'ownership by the right of conquest', i.e., ownership through violence and the gun, and by violence and the gun it is maintained. And those who created it, and those who sustain it, are the real men of violence – they are the gunmen, they alone are the terrorists.

This terrorist State I reject in its entirety. I reject in particular its judiciary. In principle it is illegitimate, in practice it has a despicable record of injustice, corruption and sectarianism.

Refusing to recognize the court is the policy of the Irish Republican army. I will immediately be suspected of being in sympathy with the IRA. Well, let's clear up this 'suspicion'. I want to state publicly and unequivocally that I am in sympathy with the IRA. Indeed, sympathy is too weak a word.

Many people may wonder why I should want to publicly proclaim my convictions. The answer is simple. My conscience forbids me to be silent, and if I did not now speak out, I could never live with myself because for the rest of my life I would know that I had been a coward . . . no matter how hard I tried to justify my silence as prudence. I would know that I had been deceitful and treacherous to the patriots who were sacrificing their lives for the freedom of Ireland. I cannot join them in the fight for the freedom of my country, but the very least I can do is to speak up for them when they are being slandered and vilified by unscrupulously vicious propaganda.

The oppressors of Irish freedom call the IRA terrorists and murderers, but I call them by their proper titles: I call them freedom fighters, I call them heroes, and I venerate their dead as martyrs for Ireland. And I know that any true Irishman or indeed any informed, honest and fair-minded person thinks and feels the same way.

I could not live with myself, if by my silence, I traitorously stabbed these patriots in the back. I abhor the deceit and hypocrisy that condemns these men and women who are sacrificing their lives for the freedom of Ireland. I could not bear to be even remotely associated with such deceit and hypocrisy – and my silence would associate me. It is only expected that the violent men who are opposing Irish freedom should condemn the IRA freedom fighters, but it is unforgivable when many so-called Nationalist spokesmen also condemn them.

Yet, in the light of history, condemnation from the latter is not surprising for every struggle for Irish freedom has been traitorously condemned by this sort of people. (And yet our patriots, despite 'this unkindest cut of all', still fought on because they were, and are, men and women of courage, integrity and dedication.) And of this I am certain: that when our patriots free Ireland, and free it they surely will, these very people will be the very first to jump on the bandwagon and salute the men and women they now condemn. They did it before and they will do it again.

To praise Tone, Pearse, Connolly, Sean Treacy and Cathal Brugha and all the others, on the one hand, while on the other, condemning those (and here I make no distinction between the Provisionals and the Officials) is treachery and deceit of the lowest kind. How I detest such chicanery. It revolts and disgusts me, and I will have no part of it.

I finalized my decision to speak out as I stood by a lonely grave. It is the grave of a man who was the personification of nobility, courage and integrity: a typical member of the IRA. He is a man whose memory I honour and of whom I

am deeply proud: my brother Patrick who died for Ireland
in 1958.

The day before the court hearing, I was being driven by the late
Dave O'Connell, a top IRA man and political strategist, from
Dublin to Monaghan. I read my statement out loud for him to hear.
When I had finished, he pulled the car off the road, clearly very
moved. 'I never thought I'd see the day when a priest would have
the balls to say what you have said.' And with great embarrassment
he silently sobbed for about five minutes. 'If nothing else, it's worth
it, just for this,' I thought, as memories flooded back into my mind
about how the priests at St Michael's were so scared of being
associated with the IRA that they would not even perform a basic
act of Christian charity or human decency, except Fr Clerkin.
Dave pulled himself together and in his signature Cork accent – at
once authoritative, yet almost roguish – said, 'Don't tell anyone I
cried. It would be bad for my image if the Brits knew.' His secret
was safe with me. Dave died in Dublin in January 1991, aged fifty-
three. Sadly, Sinn Féin split in 1986 and Dave broke from Gerry
Adams and Martin McGuinness. However, no one can diminish
Dave's stature, integrity and heroism. I had deep respect for him
and held him in great affection. On my annual pilgrimage to
Glasnevin Cemetery, 'where the Fenians sleep', I always kneel and
say a prayer at his grave in the Republican Plot.

When Frankie saw my statement, he told me I would be
interned, which I was quite prepared for. In fact, I would have
welcomed it, for as Thoreau said: 'Under a government, which
imprisons any unjustly, the true place for a just man is also a prison.'[5]
But I was neither interned for my statement, nor imprisoned for
not paying the fine.

I knew that the British government and its whole intelligence
operations would not stand idly by, even though they had not
publicly moved against me. I knew they would exert huge
pressure on the Catholic hierarchy in Britain and Ireland, and
through them on Fr Shepherd. After all, the British government
had succeeded in 1870 in getting Pope Pius IX to excommunicate

the Fenians, both in Ireland and America. No matter how badly the British treated Irish Catholics, the Vatican always listened to them on Ireland with the aid of the Irish Bishops. 'Twas enough to make a Kinawleyman a Protestant!

However, I continued to speak out but, again, never from the pulpit. Finally that letter, dated Friday 15 April 1972, with which this book opened, arrived from Fr Shepherd telling me to pack my bag for Clapham in London. 'I do not want anyone to know your immediate destination, nor your proposed transfer from Perth, I once again forbid you to make any communications to the Press or Media either per se or per alium, or to call on anyone en route or before departure.'

I was blessed with the insight to see that for what it was: an unconscionable, almost racist missive, which in fact meant: do not fraternise with any Irish person on the way to your ecclesiastical house arrest, on behalf, in effect, of Her Majesty's government.

The racist implication become clear if one imagines a white Church superior telling Martin Luther King, Jr (not that I'm comparing myself to that great man) that he must not associate with any black person, especially one engaged in the Black Freedom Struggle. James Joyce said of Ireland that 'Christ and Caesar are hand in glove' but that applies even more so to England, as I was soon about to learn.

I felt no moral obligation to obey this patently unjust and politicised diktat. Charlie Shepherd was simply implementing that British soldier's ignorant decree: 'You have no rights . . .' I am sure Charlie saw himself as protecting the Redemptorist Order but the only way he could do that was by pleasing the British government. So the end result was the same.

But let me contrast Charlie's letter with the one I received on 19 April from a local Episcopalian priest in Perth. You be the judge as to which is the more Christian:

Dear Father,
Whilst I was at the altar celebrating the Liturgy this morning, I thought about you and the difficult situation in which you

find yourself at present. I would like you to know that this vivid thought prompted me to include you in my prayers and intention in the Eucharist.

I would also like you to know that I think that I can sense – and to some extent share – the anguish which you feel about the situation in Ireland. I suppose it will always be difficult for the priest transfixed by the knowledge that he must be an [intermediary] representing God to his people and the people to God – and yet, burning within with a great desire to move into an area of what seems like worldly action for a cause which he knows in his heart of hearts is right. I use the word 'transfixed' for it seems to me that in this kind of situation, the priest is nailed to the cross, a cross which is that well-nigh unbearable tension between his priesthood, as conceived of in spiritual terms, and his (dare I use the word?) priesthood as he sees it in worldly terms. But of course, this is what the priesthood is all about. It is surely more than offering the Eucharistic sacrifice and preaching the Word (though it is that too) – but a living of this tension between the spiritual and the physical, between this world and the 'other' world. The priest who lives this tension in his own life is stretched on the Cross with his Master.

Take heart, Father. There are many who will understand and pray for you – as I do. I hope that when 'things are blown over' you will be able to come to visit me and have another 'natter'.

On Friday, I will be celebrating the Liturgy at our cathedral at 8 a.m. I will pray especially for you. In our calendar and Ordo, it is the double feast of St Maelrubha (Abbot of Applecross and Bangor) and St Anslem, Archibishop of Cantebury – a Celtic saint and one from an English See: perhaps there might be some significance in that – reconciliation – ?

With every prayer and blessing
Yours in Christ,
Reverend John Ross.

I flew down to London. Frankie was in Parliament and naturally I needed to talk to him about the whole thing. Incredibly even at that period (the week of 16 April 1972) I was able to check in my bag at the House of Commons cloakroom. Then I remembered that in my bag there was an alarm clock, set to go off at 5.30 a.m. and it was now nearly 5.30 p.m. and I was concerned my clock would not distinguish between a.m. and p.m. So I hurried back to the Clerk and told him not to worry if the alarm went off. 'Don't worry, Reverend, that will be no problem,' said the very nice Englishman.

It was there I met Bernadette Devlin, MP, for the first time. She had been elected the year before Frankie and he and she fought the good fight in 'the belly of the beast'. I had, of course, great admiration for her fearlessness, courage and eloquence. But I was not expecting someone with such a formidable public persona to be so charming and gracious. And thus she has been each time I've met her over the years. She and Frankie (and sometimes Gerry Fitt, MP for West Belfast) had to fight lonely battles. The day after Bloody Sunday (30 January 1972 when British paratroopers killed thirteen innocents at a non-violent march in Derry) Bernadette punched out the Foreign Secretary, Reginald Maudling, in the House of Commons for trying to cover up the act of State terrorism. Years later, in an interview with the London magazine, *The Big Issue*, Bernadette would recall: 'I walked over and clattered Maudling ... Big Davison, a conservative, hit me and Frank McManus floored him.'[6]

That evening I went to St Mary's, Clapham, the Provincial's headquarters. Fr Shepherd told me he wanted to see me first thing in the morning. At the appointed time, I went to his office (which, ironically, my brother Jim would later occupy as Provincial for three terms, 1990 to 1999). Charlie was in no mood for chit-chat. He got right to the point: 'Unless you give a promise, without mental reservation or equivocation, never to criticise the government again on Northern Ireland, I will suspend you from all public priestly work.'

I deliberately paused for a very long time before replying so that he would know that I was as serious as he was. My reply was slow and steady: 'Father, in conscience and with all due respect, I cannot make such a promise. While I do not intend to speak out all the time, I cannot make a promise to be silent in the face of injustice because that would make me as guilty as the British government and British army.' Then he lost it: '*You are in the English Province and you will not criticise the English government.*' Well, despite my intention to maintain a controlled demeanour, the Kinawleyman reasserted itself and I gave it back to him in kind: 'For as long as your government oppresses my country, I will not be silent.'

He jumped out of his chair, declared he had not called me in for a discussion and told me to pack my bag for Chawton (to Alphonsus House, the Redemptorist publishing house, which had no parish) in Hampshire, about 56 miles southwest of London.

As I headed for the door, I turned and said, 'Does this mean I am being silenced [in the canonical sense of not being able to function as a priest]?' He snapped, 'Nobody said anything about silencing.'

So that meant I could say a private Mass in Alphonsus House and, as there was no parish attached, the issue of public Masses did not apply.

I would come to refer to Chawton as 'my ecclesiastical Long Kesh', after the prison of that name the British were operating in the North.

Charlie Shepherd would telephone me every week or so to see if I would recant. 'In good conscience, and with all due respect, Father, I cannot . . .' But he would often slam down the phone before I could complete my mantra.

The fact that Chawton had no parish seemed a logical place to sequester me, but it had one ironic disadvantage: it was only about 9 miles from Aldershot. On 22 February 1972, the Official IRA had bombed the 16th Parachute Brigade headquarters at Aldershot in retaliation for the Parachute Regiment's murderous attack on the peaceful march on 30 January 1972 in Derry – the atrocity and act of State terrorism known as Bloody Sunday. Five women and one Catholic priest, a chaplain, were tragically killed in the IRA attack. The priest, Fr Gerry Weston, thirty-seven, had been a regular visitor to Alphonus House and was a good friend of all the Redemptorists there. So that made the situation very poignant for all of us. Yet I must say everyone in Alphonsus House treated me very kindly, though they must have wondered what they had done to deserve this turn of events.

However, my forced ecclesiastical quarantine gave me time for serious reflection and prayer. The library wasn't too bad. It had a copy of *Justice in the World* (mentioned in the Introduction). I went to the local library and got a copy of Martin Luther King, Jr's 'Letter from Birmingham Jail' – his magisterial response to the top eight Birmingham Church leaders, including the Catholic Bishop of Birmingham, who had publicly censored his protest actions:

> I have almost reached the regrettable conclusion that the Negro's great stumbling block in his stride toward freedom is not the White Citizen's Counciler or the Ku Klux Klanner, but the white moderate, who is more devoted to 'order' than to justice; who prefers a negative peace which is the absence of tension to a positive peace which is the presence of justice; who constantly says: 'I agree with you in the goal you seek, but I cannot agree with your methods of direct action'; who paternalistically believes he can set the timetable for another man's freedom; who lives by a mythical concept of time and who constantly advises the Negro to wait for a 'more convenient season'. Shallow understanding from people of good will is more frustrating than absolute misunderstanding from people of ill will. Lukewarm acceptance is much more bewildering than outright rejection . . . Before closing I feel impelled to mention one other point in your statement that has troubled me profoundly. You warmly commended the Birmingham police force for keeping 'order' and 'preventing violence'. I doubt that you would have so warmly commended the police force if you had seen its dogs sinking

their teeth into unarmed, non-violent Negroes. I doubt that you would so quickly commend the policemen if you were to observe their ugly and inhumane treatment of Negroes here in the city jail; if you were to watch them push and curse old Negro women and young Negro girls; if you were to see them slap and kick old Negro men and young boys; if you were to observe them, as they did on two occasions, refuse to give us food because we wanted to sing our grace together. I cannot join you in your praise of the Birmingham police department'.[7]

I am still amazed, almost fifty years later, how comparable the Black Freedom Struggle is to the Irish struggle.

I also decided to contact one of the priests who had taught me 'the new theology' in Hawkstone. So on 9 May 1972, I wrote asking him for his guidance on the theology concerning the 'conflict of conscience' – the possible conflict between conscience and authority. I stressed I did not want him to take a position on my stand, nor make judgments about the Irish situation, but to clearly explicate the theological principle. He wrote back saying that a good Redemptorist can never have a conflict of conscience! That was a total contradiction of both the new and the 'old' theology. Not *Pax Christi*, but *Pax Britannica*. Rule Britannia. And I was supposed to be the one being political.

Because of my rather unique position, I had to make a serious study of the subject. I knew that first of all, one had an obligation to have an informed conscience – to seek out all the available teaching on the issue, to study it sincerely and objectively and, above all, pray that one was not deceiving oneself, because all of us can have a 'self-serving' conscience. The Second Vatican Council, in its document *Gaudium et Spes* (Joy and Hope), told me that 'conscience is the man's most secret core, and his sanctuary'. So I knew if I betrayed my conscience, I would be betraying my truest self – the inner me who stands naked before the all-seeing eye of God.

I knew very well how the deal would go down: some good

Catholic MPs (and I hoped it wasn't Frankie or Bernadette Devlin!) would contact Cardinal Heenan, saying it was very bad for the Church to have a young Irish priest saying such awful things about the British government and wasn't there something His Eminence could do about it. The Cardinal would then call Charlie. Indeed, Charlie admitted as much to me – well, he let it slip out and then couldn't take it back.

I also knew there was another fundamental principle involved in making a conscientious protest: you take your punishment without whining and you do not, after the fact, unfairly look to involve others in the consequences of your action. Again, I found solace in Martin Luther King, Jr: 'An individual who breaks a law that conscience tells him is unjust, and who willingly accepts the penalty of imprisonment in order to arouse the conscience of the community over its injustice, is in reality expressing the highest respect for the law.'

I finally wrote to Fr Shepherd on 16 May 1974:

> I have thought things over – but, it was all well-charted ground. I am unable to see things in a different light. The actions I took were not impetuous: they were studied and calculated, and prayed about. I am totally convinced that what I did was right, and that I was bound to do it. Therefore, in principle I could never give an absolute unconditional promise never to speak out again . . . Before God, I do not believe that my actions were motivated by anything base or ulterior. In fact, from the very nature of the case, I have patently nothing to gain but everything to lose. Indeed, from the way things look at present, I know that I may very well have (if I may speak like this for a moment) ruined my 'personal career'.

I went on to acknowledge that I had put him in a difficult position but stressed that any apparent clash between my loyalty to the Province and my conscience was only that, i.e. apparent: '. . . because when a man stands up for what he knows is right, then he is not being disloyal to any side: he is being loyal to the truth, which can never "compete" against any value or good'. But I knew the die was cast. There was no way I would be allowed to continue working in Britain or Ireland.

I would have liked for Fr Shepherd to acknowledge the moral integrity of my conscientious protest, but he never did. He insisted as seeing it 'formal disobedience', maybe because it was easier that way for him, or because he was just plain scared or because he was incapable of respecting a conscience that disagreed with his. Religious superiors can easily fall into the sin of thinking they speak for God at all times and in all ways. They don't. That's why we have this thing called conscience. No authority, no superior, can take its place.

Soon the whole world was my parish. Fr Shepherd gave me all sorts of choices: go to Rome for further studies in Eucharistic theology, or any place in continental Europe, Canada or America. South Africa would have been the usual 'dumping ground' for the English Province. But an Anglican priest had recently been deported back to England for speaking out against the apartheid system. And there was no way someone like me would be allowed into that country.

I chose America. I checked out which Redemptorist Province in America was the most Irish. If I was going to be 'transported' (the very resonant word that was used for the exiling of political prisoners to Australia, up until 1868), then I might as well go to an area where I could do the most good. I chose the Baltimore Province, because that included New York, Boston and, most importantly of all, the nation's capital, Washington, DC.

Charlie now became very cooperative, doing everything in his power to facilitate my 'transportation'. On 16 June 1972, he wrote to the Provincial of the Baltimore Province, Fr Joseph L. Kerins, at his headquarters in Brooklyn, New York.

'Fr Sean McManus aged 29 [*sic*]. This young man is an excellent priest and a very promising missionary on the Parish Mission. Unfortunately, owing to his Irish origins, he has foolishly become implicated through newspaper articles & a TV appearance in the very sad political impasse in N. Ireland . . . Would it be at all possible for you to take him and let him work on the Parish Mission band in the Baltimore Province? . . . I am not trying to unload a bad priest on anyone, but one who has been foolish and stubborn in this particular Irish problem.' (Notice here, the strange distancing, probably unconscious, but typically British . . . 'the Irish problem' – as if it had no connection to Britain or that the British Army was not in the North doing terrible things.)

I acknowledged earlier that the average British person knows little about Northern Ireland. But is that really a good enough excuse? How long can a well-educated people be excused for not knowing what their government, army and 'tax dollars' are doing in another country? Is it ignorance or indifference? And how could the Churches in Britain ignore the mistreatment of Catholics in Northern Ireland? Is it because they did not want to become 'involved in politics' or is it because they were being profoundly political? Was their silence prudence or betrayal?

How could ecclesiastical silence be reconciled with the clarion call of *Gaudium et Spes* issued by the Second Vatican Council in its very opening lines: 'The joys and the hopes, the griefs and the anxieties of the men of this age, especially those who are poor or in any way afflicted, these are the joys and hopes, the griefs and anxieties of the followers of Christ. Indeed, nothing genuinely human fails to raise an echo in their hearts.'

In August I went home to Clonliff to prepare for my exile to America. So far, 1972 was proving to be one of the worst years of the Troubles. Danger was palpable all over the North. And it visited Mother. She was home alone one night. A gunman blasted her bedroom window but mercifully she escaped injury. She was sixty-nine at the time. And to make it all the more painful, the man who tried to kill her was a local Protestant whom we had known all our lives, and whom we had always treated with friendliness and kindness (as we had treated all our Protestant neighbours).

Now let me tell you the follow-up to this incident in two parts. The first and most important part is about my Mother's forgiveness; the second is about the nature of the State of Northern Ireland.

About two nights after the shooting (while we still did not know who the shooter was) I was sitting home with my mother. There was a knock on the door, and as we were not expecting any visitors, I signalled to my Mother not to move and went to the door. Outside there was standing the tallest policeman I had ever seen in my life, indeed the tallest person I had ever seen. I then saw there was someone hiding behind him whom the policeman then brought forward. The policeman said: '[first and last name] has come to apologise for shooting at Mrs McManus.' The man then, sheepishly said, 'Hello, Fr Sean,' casting his eyes down.

I brought them both into the kitchen and the Protestant gunman said, 'Mrs McManus, I am sorry for shooting at you. Will you forgive me?' Without hesitating a split second, Mother reached out, grabbed his hand in hers and said, 'Of course, I will [first name]. God love you.'

I have told that story to very few outside the family because it is so profoundly personal and precious, and also because it is difficult for me to get through it without crying.

And now to the second, less edifying, part of the story: can you imagine that, had a Catholic tried to kill the mother of a Protestant MP, the police would have brought him to that woman's house to apologise? Nothing can tell you more about the nature of the State of Northern Ireland than this. Why would the police do such a thing? Certainly it had to come from the very top, as no local policeman would take it upon himself to do such an extraordinary thing. Local people immediately saw it as an attempt to get the court to go easy on the gunman. But the far more serious question was why would the police go so far out on a limb for an ordinary working-class Protestant? What was the purpose of their damage control? What were they trying to contain or hide?

We have never been given an explanation. But we all, like Mother, forgave the gunman, whom we felt had been used as a patsy, like so many other working-class Protestant gunmen.

6

Bound for America

I know how men in exile feed on dreams.
Aeschylus

I have never met an emigrant from Ireland who did not know the exact date of their arrival in America. It is a big day in their lives – truly a transitional moment in every sense. My big day was 2 October 1972. I flew out from Dublin on Aer Lingus with a stop in Shannon Airport. At the airport I telephoned Celia to get the momentous news that Carmel, Frankie's wife, had just given birth to a lovely baby girl, Emer. I ran back to the plane, my homesickness abated by the good news. Needless to say, I never have a problem remembering Emer's birthday.

Ironically, I wasn't back on the plane ten minutes before the woman sitting next to me brought up Frankie's name, totally of her own accord, having no idea who I was. When she heard I was from the North, she immediately started talking about the Troubles. I knew immediately she had to be living in America because most people from southern Ireland did not want to talk about the North. She was a nice, middle-aged woman, originally from Dublin, who had spent most of her life in America but was now living six months in Ireland and six months in America. 'God bless us,' I thought, 'she must be a millionaire.' Anyway, she proceeded to tell me something which was not 'generally known': that Frank McManus and Bernadette Devlin were secretly married; and there was nothing wrong with that; that they were properly married in the Church (an acknowledgement of my clerical collar); but the marriage had to be secret because a husband and wife could not serve in the British Parliament at the same time.

Keeping a straight face, I asked her the source of her information. She implied she knew some very well-connected people. 'Well, now, I don't think that's quite right,' I said, looking for a way to let her down gently. But she would have none of it, and dismissed my mild protestations with a wave of the hand and changed the subject. It was my first introduction to how some Irish Americans (even Irish born) have very definite views about Ireland that may not be exactly correct.

I will never forget my arrival at JFK Airport in New York. I was a little apprehensive. I had never seen so many people, racing like crazy. I see some sort of uniform, a gun in a holster and instinctively I tighten. Then I see it is a black man in uniform and somehow that made it all right. It had been my first sight of an armed policeman, other that the RUC.

I got a cab and headed for the Redemptorist headquarters on Shore Road, Brooklyn. And, would you believe it? The cab broke down, in the worst looking area I had ever seen in my life. I immediately thought it was a set-up. I was relieved the driver was an African American, but what if the British had paid him to 'break down'? That may all sound melodramatic now, and it may have all been in my head, but the reality was that the British were regularly setting up people for assassination in the North.

But my driver waved down a passing cab, and I made it safely to the Redemptorist headquarters. When I had settled in, I went to the common room where about five or six Redemptorists were watching TV news. They welcomed me kindly and offered me a seat. I took out a pack of cigarettes, and in my good mannerly way, offered one to each priest. They laughed and declined. I had learned my first etiquette lesson in America: it is not considered

cheap if you do not offer a cigarette, as everyone smokes their
own. (But you better unlearn that when you are back in Ireland.)

As we watched the news (each smoking his own cigarette),
Kissinger comes on. He has just returned from the Middle East.
He is asked if America has plans to take over the Arab oil fields.
That would only be done if America's national interest were at
stake, he droned. I wanted to shout back at the TV, but I was just
off the boat, so to speak. I glanced around the room expecting
a reaction to Kissinger's British–imperialist-type declaration but
it hadn't even raised an eyebrow. I had learned my first political
lesson: America is permanently in danger of making the same
mistakes as the British – the hubris of empire.

My most vivid first impressions of America came the
following morning as I jumped into the shower in my room.
The water took lumps out of me. I couldn't believe its force. In
the Redemptorists' showers in Britain, you almost had to beg
the water to trickle out. When I grabbed the towel, I couldn't
believe its size, softness and absorbency. The towels in the London
Province, by contrast, were like glorified dishcloths that became
soaked on the first contact with your wet back. When I stepped
out of the bathroom, it appeared that my feet almost sank up to
my ankles in the lush carpet. Coming out of the showers in Britain
was always the worst part. You stepped on cold floor, covered with
linoleum, if you were lucky, and froze until you had dressed again.
Not in the good old USA. I could have been quite comfortable
in my room with just the big towel around my waist. (Mind you,
the rooms in the Redemptorist houses throughout the Baltimore
Province were not as nice, and did not have their own bathroom.)
After Mass and breakfast, I met with the Provincial, Fr Joe Kerins.
I knew immediately I was in the presence of a remarkably fine
man. Things even got better when he knowingly said, 'One of my
uncles in Kerry was in the IRA.' (Put that in your pipe, Charlie
Shepherd, and smoke it, I thought to myself.)

Then he completely bowled me over when he said, 'Here's
your file.'

'What do you mean?' I asked.

'It is a copy of all correspondence regarding you – including Fr Shepherd's letters,' he explained.

'And do I get to keep this file?'

'Yes, in this Province, we have a policy of total openness. It is the right of every Redemptorist to see every letter that is written about him.'

To me, this was extraordinary and revolutionary. I had been so used to British men telling me I had no rights. God bless us, I thought, this is a great country altogether.

And that is how I got a copy of the letter from Charlie Shepherd, to Fr Kerins, that I quoted earlier. Over the next few years, Fr Kerins would keep sending me copies of letters Fr Shepherd would write about me, as I kept denouncing the British government – the more I denounced, the more angry and personal Shepherd's letter became. And I'm sure he had no idea I was being given copies of his letters.

Fr Kerins told me they badly needed a young priest in Sacred Heart of Jesus parish, in Baltimore, especially for youth work. I suspected that Baltimore was selected because it was not as Irish as New York or Boston. He told me to take some time for myself, and visit my brother Thomas in upstate New York and my sister Alice in Reading, Pennsylvania.

He also told me that he was sure I would want 'to meet my many admirers in New York City'. And with a big smile, he handed me a copy of the *Irish People*, which I had never heard of, but which announced to great acclaim there was 'an Irish rebel priest' in town.

A delegation of ardent Irish men and women came to Shore Road to escort me into the city. I stayed in the apartment of a man from Ballinamore, County Leitrim, who had been in the IRA with Patrick, and had soldiered alongside him. He was a labouring man. Yet, when he showed me into my room, he pulled out two drawers from a cabinet, and said if I needed any vests (T-shirts), there were plenty there. And was there ever! I had never seen so many gleaming white T-shirts, all neatly folded, maybe even pressed. Now, I had come to America wearing one T-shirt and one in my bag. 'God bless us,' I thought, 'this man must be rich indeed.'

My Ballinamore host could not wait to take me to meet Seán Cronin, who was Chief of Staff of the IRA after Patrick was killed. He was then a journalist in New York City. Seán was very pleased to meet me as he had great respect for Patrick. He told me I could do a lot of good work for the Cause, but to watch my back, as both the London and Dublin governments would try to bring me down. I soon met all the leaders and activists in Irish Northern Aid, AOH and general Irish organisations in New York City. They were fiercely anti-British and furious at the quisling attitude of the Free State government. Suddenly, I felt very much at home.

When I arrived at Sacred Heart of Jesus, in the section of Baltimore called Highlandtown, the first thing that struck me was that there were absolutely no people on the streets, although it was mid-afternoon. The next thing I spotted were the famous marble steps that lead up to each row house, and which the housewives kept as clean as their own very white teeth. Highlandtown was mostly German and Polish, hardly any Irish.

After the Masses on Sunday, my reaction was that apart from superficial differences, Sacred Heart could have been like any city parish in Belfast, Dublin or London. I was sad, however, to see only a few black faces – the great weakness in the American Catholic Church. How often over the years would I reflect on that telling quote of Martin Luther King, Jr about eleven o'clock on a Sunday morning being the most segregated hour of the week!

Right away, I arranged a meeting with the officers of the parish CYO (Catholic Youth Organisation) – a group of lovely young girls, aged fifteen to seventeen, I guess. They were delighted to have a young priest for their group. The TV show *Charlie's Angels* was very popular at the time, so they took to calling themselves 'Fr Sean's Angels'. When I told them I was from Ireland, they nodded their heads. But at the end of the meeting, the president, a very bright young lady, said, 'Fr Sean, where is Ireland, near Canada?' My first lesson about Americans and geography. And there was I thinking Ireland was the centre of the world, with everybody knowing about it.

I quickly got the run of the parish, and did my work with gusto. There was hardly any Irish activity in Baltimore and none on the North. But I was determined to quickly change that. The word got out that I was in town and a group wanted me to speak to them. I made them feel guilty that they were ignoring their homeland and told them they were aiding British oppression in Ireland by their silence. Soon there was an active chapter of Irish Northern Aid in Baltimore and Washington.

As the only young priest, I was doing a lot of good work in the parish. All the other priests were over fifty, with most in their seventies. I loved the people. I had never met any nicer people than these German and Polish folk – all patriotic Americans and deeply committed Catholics. I was humbled by their devout Catholicism and surprised at how strongly Catholic this big country was.

I was getting on with my work, reinvigorating the parish with no thought that I would see Ireland in the near future. But just as I thought I was out, they pulled me back in.

A month after I arrived in Baltimore, Seán Mac Stíofáin, Chief of Staff of the IRA, was arrested in Dublin on 19 November 1972, and immediately began a hunger and thirst strike. On 25 November, he was sentenced to six months' imprisonment. The previous day, Irish Northern Aid leaders in New York had appealed to me to come and speak at protest meetings in New York, and to go to Ireland because Mac Stíofáin had asked for me.

I tried to reach both my Rector at Sacred Heart and Father Provincial in New York. They were unavailable so I left a message for them that 'I had presumed permission' (the theological principle that states one can, in an emergency, legitimately and in good faith presume the superior would grant permission if he were present). I travelled to New York and spoke at the hastily called public meeting at the Irish Institute. The other two speakers were Seán Cronin and Congressman Biaggi. The meeting was followed by an all-night vigil outside the Irish Consulate.

Jack McCarthy, the crusty but admirable leader of Irish Northern Aid, arranged my flight to Dublin.

When I picked up my luggage at Dublin airport, I asked the

luggage handler if Mac Stíofáin was still alive. 'Unfortunately, he is. It would be far better for the country if he died.' He clearly thought because I had a clerical collar on that I would be supporting the Dublin government. I gave him such a withering look he scurried off. I stayed at the home of friends, a fine elderly couple from Kerry. Their house was a veritable hotel for IRA leaders like the late Joe Cahill.

I spoke at a massive rally, which my brother Frank also attended. On Sunday afternoon, 26 November, I visited Mac Stíofáin in the Mater Hospital, to which he had been transferred from prison because of his deteriorating condition. As I walked into the hospital ward, a group of Special Branch men grabbed me and pinned me with my back to the wall. I had never seen such fury or hatred in anybody's eyes as the man who held me by the throat. I said, 'You fellows are worse than the British Army. Why are you doing this?' The lead guy hissed, 'One of you f★★kers tried to shoot me.' 'What do you mean one of us f★★kers tried to shoot you?' I demanded.

Then I learned why they were so (understandably) agitated. A short time before I had arrived, an IRA team, disguised as priests, had tried to rescue Mac Stíofáin and had got into a shoot-out with the Special Branch. Two IRA men were wounded and four caught. I had been oblivious to all of this, and had innocently blundered into an explosive setting. IRA leaders had known in advance that I was going to be visiting Mac Stíofáin but had not said a word to me – and I guess that was also understandable.

Finally – with bruised neck, but none the worse for wear – I got into Mac Stíofáin's room. I was stunned to see how terrible he looked on his eighth day of hunger and thirst strike. The last time I saw him he was a vigorous, strong man. But now he was a shadow of his former self. It was evident he was in a most critical condition.

That night or early morning the following day – to avoid any further rescue attempts – Mac Stíofáin was transferred by helicopter to the Irish Army's main barracks in the Curragh, about 30 miles from Dublin. Dave O'Connell, a top IRA man, told me it was vital that I got into the Curragh to see Mac Stíofáin, as the Republican Movement would have no other point of contact.

Friends drove me to the Curragh and I tried to see Mac Stíofáin the evening of Monday 27 November, as it was getting dark. The Free State Army had the entire area cordoned off. I asked to speak to the lead soldier, a surprisingly young man. He was absolute: It didn't matter if I were the Pope. I was not getting through, he told me with just too much relish. 'How does it feel to be doing England's dirty work?' I blasted. Sticking out his chest he boasted, 'It feels great. It feels great.' I think if I had not been a priest, I would have decked him on the spot.

The following morning, I returned to the Curragh military hospital and waited outside with Mrs Mac Stíofáin and her daughter, Marie. They were eventually allowed in.

Then I went to a soldier guarding the door and asked him if I could use the bathroom. He refused. I told him it was an emergency and if I could not use the bathroom, I would go behind the trees at the bottom of the field. He then earnestly pleaded, 'Father, please don't. We have orders to shoot anything that moves down there.' At least he's a decent sort, I thought, compared to the blackguard from the night before.

Sometime later, the top brass summoned me in: 'It's an emergency.' They rushed me to where Mac Stíofáin was caged, literally: his bed was inside a huge cage. From inside the bars, Mac Stíofáin's daughter was screaming, 'Fr Sean, Fr Sean, my father is dying.' Mac Stíofáin was having some sort of seizure, shaking violently. However, he survived and came off his thirst strike, and afterwards off his hunger strike.

Later on, when the emotion and high drama had subsided, I slipped up to Fermanagh to see my mother. In retrospect, it was probably a risky thing to have done as the Orangemen were out for my blood.

When I was returning to America, Dave O'Connell drove me to the Dublin airport. He assured me he had given a full report to Irish Northern Aid leaders in New York about all the details of my efforts.

The same luggage handler was there. I had been on TV so much that he could not fail to recognise me. A look of sheer terror came over his face, scared that I might have passed on his vicious comment about Mac Stíofáin to the IRA. I had not, of course, as I did not want him to suffer any retaliation. I went over to him and assured that I had not told anyone. 'Oh, thank you, Father, thank you, Father. I didn't mean it. I'm a good Republican meself.' You've never seen a more relieved man.

Years later, a Redemptorist friend told Jim and me this story in Washington. He was based in Clapham with Charlie Shepherd during the Mac Stíofáin hunger strike. They were in the common room watching the TV news and the hunger strike was covered. Charlie turned around and intoned to all in the room, 'Thank goodness Sean McManus is safely in America.' And at that very instant, I appear on the TV, large as life, not safely in America but in Dublin. Charlie got such a shock he almost fainted.

When I arrived back in Baltimore, I wasn't sure of the reception I would receive at Sacred Heart of Jesus. The national and Baltimore media had covered my activities and everyone in the parish had been excited to read about their 'young new Irish priest'. I did not receive one negative comment from the parishioners, only, 'right on, Father, way to go' from those lovely German and Polish Catholics.

Parishioners are one thing, but what about the powers that be?

Fr Kerns – the noblest of them all – would provide me with another file of all correspondences relating to my Irish visit. God bless us, I thought to myself yet again, this is a great country altogether.

On 1 December, while I was still in Ireland, the Rector of Sacred Heart had written to Fr Kerins: 'My reaction about this whole affair [the Mac Stíofáin hunger strike] is that Sean is welcome back here at Sacred Heart, as far as I am concerned. My motives for saying this perhaps are not unselfish in that he is filling a need here for someone in the younger age brackets . . . I honestly don't think he has caused any serious embarrassment or problem to us here.'

Fr Kerins replied on 6 December: 'I certainly would have no objections to his return to our Province. I would agree with you that he had a valid reason for going to Ireland . . .' And then this splendid human being instructs the Rector: 'It might be well if you ask [Sean] if he had to borrow the money for his travels. I would not want him to be saddled with a debt or have to approach his own Provincial [Charlie Shepherd] for funds in this situation . . .'

Then on 10 December (ironically, International Human Rights Day), Charlie Shepherd wrote a letter to Fr Kerins decrying my disobedience in 'presuming permission' and the harm I had done to both the English and Irish Provinces. I did not mind his attack on me. I was fair game. But Shepherd – abandoning even the slightest pretence at objectivity and fairness – took out his anger on my brother Jim. He complained: 'I have heard his brother, Fr Jim ([at] Hawkstone) has been in touch with Baltimore [Sacred Heart]. He is just as politically minded as Sean, but more cautious in the way he goes about things. The point of the matter is that at least 75% of this Province are heartily fed up with the two of them, especially with Sean, in the complete disregard they show for the feelings of the people of this country, where they received the opportunity of their priesthood and the chance of exercising it.'

And there you have it, the classic blackmail. You must not oppose England's injustice in Ireland lest you upset the feelings of the English people. So forget human rights. Forget democracy. Forget even the teaching of the Catholic Church on justice. Anything that disturbs order in Her Majesty's realm is sinful, inconsiderate and to be crushed. Remember that quote, given earlier, from Martin Luther King, Jr about how the greatest stumbling block to justice is the nice, respectable 'moderate', 'who is more devoted to 'order' than to justice; who prefers a negative peace which is the absence of tension to a positive peace which is the presence of justice'.

Contrast Fr Shepherd's myopic moral view with that of the greatest Redemptorist moral authority, after St Alphonus, the famed German moral theologian, Fr Bernard Haring: 'One of the most important criteria for determining a genuine priestly vocation is a deep rootedness in, and practice of, the virtue of non-violence. If strength and resolve to become witnesses to justice, peace and non-violence do not flow from our Eucharistic celebrations, then we must fearfully and sadly conclude that far too many priestly and lay Christian vocations are not sufficiently authentic.'[1]

As regards Fr Shepherd's gratuitous swipe at my brother: Jim was and is one of the most respected and productive members of the London Province and would go on to be himself elected Provincial, not just once but three times for a total of nine years (1990–1999).

The ever unflappable Fr Kerins replied to Shepherd on 18 December: 'Despite your own evident displeasure at this development in his life, I would have to frankly let you know that in my judgment the presumption on his part was valid.' Still Charlie Shepherd would not let it go. He must have thought the natives in the former colony (these United States of America) were getting uppity. On 17 January 1973 he replied to Fr Kerins: 'I do understand that in your country you have learned to live with protest, especially made in the name of conscience, which over here is still something of a novelty.' A novelty? Charlie was here personifying what Thomas Merton (1915–1968) – the Trappist monk who was at the time one of the most incisive spiritual thinkers and prophetic voices – deplored: 'One of the grave problems of religion in our time is posed by the almost total lack of protest on the part of religious people and clergy in the face of enormous social evils. It is not that these people are wicked or perverse . . . but simply that they are no longer fully capable of seeing and evaluating certain evils as they truly are: as crimes against God and as betrayals of the Christian ethic of love'.[2]

Fr Shepherd concluded his letter with a parting shot: 'Let us hope that Fr Sean won't want to dash over – on the grounds of conscience – to console other leaders of the IRA if the Dublin legislation puts more under restraint.'

This from the man who was supposed to be non-political!

This from the man who warned me never to express political opinions! The 'Dublin legislation' allowed the imprisonment of any suspected IRA member just on the word of a senior policeman. This type of double standard has, unfortunately, a long history in the Catholic Church, and ranks, in my mind, as almost a heresy. It is the belief that the politics with which the religious superior agrees – i.e. the status quo – is not politics at all but in effect, the divine order. Therefore, the Churchmen conclude (and always on behalf of God) that a person is only political if he opposes this 'order'.

An example comes to mind. In 1961, Fr Phil Berrigan (whom we will meet again in Chapter 8) was forbidden by the Superior of the St Joseph's Society of the Sacred Heart to be the first priest to become a Freedom Rider – the heroic Americans who risked their lives in the Deep South to challenge racial segregation in interstate travel, then still rampant despite having been declared illegal by the Supreme court in 1946.[3]

Can anyone now seriously argue that Fr Berrigan's Superior was right? That it was better for the Church that a priest would not give witness to God's love for the poor and oppressed by joining the noble Freedom Riders? That Superior was, I'm sure, a good man, but he was playing it safe, wanting to protect his Order from controversy and hassle. But, I'm bound to ponder, how did it come to pass that priests – who were supposed to give up everything and risk all for God's Kingdom on earth – became the ones not supposed to risk anything?

7

Formation of the Irish National Caucus

The imagination, courage and energy of an immigrant Northern Ireland Catholic priest made the dream of an Irish-American lobby a reality.

Joseph E. Thompson[1]

Once the hullabaloo over my visit to Ireland for the Mac Stíofáin hunger strike died down, I was back to my good work in the parish. I said Mass, preached, administered the sacraments, visited the sick, comforted the dying and instructed the young – all the ordinary, wonderful work of any parish.

But the Baltimore media kept me in the news. I gave interviews on TV, radio, spoke at colleges and to all sorts of groups.

The months sped by and it was soon the summer of 1973. I was entitled to go home on vacation, but gave it up to go on a speaking tour for Irish Northern Aid. On 8 July I went to Cleveland, Ohio; 10 July to Detroit, Michigan; 12 July to Chicago, Illinois; 14 July to St Paul, Minnesota; 15 July to Portland, Oregon; 17 July to San Francisco, California; 18 July to Los Angeles, California; 19 July to St Louis, Missouri; 21 July to Dayton, Ohio; 23 to 27 July back to New York to speak all over the city and State. I was so impressed and touched by the dedication of Irish Americans. And that feeling has never left me.

I wanted to put Baltimore on the map as an Irish city. All the publicity I had received greatly helped. But I wanted to get the Irish on the move. What better way than a march to the nation's capital, 45 miles away? So I announced we were going to have 'An Irish Freedom March' and then set to organising it with a small group of very enthusiastic men and women. The bets started immediately on who would be able to walk the full 45 miles.

And here is when I established a principle that would be the guiding one for the rest of my work with the Irish National Caucus. Others immediately thought I would be leading them to the British Embassy. No, I insisted, Irish Americans have no influence with the British Embassy but they do have with their own government. The proper role of Irish Americans is to change American foreign policy, to end the historic 'hands off Northern Ireland' policy. So the march would be to the White House to protest the silence of the American government about British oppression in Ireland. I immediately got opposition. The intrepid Jack McCarthy, who by now was a good friend, was on the phone in high panic: 'Fr Sean, Fr Sean, we cannot be seen to be criticising America. We should only criticise England.'

I explained that if we only criticised a foreign government, we would be giving a pass to all politicians in America, and they need never listen to us: 'Jack, if you were still living in County Cork, you could criticise England. What is the point of being an American unless you mobilise America to put pressure on England?' But Jack was really scared that the march would be seen as anti-American. And of course, he would be right, if marching on the White House was anti-American. (In the same way Jack was right to tell Republican speakers from Ireland not to confuse Americans by mentioning 'socialism' as they would be branded communist.) 'Jack, there is nothing more American than petitioning your government for help, and for having input into its foreign policy. We will march from Fort McHenry, birthplace of the star-spangled banner and site of a famous victory against the Brits, with both American and Irish flags flying proudly for 45 miles. I will be the only one with the bullhorn, calling out the question: "What do we want?" And all of you will respond: "England out of Ireland." What better message, Jack, to carry to the White House?'

I could feel Jack was softening up. And I clinched it by asking him to be in charge of supplying American flags. He was delighted. It was as if he was back in his youth and being given his first assignment to go and fight the Black and Tans, 'like the boys from the County Cork'. And that great-hearted Irish patriot went on to deliver two busloads of people for the last leg of the march to the White House.

I invited Bishop Thomas Drury of Corpus Christi to attend one of the planning meetings – a small group of about ten. He urged us to see the march as a pilgrimage that the Irish should be proud to march in, 'even with pebbles in their shoes'. Years later, when I got my FBI file, through the Freedom of Information Act, the exact quote from the Bishop is filed in the report, by the informant at the meeting. Needless to say, with my background, I was totally conscious that there would be informers everywhere – FBI, British government, Irish government, etc. I was equally aware that there was nothing I could do about it, except to make sure they would never gain control of my work.

The plan was to split the journey into two. We would stay overnight in Laurel, Maryland, the halfway point, in St Mary's church hall, sleeping on the floor in sleeping bags. The pastor, an Irish-born priest, insisted that I would use the spare room in the rectory. I was a bit concerned about this, as I did not want it to affect the morale of the 'troops' – seeing the leader defecting to a comfortable bed while they slept on the floor. But once they all assured me that I should accept the courtesy of the parish priest, I agreed I would.

We had invited my brother Frank to speak at the rally outside the White House. One morning my sister Alice woke me with a phone call: 'Frankie has been shot.' Alice had forgotten how back home when people said someone was shot, it meant shot dead. And for one terrible moment, that's what I thought she was telling me. 'But, he's okay, just a slight wound in the leg,' she added. I'll let Frankie tell the story himself:

> At about 10.30 p.m. on the night of 18 September 1973, I
> was travelling home alone. I was not paying any particular
> attention to road users behind me. As I turned left off the
> main road, I heard my car being hit. Road works were
> taking place at the time, and I immediately thought that I
> had hit loose stones at the side of the road, and I did the one
> thing that I should not have done, I stopped and got out of
> my car. It was only then that I realised that I had been shot.
> As I turned left, the car behind me carried on, effectively
> creating the two long sides of a triangle. The gunman was
> obviously an expert. He fired three shots, two of which hit
> the car and one of which hit the front of our new home.
> One of the shots pierced the driver's door, and shot me just
> where my right thigh made contact with the seat, causing an
> unpleasant but essentially a superficial flesh wound.[2]

I assumed that Frankie would not be able to travel to Washington.
But he did, marching a good distance, with limp and walking
stick, which added to the urgency and drama of what we were
about.

The Washington Post gave the march reasonable coverage under
the headline 'Irish Americans Urged to Enlist Aid of Countrymen
Against British': 'With sore feet and soaring enthusiasm, 250
persons ended a 45-mile "Irish Freedom Walk" at Lafayette
Park yesterday, where they were urged by [Frank McManus] a
member of the British Parliament to enlist the support of other
Irish Americans in their quest to oust British troops from Ulster.'
(Sunday 15 October 1973).

The following year, as promised, we had another Irish
Freedom March, this time to the British Embassy. The Embassy
sent word that they would receive a delegation, but I refused to
accept their offer, which was meant to co-opt the march and
show how reasonable they were.

Any chance I could get I would go into Washington to speak

to Members of Congress to tell them about the great injustices Her Majesty's government was inflicting on the Catholics in Northern Ireland. As I walked through the Halls of Congress, I would run into all sorts of ethnic groups lobbying for their homelands – Jewish Americans, African Americans, the Poles, the Greeks, etc. But there was one group noticeably absent. And they were one of the largest, best educated, affluent and politically connected: Irish Americans.

I just could not believe it. There was no Irish lobby or office on Capitol Hill. I knew that would have to change. In the meantime, my immediate priority was to get Congress to officially show concern for the violation of human rights in Northern Ireland.

One of the very first people who offered her help and expertise was Bernadette O'Reilly (later McAuliffe) whose parents were from County Cavan. Bernadette was the personal secretary for Silvio O. Conte (R–MA) and, therefore, was very familiar with the workings of Congress. (Just a note of explanation here, US Senators and Representatives – Congressmen/women – in the Houses of Congress are identified as 'R' or 'D' (Republican or Democrat), followed by the state they represent: Conte was from Massachusetts.) Fred O'Brien, an attorney with US Customs also offered to help.

One of our first efforts was to arrange for brother Frank to be called to testify before the House Foreign Relations Subcommittee on Human Rights, chaired by Congressman Donald M. Fraser (D–MN). We met with the Director of the Subcommittee. He explained that the practice was not to have someone testify for a foreign government: 'Don't worry,' I said, 'Frankie will not be testifying for, but *against*, the British government.' That sealed the deal. Then we convinced him to invite Ruairí Ó Brádaigh, then president of Sinn Féin (like Dave O'Connell, Ruairí unfortunately would split from Gerry Adams in 1986 and form Republican Sinn Féin, of which he is now president. Ruairí was in the IRA with my brother Patrick and they soldiered together so I have always had respect for him).

The hearing took place on 9 October 1973. Frank and Ó

Brádaigh gave powerful testimonies – much to the shock and chagrin of both the British and Irish Embassies. Congressman Conte and Tip O'Neill, then Democratic Majority Leader, held a reception in their honour, which Bishop Drury also attended. Before the reception, Tip chaired a press conference with Frank and Ó Brádaigh. He complained bitterly that he never got information about the Troubles from the Irish Embassy and promised 'if the good Father [yours truly]' kept him informed, he would do everything he could to help. That, of course, was further proof to me that an Irish lobby had to be launched on Capitol Hill.

By now I was getting to know Tip quite well. He was very friendly, in the way all Catholic Boston politicians are to priests. I remember later when he called a number of Congressmen together in his office for a publicity photograph for the Irish National Caucus, he put his hand on my right shoulder and said to the late Congressman Joe Moakley (D–MA): 'Look at those big shoulders, Joe. He's got them from loading guns in the coffins they ship to Ireland.' And they had a great laugh at that. Personally, I resented it but did not say anything. I have always hated frivolous stereotyping of the Troubles – a sure sign of superficiality, with no sensitivity for the deep pain and anguish.

But I would quickly learn a basic Washington law – 'For every action, there is an equal and opposite reaction'. It may be Newton's third law of motion, but it is Capitol Hill's first law. Our initial successful foray in Congress would now force the Irish Embassy to organise against us. Isn't that ironic? They had not been lobbying to get the Congress to put pressure on the British, but they would lobby against us. And of course, so would the British Embassy, but it would let the Irish Embassy lead the public charge, as would be later admitted by Ambassador Peter Jay, son-in-law of James Callaghan, Britain's Labour Prime Minister from 1976 to 1979.

Tip would later, as Speaker of the House, give me the cold shoulder but in the meantime, the Irish Embassy provided him with the perfect cover. He would put that big hand on my shoulder and say, 'Fr Sean, how can I be more patriotic than the Prime Minister of Ireland?' My response was always the same, 'That wouldn't be hard, Tip.'

But anyway, buoyed up by the success of the Congressional hearing, I knew I had to give a name to the work I was doing, which was simply not being done by any other Irish group, no matter how worthy. My basic conviction was that the primary role of Irish Americans should be to influence American foreign policy on Ireland – to change the long-standing 'hands off Ireland because we must not offend the British'. My operating principle was: 'Human Rights for Ireland is an American Issue'. It became one of the first mottos of the Irish National Caucus. Our job would not be to raise funds for Ireland or to relate to a particular group, party or government in Ireland. And we would most certainly not be controlled by any entity in Ireland, North or South. In other words, we would have 'no foreign principal'.

My initial thought was to get others to head up the new organisation, but I quickly realised that if I did not do it, it would not be done. So on my birthday, 6 February 1974, I founded the Irish National Caucus and signed up as officers Bishop Drury, Bernadette O'Reilly and Fred O'Brien. Bernadette did invaluable work for us until the opening of the Caucus office on Capitol Hill on 10 December 1978.

Amazingly, some books have said the Caucus' origins were unclear, yet no organisation ever had such clear origins. I founded it, and put out a press release announcing it. The late Jack Holland in his book *The American Connection* states, 'Though the Caucus's beginnings are a matter of dispute, even among its own members . . .' Strangely, Holland, who had taken up residence in the US by that time, never called me to ask how the Caucus started. Even more oddly, in over thirty years of writing about Irish American activity, Holland never called me except once – on the death of Seán Mac Stíofáin in 2001. Holland then proceeds to make the ridiculous claim that, 'Mike Flannery, the founding father of Irish Northern Aid . . . was among those involved in its formation'.[3] Nothing could be further from the truth. Indeed, Flannery was always opposed to the formation of the Irish National Caucus, feeling that there was no need for any other Irish organisation because Irish Northern Aid could do it all – something that most evidently was not true.

I then turned my attention to the AOH (Ancient Order of Hibernians), which by this time was very familiar with me. Up until 1974, the AOH was only nominally involved in the Northern Ireland issue. It followed the Dublin government line, which was 'do not support the IRA and do not criticise the British lest it give aid and comfort to the IRA'. A non-policy, which in fact aided and comforted the British government.

But there were many members of the AOH who vehemently disagreed with this appeasement of the British government, and they wanted me to 'convert' the AOH. In 1974, two AOH stalwarts, the late Dave Burke from Massachusetts and Liam Murphy from New York, arranged for me to address the AOH National Board meeting in Washington, DC in advance of the National Convention in Anaheim, California. I spoke very strongly, denouncing the weakness of the Irish government and urged them as proud Americans to stand up for American values in Ireland. 'I believe,' I told them, 'that Ireland too has the right to be one nation under God with liberty and justice for all.'

Dave Burke and Liam Murphy were ecstatic – they could see the AOH change before their eyes as I spoke. Jack Keane, who was running to be the new AOH president, was particularly moved, and immediately proposed that I would be invited to give the keynote address at the National Convention. His proposal was unanimously accepted.

Reminiscing on those days, Jack Keane, on 30 May 2008, said: 'At that time I was trying to get the AOH to take a firmer stand on the North of Ireland. The perfect instrument came along in the person of Father McManus. He electrified the National Board Meeting and then the entire Convention. From that moment we made sure the AOH would be intensely involved.'[4]

Jack Keane was elected president. He appointed Bishop Drury to be the National Chaplain and appointed me Deputy National

Chaplain. It would be safe to say that now the AOH had indeed been officially converted. Liam became the editor of the AOH paper, *Hibernian Digest,* and kept up a steady Irish Republican drumbeat. Dave went on to become, without doubt, one of the most dedicated and productive leaders the AOH ever had. Tom McNabb, New York, would follow Jack Keane as president. Since that time, the AOH has retained an activist and excellent position on Northern Ireland.

On 28 September 1974, Jack, in keeping with a promise made to me if he were elected AOH president, called a meeting in New York of all the major Irish organisations and they unanimously endorsed the Irish National Caucus.

However, while I appreciated their endorsement, I made it clear that the Irish National Caucus would continue to be an independent organisation – that they had endorsed us but we had not endorsed them, and we would not be getting involved in their internal business (or feuds). I also made it crystal clear that while they could have reasonable input, they could not control us in any way. I knew, of course, there would be immediate attempts to destabilise and marginalise us – by the Irish and British governments, and maybe the American government. I knew what to expect – agents, informers, 'useful idiots' [those who would be helping the British without even knowing it], malcontents, people who simply did not like me or people whom, through my own fault, I rubbed the wrong way. But hey, welcome to Irish American politics!

Later the following year, on 18 February 1975, the Executive Council of the AFL-CIO (American Federation of Labor and Congress of Industrial Organizations) endorsed the Irish National Caucus after I addressed a luncheon meeting of about 300 Union members in Bal Harbour, Florida. The then president, the famed George Meany, sent Lane Kirkland, Secretary Treasurer, to deliver the endorsement.

8

Caucus Baptised in Blood at British Embassy

To sin by silence when they should protest makes cowards of men.
Abraham Lincoln

Organising politically did not mean that I would cease my activist 'street politics'. Both were needed – and necessitated by developing circumstances. I decided that the first action of the Irish National Caucus should be symbolically at the British Embassy.

In Baltimore, I got to know the late Phil Berrigan (1923–2002), the former Josephite priest and anti-war activist, and his wife Liz McAllister who had founded Jonah House. Phil was one of the most remarkable men I have ever met. He was a bigger, better-looking version of Paul Newman. I've never known a man with such physical presence. I confided in them that I wanted to do a non-violent action at the British Embassy in Washington, and I needed their advice on how to pour blood all over the premises, and how to contain things in a non-violent manner so that nobody would get hurt – except the pride of Her Majesty's government.

I could not have consulted a more wise or seasoned source than Phil. He tutored me in the technique – and non-violent resistance is most certainly a technique as well as a principle. He explained it was vital for me at all times to maintain control of the situation – through the unique calmness that descends on one if non-violence is done correctly. I had explained to him that the British tended to lead with their fists, and I was concerned that things could spiral out of control, and lead to one of my group being shot by Embassy security or the many British agents housed there. Phil explained that the more I knew about the layout of the British Embassy the better, so as to minimise surprises or confusion.

One of his group, a mother of a four-year-old boy, kindly offered 'to case the joint' – to visit the British Embassy and give me an intelligence report. When she visited the Embassy, she would prod her son to send him to different corners of the embassy so that she would have an excuse to follow him. What a gal! And she didn't have one drop of Irish blood. She then drew a perfect sketch of the layout of the inside of the Embassy.

Now about the blood. How were we to get it? 'Leave that to me,' said Phil, 'I know a doctor who does that for us when needed.'

The doctor drew two pints of blood from me, on two separate occasions. A local man gave another pint. And the late Mitch Snyder (1946–1990) gave one pint. Mitch, a Vietnam vet, had been converted (back to active Catholicism) in Danbury Prison, Connecticut, by Phil Berrigan and his Jesuit brother, Dan. And he would go on to dedicate his life to the poor and homeless in Washington as the driving force in the Community for Creative Non-Violence (CCNV). In a celebrated hunger strike he forced President Reagan to hand over a federal building for the homeless, now called Mitch Snyder Place. In 1986, Martin Sheen, also a disciple of the Berrigan brothers, would make a TV biopic about him, *Samaritan: The Mitch Snyder Story*. Sadly, this great man who had 'given his blood for Ireland', hanged himself on 5 July 1990.

I decided I needed only three colleagues, as anything more than four people would be a bit unwieldy. I felt there should be two men and two women. And I knew I would have to pick carefully and diligently. They would have to be totally reliable and prepared to go to prison, maybe for several years, without regrets or recriminations. I was proud of my choice: the late Maureen Armstrong of New York, from County Monaghan, a grandmother in her late fifties; Joe Mitchell, sixty, a warehouseman of Queens, NY, from County Meath; and Mary Baggarly, twenty-eight, of Maryland, a housewife and mother of two, from the Bogside, Derry. A fiercely and fearlessly strong Irish patriot, Mary was a 'Stickie'[1] when I met her, but I converted her from the error of her ways.

We were all set. But there was no point in having a protest in the British Embassy if nobody knew about it. So I alerted trusted reporters, telling them they could enter a few minutes after us.

At exactly 11.58 a.m., Friday 24 April 1974, Jack O'Brien of Maryland (who also had been a Stickie until I converted him), drove the four of us to the front of the British Embassy (Chancery, technically; the Embassy is the residence of the Ambassador, a bit further down Massachusetts Avenue, NW).

I jumped out of the car, and immediately a young man headed towards me. I thought he was on to us. In an exaggerated display of coolness I looked up at the sky and said, 'What a beautiful day.' 'Indeed,' the young man replied with a smile. We headed for the big glass doors, and again I was alarmed as another young man hurried to the door – but only to open it. 'Good morning, lovely day,' I said and with that all four of us made it safely in.

Phil Berrigan had drilled it into me to immediately 'disarm' the first point of contact – to engage the guy at the security desk in a friendly, one-to-one, eye-to-eye dialogue. I headed straight for the desk, while the other three remained by the inside of the door. 'Good afternoon,' I beamed, ''Tis a grand day.'

'Indeed it is,' he replied.

'My name is Father McManus.'

'Oh, yes, Father.'

'I'm based in a parish in Baltimore.'

He folded his arms and looked very interested.

'I have come with some friends to the Embassy . . .'

'Yes, good.'

'To express our concern about Northern Ireland.'

That changed everything. He unfolded his arms, shot up in his chair and grabbed the telephone. He had the phone up to about his shoulder when I positioned our statement right in front of his face, and urged, 'Please read this' – never once breaking the eye contact that Berrigan had warned me was so crucial.

He put the phone down and read the opening sentence: 'Our action – the pouring of blood . . .' His mouth fell open. He jumped to his feet, put one foot up on the chair behind him and held the arms of the chair with both hands and sank back staring at me. 'Just a moment, just a moment,' he gasped and grabbed the phone. I leaned over towards him and in my best Confessional manner I whispered: 'Look, it is very important that you remain cool, otherwise you will cause panic. Remain calm. Do not be afraid. We are non-violent people. We will not hurt anybody, I assure you.'

I gently motioned with both hands for him to sit down and he did, never taking his eyes off me, in sort of a trance. Berrigan and his people told me to be prepared for that to happen. I then told the man I was going to open my coat and for him not to be afraid. 'In this pocket,' I said, 'there is a bottle, which I am now going to slowly take out.' His eyes followed my hands. 'In the bottle is some blood. My friends and I are going to pour blood all over the Embassy. But stay calm and do not scare people.'

I then turned to Joe, Mary and Maureen and gave them the signal to begin pouring blood.

And then for the first time, I think, the man realised what was happening. He jumped up and shouted: 'Stop there, sir. That is forbidden. I am sorry I cannot allow you. This is an Embassy.' As I turned away from him, he shouted, 'Get someone. It's the Irish.' (You're damn right, I thought to myself. It is the Irish.)

It is amazing how quickly blood diffuses and spreads. Squirted methodically from 'squeeze' bottles, Mary and I had the entire front of the glass building covered in no time. (The night before I had called Mary to express concern that we did not have enough blood and asked her to make some blood-substitute – ketchup, etc. – and that we would explain to the media that we had made some extra blood substitute as a backup.)

Meanwhile Maureen and Joe were doing their thing, as planned. The *Baltimore Sun*'s reporter, whom I had brought with us, would describe Maureen as, '. . . neat as a pin, no make-up, and no nonsense grandmother'. Joe, he wrote, was 'a soft-spoken law-abiding . . . man with a steady hand and a narrow tie'.[2]

Both stood in the middle of the Embassy holding a Union Jack, which Mary had bought the night before for $15. 'That hurt,' she told the *Baltimore Sun*. Maureen and Joe proceeded to pour blood all over the Union Jack, which for centuries has been soaked in Irish blood. Suddenly, the head of the chancery, John Graham, probably in his fifties, charged Maureen from the back, bowled her over, grabbed the flag and ran part of the way up the stairway, stopped and turned around, clutching the flag to his chest. It was a cowardly, violent British assault on a non-violent Irish grandmother.

As Maureen lay moaning on the ground, we knelt beside her and I grabbed hold of all of them and said, 'Remember, we had vowed nothing would make us retaliate. If we do, we will destroy our entire protest.' We had role-played and mentally disciplined ourselves that no matter what happened we would not be violent. We helped Maureen to her feet, and continued our business, calmly and serenely.

Mary and I opened the glass doors and poured blood on the outside and on the doorsteps. As I stepped back in, a distinguished grey-haired man came towards me to usher me out. 'You can't, you can't possibly . . . this is the British Embassy,' he said. I gently patted him on the shoulder and ever so soothingly said, 'You do not understand. This is a non-violent protest and it is precisely to do this that we came.' He stared at me in complete astonishment. Then he saw that Mary was still outside, so he ran and held the doors closed against her. I tapped him on the shoulder, and with complete authority in my voice, ordered, 'Excuse me, let the lady into the Embassy.' And incredibly, he did. He looked at me apologetically and said, 'Okay, okay', and then walked away. Again, the amazing power of non-violence!

When we had finished pouring the blood, we calmly

reassembled in the middle of the Embassy. We quietly stood there while all around us the Embassy was in chaos. A feeling of complete harmony and tranquility descended upon me. It was a beautiful moment, which the Berrigan people had told me to expect if our motives and techniques were pure. The other three, I could tell, were experiencing the same serenity, although flushed and smiling from our success.

We waited for the confrontation. It had been agreed that I alone would do the talking, no matter what happened, so we could contain the situation in a disciplined manner – another essential ingredient of the successful non-violent action. If each of us were tricked into speaking to different members of the Embassy the coherence of our protest would be shattered.

While we waited, Embassy people started pouring out from everywhere. Employees were hanging over the banisters of the big spiral staircase in the lobby, staring down. Dozens of people began forming a semicircle around us. In a calm but loud voice (well trained in Hawkstone for the parish missions in Britain) I called out. 'Would you all be quiet, please?' There was instant silence, a palpable hush. 'Please do not be alarmed. This is a non-violent protest. We come in peace. We will not do you any harm.' They all stared in astonishment. Then a pompous little man in a dark suit pushed his way through the crowd. His face was deathly white and he was bubbling with venom, 'Mister, are you in charge?' He fairly spat at me. I calmly demanded, again with authority, 'Who are you?' It had the expected result. He was astonished at the temerity of this intruder asking him who he was. He prodded both hands to his chest and in complete exasperation spluttered, 'Who . . . who am I? I'm the head of security.'

'Fine,' I replied, 'I will talk to you. My name is Fr McManus. This is Joe Mitchell, this is Mary Baggarly, and this is the lady whom one of the Embassy officials assaulted, Maureen Armstrong.' The three courteously nodded.

'There was no assault here,' shouted an official to my left. 'Yes, there was,' said a reporter, 'and we have a photo to prove it.' Then an Embassy official tried to grab the camera. 'Take your f***ing hands of my camera, buddy,' the reporter said with explosive force and for a moment I thought there was going to be a fistfight. I remember thinking: wouldn't it be ironic if, after all our non-violent role-playing, the press starts a riot in the Embassy?

I turned back to the little security man who was wailing away, 'I have got a responsibility . . . I have got to do my duty.' I said reassuringly and softly: 'We understand; no need to give explanations. Of course, do your duty and we will do ours.' He just could not handle it and was going to start wailing again. 'No, no,' I said, 'it's all right, be calm, there is no need to worry. This is a non-violent protest and we will not harm anyone.'

He made an obvious effort to control himself, then very officiously pulled out a little notebook and said to Mary, 'Okay, madam, what's your address in Ireland?' Do not answer that, Mary,' I directed. He almost pleadingly said, 'But I've got to have . . . I've got to have . . .' I gently leaned towards him and said, 'We are not answering any of your questions like that. We will answer all questions at the appropriate time and place.' The poor guy just gave up. He put his little book into his little pocket and walked off, dejected and defeated.

An ashen-faced individual was hovering around the periphery of the semicircle going nuts. 'He is sheltering behind his collar,' he was screaming. I turned to him and demanded, 'Do you want to speak to me?' It stopped him dead. Then he started up again, arms flailing: 'He's a priest. He does not have to tell the truth.'

'Do you work here?' I asked. 'Yes,' he hissed. 'It appears you are giving vent to religious prejudice, which ill becomes the British Embassy. And how could I be sheltering behind my collar when I'm completely at your mercy?' He stared at me in total exasperation and then darted off.

Then I began to address the crowd again: I realise that we have caused you embarrassment,' I began. 'We are not embarrassed,' someone shouted from my right. I turned around. A tall, well-groomed young man was glowering at me. 'What nationality are you?' he asked. I quietly stared him in eye, and wondered if the same tactic would work again. 'Who are you?' I asked. The simple question stunned him by its impertinence. I could see he was trying to regain his poise. 'I am Baker Bates, the Embassy information officer,' he said. 'What are you doing here?'

I replied we were conducting a non-violent protest against British mistreatment of political prisoners and the assassination campaign of the British Army. Thinking he had a trump card, he shot back, in a perfect English accent, 'I am from Northern Ireland. Have you ever been to Ireland?'

(There was I thinking the British Embassy would know all about me!) 'My home is in British-occupied Ireland,' I conversationally replied. He was not expecting that. 'Well, it's a pity you just missed John Hume,' he sniffed. 'Was this done to offset the good John Hume did here? Did you know he was here?'

We, of course, had no idea Hume had just been there and I told him so. He very illogically responded, 'So you're saying this was not a planned protest?' I replied, 'Not at all. It was a very planned protest.'

'Yes, indeed,' he shouted. 'You even brought your own hired press.' Then whirling on his heels, he snapped, 'Okay, Jack, you have made your point.'

'Thank you,' I replied, 'you are most courteous.'

Then I turned to the next official, a young man with fairly long, well-styled hair, who clearly wanted to have a go at me. 'Now it's your turn,' I said to him. He let loose, 'I suppose you also brought rubber bullets with you, Fr McManus?' (I had shown rubber bullets on TV all over America to illustrate that they were not harmless little pellets but six-inch projectiles of hard rubber that had killed children and blinded people in Northern Ireland.)

'So you know me?' I said.

'Yes, I've seen you on TV and I read the *Irish People* every week,' he said. Then he, too, started up about John Hume: 'John Hume says that all the money of the Irish Northern Aid Committee goes to the IRA. It all goes direct to Joe Cahill.' I asked, 'What has the IRA and Northern Aid got to do with this protest?' He replied, 'This is an Irish Northern Aid protest.'

'Please don't speculate. Read our statement and you will see what it is.' He would have none of it. 'You are the spokesman for Irish Northern Aid,' he persisted. 'No, I am not,' I said. 'But I've heard you speak on their behalf,' he shouted. 'Yes, I have spoken on their behalf, but I'm not their spokesman,' I tried to reason.

He finally agreed to read our statement. When he came to the part about political prisoners, he went on again about John Hume. (The British Embassy for years always paraded out John Hume to cover up their misdeeds.) 'John Hume says there are no political prisoners in Northern Ireland.' I looked him straight in the eye and earnestly said: 'I am prepared to discuss Northern Ireland with someone in the Embassy who knows something about it, but you quite obviously know nothing about it.' The gentleness with which I said it puzzled him, I could tell. I kept calmly looking him in the eye until he felt uncomfortable and finally walked away.

Baker Bates came back, a little bit more in control of himself: 'Fr McManus, you have made your statement. Now why don't you leave?'

This was unexpected. And the Berrigan people had warned me about the unexpected, as that is when things can unravel. We had expected to be immediately arrested, and clearly the Embassy did not want that. I needed to play for time so as to be able to talk to my three colleagues. I glanced admiringly around the fine building, and said to Baker Bates, 'I've never been in the British Embassy before. I think I will stay a while.'

'So it's a sit-in, is it?' he snapped, and took off like a scalded cat. I huddled with Joe, Mary and Maureen and explained we would have to do a sit-in, which we had not planned, because they were not going to have us arrested. I told them to do exactly as I did.

The Executive Protective Service, the uniformed branch of the Secret Service, soon arrived. The moment the lead officer saw me he smiled broadly. I immediately knew he was Irish Catholic. I told them that we were concluding our non-violent protest by a sit-in. We would not resist in anyway but they would have to carry us out. I then signalled to Maureen, Joe and Mary to sit down. The smiling officer said to me as he and another lifted me off the floor, 'I had a nice pint of Guinness in your country, Father, a few months ago.'

'Which part?' I asked. 'Mayo,' he grunted as he held me. 'My mother is from Mayo and my father is from Galway.'

It was only in the police station that we realised the extent to which Maureen had been hurt. Her left arm and back were badly bruised by the body-slam of the Embassy official. She did not want to go to hospital and leave Mary in prison by herself. But we insisted.

We refused to sign the 'citation form', which would have entitled us to get out. Instead, in solidarity with the political prisoners, we spent the night in prison – Mary in the Women's House of Detention and Joe and me in the DC Central Cell Block.

I got on the metal bed, no blanket, put my shoes under my head and slept soundly throughout the night. The following morning, I was handed a sandwich through the bars of my cell. It was just a piece of ham between dry bread but no food ever tasted so good (I had not eaten for several hours before being arrested and was now starving).

Afterwards I was moved from my cell to a holding area – a huge, cage-like structure with dozens of young black men. I think I was the only white man in the cage (although I never think of myself as white, just Irish). They were astonished to see me, in my black suit and clerical collar: 'Hey, Preacher-man/Reverend/ Father, what you in for?' they asked as they swarmed around me, all excited. Before arraignment, I was greeted by a nice surprise, a press release from the Fellowship of Reconciliation, one of the oldest Christian non-violent movements. It read:

> The following is the text of the statement that two leading representatives of the organization Fellowship of Reconciliation (F.O.R.) issued in response to the non-violent blood-protest that Fr Sean McManus led at the British Embassy on Friday, April 24. The statement was hand delivered to Fr McManus while he was in prison.

> We British visitors to Washington welcome such dramatic non-violent protest against the military policy of the British Government in Ireland. Blood given for justice in Ireland is a supremely good investment.

This statement was released by Rev. David Harding, a Methodist Minister, who is Secretary General for Fellowship of Reconciliation in Britain; and by Mr Guy Otten, who is a member of the International Executive of Fellowship of Reconciliation.

Later that morning, we were arraigned, charged with 'protesting within five hundred feet of an Embassy'. The British Embassy did not press charges and the judge told us we were free to go.

We were well pleased by our good work. It sublimely confirmed to me the transcendent power of non-violent action – and demonstrated that the British government cannot simply handle it, as Gandhi knew so well.

All the News That's Fit to Print – Or Not

In wartime, truth is so precious that she should always be attended by a bodyguard of lies.
Winston Churchill

My arrest at the British Embassy – plus all the previous publicity and consciousness-raising my activity had generated – gained huge support for my work all across the United States. Therefore, when I stressed the need for the new approach of the Irish National Caucus, people listened and trusted my judgment. Furthermore, the new approach could not be dismissed as being 'soft' because, as the action at the British Embassy proved, we were prepared to go to prison. I was, of course, aware that my actions could be seen as 'radical' – a real taboo among many Irish Americans. Being 'radical' was almost as bad as being a communist. So I had to walk a fine line, which some very conservative folk believed I crossed often.

But without resources and money, I knew of no other way to spread the word. One had to break the unbelievable conspiracy of silence in the media and US Congress.

To give one passing example of media bias: After my brother Frank was shot, *The New York Times* reported that he had been shot by the IRA because he was not sufficiently militant. Now, how do you suppose they got that ridiculous piece of information? I called the *Times* from Sacred Heart in Baltimore and asked to speak to one of the editors responsible for publishing the item. I began by protesting the story and he countered by saying, 'What would a priest in Baltimore know about the incident?' I told him I was Frank's brother. He countered by saying their information was good and that they were standing by the story. If such a prestigious newspaper as *The New York Times* can be so obtuse on Northern Ireland, what could one expect from the general American media that simply kept churning out the same old British line?

In fact, my very first letter to the American media was to the Baltimore Archdiocesan newspaper, *The Catholic Review*. The well-known priest, sociologist and novelist, Fr Andrew Greely, had written in his column that the IRA was in business for the thrill of killing and being killed. This from a man who prided himself on his Irishness and knowledge of all things Irish. Just how do you suppose he came by that conviction? Years later, Greely would become an outright defender of the IRA. A few years ago, I met him on two occasions at the White House for St Patrick's Day celebrations. On both occasions I reminded him of his ridiculous letter and each time he totally ignored what I said, making absolutely no response.

And in speaking of *The Catholic Review*, I recently checked its website where it reviews its own history and its 'campaign against the Ku Klux Klan in the 1920s or its calls for justice in Central America in the 1980s'. What about justice for Catholics in Northern Ireland? No campaign for them! So it was not just the secular media that was complicit in British oppression of Catholics, so were the Catholic media, with some exceptions – and so were the US Catholic bishops, with very few exceptions. More of that later.

So with that sort of media indifference, what could one do? If the American media were not going to announce the news, I would have to announce it myself. A case in point: on 15 October 1974, the political prisoners – incarcerated without charge or trial – burnt Long Kesh to the ground in protest at the inhumane conditions. That did receive media attention, but the resulting British punitive action, including forcing the prisoners to sleep in the open air, covered only by sheets of polythene did not. I tried, to no avail, to get the media to cover that inhumanity. So I decided if they were not going to announce it, I would do it for them.

At that time, ABC nationwide news was announced live, at least in part, from its studio in Washington, DC by Howard K. Smith. I decided to interrupt the live newscast and tell America, all 100 million of the estimated viewers, about the mistreatment of prisoners in Long Kesh.

Again, I decided four was a good number for the action. And, again, I turned to Mary of the Bogside – Mary Baggarly of British Embassy fame. I also recruited a young woman from Baltimore, Kathy Fogarty, who, with her father, had become very active. The third person was Sean Walsh of Washington who had recently joined the Irish National Caucus. Naturally, we had to 'case the joint'. In particular I had to know exactly when Howard K. Smith was broadcasting live otherwise my protest would not be carried.

Days well in advance, I went to the ABC studio and introduced myself to the appropriate persons. I told them that I was visiting from Ireland, where I was in religious broadcasting, and I wanted to learn from the real professionals of ABC, and could I perhaps come back and observe from within the studio how these great experts did it? They graciously accepted. While I was talking to them, Sean Walsh was casing the joint, even using his credit card to slip the lock to enter the broadcasting room, then not in use. He even made a date with the young receptionist who would have to buzz us in when we came back for our action. He took her to dinner the night before the action.

On Tuesday 22 October 1974, the four of us headed to ABC News. They recognised Sean and me, and brought us in. At first I was escorted into the glass control booth, with all the TV monitors, etc. I was initially concerned because it cordoned me off from the actual studio where Howard K. Smith was seated. But I quickly realised it was a blessing as it enabled me to know exactly what was going on, with the very helpful control-team giving me a blow-by-blow account. Otherwise, I would have no idea when Smith was going out live. The control team told me there was a commercial break coming up and that right after it, Howard K. Smith would be broadcasting. I made my move, quickly telling my three colleagues to follow me. I walked into the actual broadcast room. A technician looked momentarily alarmed, I put my finger to my lips, in the silence gesture, and nodded reassuringly that I was just going to stand nearby. He nodded back, understandingly.

I was now in a perfect position to see and to interrupt Howard K. Smith. I had given the others the exact same sentence which each of us would say, knowing we would have only a split second to get it out before we were cut off.

At exactly 6:16 p.m. I mounted the raised dais from which Howard K. Smith was reading the news live. I walked right behind him (and felt guilty at the way the poor man jumped off his chair in real shock) and proceeded to say my lines: 'Will someone please help? The British are torturing political prisoners in Northern Ireland.' Every word went out as clear as a bell, all across the United States. I then moved on, as planned, to let the three others walking behind in single file, say the same words. But they were cut off, as I feared they would.

The allegedly unflappable media went flapping like crazy. These folk, who demand that others keep their cool under the most trying circumstances, were like headless chickens. I walked out of the main newsroom, to wait for the police, reassuringly holding out my hands saying, 'Don't worry. This is non-violent protest. We will cause no harm.'

A small guy with longish hair, in his late thirties, and obviously in some position of authority in ABC, tried to confront me, saying he was not going to let me leave. I told him not to worry: we were not leaving but waiting for the police because we wanted to be arrested in completion of our non-violent act.

He then got a bit hysterical, screaming at me that I was protected by my collar. I quietly asked him if it did not occur to him that my collar might be protecting him. 'What do you mean?'

he incredulously asked. 'Well, if I were not a priest, I might have punched you out for your abusiveness,' I gently responded. That seemed to steady him up.

Then a group gathered around, all complaining about our action. I asked which of them were reporters as opposed to technicians, producers, etc. A few indicated they were. I then made the point that the first question a real newsperson should be asking is, 'Why did we do it?', not just berating us for doing it.

I further explained that we were fed up with the news always presenting the problem in Northern Ireland as a senseless conflict between Protestants and Catholics with no explanation of the vicious role of the British government. One newsman defiantly said ABC did not present the problem in simple Protestant–Catholic terms. And just as he said it, Howard K. Smith stormed among us, incandescent with rage. He roared at me: 'What are you – Protestant or Catholic?' I gave a knowing sweep of my hand to the previous newsman who had just been speaking and said: 'The top ABC man has just confirmed my point.' Smith rounded on me, 'What the hell does that mean? What are you talking about?' I explained to him that the other newsman had denied my charge that ABC presents the Northern Ireland problem as just a religious squabble. 'And Mr Smith,' I said, 'you just proved my argument.' Then he spluttered that he gave money to both Protestant and Catholic charities. 'Very commendable,' I said, 'but that is not the point. You have not exposed British government violation of human rights in Northern Ireland.' He waved his hands dismissively and stormed off to his inner sanctum.

The police finally arrived, a hefty black officer of about forty in the lead. He immediately gave me a huge smile. He's Catholic, I said to myself. 'Okay, okay, settle down, you all. What's going on?' I waited for ABC to explain what happened. The officer then inquired if the intruders had a knife or anything or attacked anybody. No, he was told. Then he burst into a huge smile and asked what all the commotion was about.

He then turned to me, 'Father, what's going on?'

'Well, Officer, in the tradition of Martin Luther King, Jr (here he broke into the biggest smile I had ever seen), we have done a non-violent action to protest ABC covering up British oppression in Northern Ireland. We interrupted Mr Smith's live broadcast. And in the spirit of Martin Luther King, Jr, we waited for you to come and arrest us.'

It was clear that the officer was enjoying all of this. 'Do you want me to arrest the good Father?' he asked the ABC officials. They huddled for a moment. 'No,' was their firm answer. 'Okay, Padre,' said the smiling cop, 'you and your friends are free to go.' And so ended my stint as an ABC newscaster.

I got hundreds of letters, even three marriage proposals! For years later people would say to me, 'Oh, you're the priest that made Howard K. Smith jump out of his chair.'

One of the last things I did in Baltimore before moving to Boston was to organise with Ed Brady and others an Irish Testimonial Dinner on 21 June 1975 for Irish Northern Aid with Limerick-born movie star, Richard Harris, as the guest speaker.

About a year before the event, I had met Harris for the first time after a live performance at a local university. After the performance, I waited for him to come out from the stage area. Out he comes, with the longest overcoat I had ever seen on a man – down to his heels – and with a stunning lady on his arm, Ann Turkel. She was the most glamorous woman I had ever seen, almost as tall as Richard and with a smile as wide as the ocean. I gingerly approached this super-couple, excused myself for interrupting, but explained I was desperately trying to help the North, and if he was interested, as rumoured, I would like to meet with him. 'I'm fiercely interested, absolutely, passionately,' he declaimed in his best King Arthur voice. 'Annie, let's cancel our appointments for tomorrow and meet with Fr Sean for breakfast.'

Richard was intensely patriotic. And we got on very well. Before the Baltimore Dinner, I had him as the guest speaker for the big Irish Northern Aid Dinner in New York. He recited the poem, 'The Fool' by Patrick Pearse and concluded by singing, without any accompaniment, 'Kevin Barry'. Needless to say, that brought the house down. Ann was especially pleased as she told me she had never seen such an outpouring of love and respect for Richard.

Ann was a lovely lady and, though not Catholic, had an exaggerated respect for priests, as is shown by the following story. At the time, the horror movie *The Exorcist* was all the rage. I had seen it in Baltimore. One evening I called Richard from Sacred Heart at their New York apartment. Ann answered the phone. 'It's Fr Sean, Ann,' I said. Well, she let out a bloodcurdling shriek. I heard Richard shout, 'Annie, Annie, it's all right.' Richard then came on and said he would have to call me back as Anne was almost fainting.

I was really worried and didn't know what to do. Anyway, a short time later Ann called back, very apologetic. 'Don't worry,' I said. 'What happened?'

She explained that they had just come in from seeing *The Exorcist*, which had deeply troubled her, and on the way back Richard was increasing her fear by telling her even worse stories that happened in Ireland – bigger and scarier, of course. Ann kept fretting that if diabolic possession could happen to anyone, might it happen to her? By the time she was walking in the door she had worked herself into somewhat of a frenzy. She says to Richard, 'I've got to call Fr Sean or I will go insane.' She grabbed the phone to dial my number, and at that very split second, I said, 'it's Father Sean'. It scared the living daylights out of the poor woman.

In the summer of 1975, the Baltimore Province of Redemptorists was making the periodic new appointments. I was assigned to Mission Church in Boston. That surprised me. Had my Superiors been unduly concerned about my escalating activity, they would have hardly sent me to the most Irish city in the most Irish state of all.

I was given the same room that de Valera used when he visited Mission Church to meet with his half-brother who was stationed there, Fr William Wheelright. (That was during the period 1919–1920.) Down the street from Mission Church was the funeral parlour owned by Gene Sheehan, an old IRA man who was a close friend of Dev and the last man on the run in the Civil War (according to Gene).

I loved Boston. What a city! No Irishman could feel unwelcome there. However, the Irish in Boston were not as militant as the New York Irish regarding Northern Ireland.

I had spoken several times in Boston so I was already well known by all the Irish with an interest in the Troubles. Mission Church parish itself was no longer strongly Irish. The neighbourhood had changed and was now predominantly black and Hispanic. I welcomed the chance to work for them, as there had been no blacks or Hispanics in Sacred Heart in Baltimore. I got to know many of them, especially those involved in social work and community activism. Some were really radical, in the good sense. And boy, did they stand by me when the Irish Consulate in Boston tried to have me silenced or moved! More of that later.

Shortly after I arrived, an old Irish-born man came to see me. He said it was great to have a young Irish priest again in the parish, that it would be like old times and that I should use the parish halls for Irish dances – not the newfangled stuff, mind you, no bands, just a man sitting in the corner, playing a fiddle.

I was touched by the wistfulness of the moment, but acutely conscious of how he was living in the past. That day was gone. The parish would never be like that again – when 50,000 people attended the Masses on Sunday during the Second World War and practically every newly arrived Irish person in Boston wanted to get married at Mission Church. I have since used this as a parable to illustrate how Unionism in Northern Ireland has changed forever: no going back to the big house on the hill where Unionists rule supreme. That day, too, has gone forever.

But I did have some Irish dances in the hall. And I took the theatre – yes, the theatre – out of mothballs. It had the best acoustics in all of Boston and a local Irish drama group put it to fine use. One of my jobs was looking after the parish's primary school, which was run by Notre Dame Nuns – all of them walking saints. All except one was over fifty. They were a group of dedicated, loving and joyful women, so totally different from the often ignorant, cruel and sexist stereotype of nuns in the media. It was a terrific school, totally integrated, black, white and Hispanic. And I loved the kids. I became good friends of the Sheehan family, who had three girls at the school. The father, Mossie, was and is an ardent Kerryman who loved to sing and was GAA mad.

Their youngest girl, Tricia, was out sick for a while. One day I was walking back to Mission Church from my hospital-chaplain rounds, and as I passed the local pharmacy I spotted a cute teddy bear in the window. And a strange thing happened, which I've never been able to explain, and which has never happened since. I found myself thinking: 'Why should I rush to New York to meet a politician (some politician had asked to meet with me) when little Tricia is sick?' I decided to cancel my New York visit, bought the teddy bear, and went to the Sheehans and gave it to a delighted Tricia. It was on her hospital bed the day she died. In a heartbreakingly short time we discovered Tricia did not have the flu, but leukaemia. I was in her hospital room with her parents when her heartbeat started to fail. The doctors swooped into the room and practically lifted the parents out, leaving me inside as they desperately attempted to revive her. I could feel death descend on the room almost like a wind, while Tricia's soul soared to God.

Even now, after all these years, I tear up as I write this. My sorrow at Tricia's death was made all the more acute because my sister Celia and her husband, Michael, had lost their young daughter, Caroline, to the same dreaded disease. Tricia was a special child, with beautiful, golden-blonde hair and a personality that lit up the room. I preached at her funeral Mass, and I think it was the most difficult thing I have ever done. But I made it through without breaking down, buoying up the grieving congregation with my tribute to Tricia, aged eleven. The power of the funeral Mass, with its message of hope and resurrection, remains one of the most visible sacramental graces of the Catholic Church. It has healed and helped millions to recover from the most awful human suffering and bereavement.

My campaigning for justice and peace in Northern Ireland did not appear as sensational as it had in a German–Polish parish in Baltimore. I continued to speak and organise chapters of the Irish National Caucus all across the United Sates. And then we made a surprise move. I organised an Irish National Caucus delegation to the Vatican.

Through the assistance of an Irish nun from Belfast, I was put in touch with a priest involved with the Pontifical Commission for Justice and Peace at the Vatican, Monsignor Maurice Bonneric, who felt it would help to raise the profile of the Troubles if an American group was to visit specifically for that reason. He guaranteed a meeting with Archbishop Giovanni Benelli, Substitute Secretary of State. The *Sunday Telegraph* said the Archbishop had 'in effect become the Pope's [Paul VI] chief executive'.[1] He was made a Cardinal in 1977. He was also on most *papabili* lists – shortlists of likely future Popes. But he died suddenly in 1982 at the age of sixty-one.

We travelled to Rome during the week of 7 December 1975. The delegation I headed up was composed of Bishop Drury, Jack Keane (president of the AOH), Brendan McCusker (chairman of Irish Northern Aid Committee), Sean Walsh and Fred O'Brien of the Irish National Caucus. Cardinal Wright of Boston welcomed us to the Eternal City by giving us dinner in his apartment. Wright, who was the Prefect of the Congregation for the Clergy, was the highest-ranking American in the Roman Curia.

Archbishop Benelli gave us a very attentive and gracious hearing. I spoke very strongly and urgently, but very respectfully. The Cardinal seemed to be very sympathetic, and emphasised the importance of America putting pressure on Britain. As we were leaving, he grasped my hand and whispered earnestly, 'The Irish National Caucus must be non-violent. In the Lord's name I beseech you to follow the path of non-violence.'

When a top Vatican official, so close to the Pope, and in the Vatican to boot, says that to a young priest, it has to register. And it did. The fact that the Archbishop listened carefully and did not automatically take the side of the British made his appeal more authentic. He was preaching *Pax Christi*, not *Pax Britannica*. In that instance, I just knew the Irish National Caucus would have to formally adopt the position of non-violence. The Caucus was, in fact, non-violent, as our actions showed, plus we had no foreign principal, but we had not formally taken a position of non-violence. I knew it was one thing for me as an individual to say the IRA had as much right to fight for freedom as the British or Americans had, but if I were to head up an organisation as a priest, then I would have to formally adopt a policy of non-violence. This became even more compelling later on when I realised I would have to go full-time into a special ministry of justice and peace if the Irish National Caucus was to succeed in its mission. I issued a press release saying we were well pleased with our visit.[2]

After the Vatican visit, we went to Dublin. Ruairí Ó Brádaigh and Joe Cahill met us at the airport. And the Special Branch went crazy. They were scurrying about the place as if aliens had arrived. We filled in Republican leaders on our Vatican visit. I gave interviews to the Irish media and told them that since the Caucus was now well established, we would be making Ireland an issue in the 1976 presidential elections. I slipped up to Fermanagh to see my family and then returned to the United States.

10

The Caucus and Jimmy Carter

*The Irish National Caucus . . . achieved its first major mark . . .
when it obtained an 'Irish justice statement from candidate Jimmy
Carter'*
Professor Paul Power[1]

As mentioned in the previous chapter, I was determined that
the Irish National Caucus would flex its muscles in the
1976 presidential election. The first Democratic candidate who
made contact with me was Senator Henry 'Scoop' Jackson of
Washington State. I travelled to meet Jackson in New York. The
first thing he said to me was, 'Well, Father, I'm of Viking stock, so
the Irish cannot be mad at me.' With a totally straight face, I said,
'You guys killed Brian Boru in 1014 and we haven't forgotten it.'
He almost fell off his chair thinking he had made the classic and
much dreaded candidate faux pas. Then I laughed and told him I
was kidding. I urged him to make a strong statement, no wishy-
washy nonsense, condemning the violation of human rights,
internment and calling for British withdrawal. He did exactly that
in January 1976.

Then one of Jackon's top operators made contact with me
during the hunger strike of Frank Stagg (1942–1976), who died
in a British prison on 12 February 1976, after sixty-two days on

hunger strike. I explained that Stagg's hunger strike was making a huge impact on the Irish in Massachusetts and that Jackson should campaign vigorously among them on his Irish position. Finally, when Stagg died, I invited Jackson's man to the public Mass I was saying at Mission Church for Stagg. We had put on a special effort to have a suitable turn-out for the Mass. Thousands flocked to honour and pray for that young Irish hero who sacrificed his life for Irish freedom.

I preached a moving tribute to Stagg. I was careful not to be 'political' as this was the Mass, not a political rally. I have always been scrupulously correct in this matter. Nonetheless, I could not preach a proper funeral Mass homily unless I properly explained who Stagg was, what his values were, and why he had sacrificed his young life.

After the Mass, Jackson's man told me I was 'a master' at presenting a difficult subject, expressed amazement at the size of the congregation and how they responded to my words. I replied that it 'was the song, not the singer' that the Irish felt deeply about, i.e. the Troubles, and all politicians ignored that at their peril. 'I bet you're now glad that Senator Jackson put out that strong statement,' I added.

Jackson went on to win the Massachusetts Democratic primary on 2 March. On 16 March, he wrote me a personal letter of thanks: 'Let me personally thank you and the Irish National Caucus for your efforts with the Irish voters on my behalf . . . Let me reaffirm my commitment to the cause of Irish Freedom so closely related to the founding of our great nation. As stated previously, I support a declaration of intent from the British Government regarding their withdrawal from Ireland and I believe that will be a concrete step towards peace with justice in Ireland, a cause for which an Irishman, Frank Stagg, died recently in a non-violent, peaceful protest in an English prison.'

That from a Cold War anti-communist senator! You knew it had to get the attention of the British (and that of the Irish government). But more importantly, it got the attention of the man who beat out Jackson for the Democratic nomination –

Jimmy Carter. (Jackson won the New York primary on 6 April but dropped out on 1 May after Carter beat him in Pennsylvania.) I sent the Jackson letter to the Carter people through Senator Joe Timilty of Boston, a good friend of mine and an ardent Irishman, who was a key man in the Carter campaign. I told Joe we wanted to meet Carter and that we would not support him unless he met with us.

But here let me digress a bit, to take care of the Queen of England. She visited Boston on Sunday 11 July and I had to make sure she got an Irish welcome. Tommy and Agnes Clifford, two good friends, and I organised the protest. Tommy drove me around the city for weeks so that I could speak to every possible Irish grouping. We had a pretty good turnout for the protest. *The New York Times* carried a photograph of Her Majesty surrounded by placards saying: 'America 1776. Ireland ?', 'Ireland Unfree Shall Never Be at Peace', 'Tyranny is Not Easily Conquered, But We Will Conquer' and 'England Out of Ireland'.[2] To my own astonishment, I was able to get right up beside the Queen – only Mayor Kevin White was between us. Sometime later when I arranged for the Mayor to meet Nora Connolly O'Brien, daughter of Irish patriot–martyr James Connolly, when she visited Boston, he smiled and said, 'Seems like I always see you, Father, when we greet famous ladies from across the Atlantic.'

Just when it seemed that a meeting was in the works, Carter's people got nervous and admitted that the British were going crazy and putting a lot of pressure on them to cancel the meeting. 'How is it going to look if Carter is seen to back down because he is scared of the Brits . . . how many votes will that get him?' I retorted. Then Al Stern, First Assistant to Stud Eizenstat, Carter's top adviser, sent a telegram to us: 'Urgent . . . Trying to reach you. Please call'.[3]

I called Stern and he assured me that Carter was not scared of the British and that the meeting was still on, even though the Irish Embassy was also opposed to the meeting. The meeting was finally and hurriedly scheduled for Wednesday 27 October 1976 in Pittsburgh – just six days before the presidential election. I discussed with Stern, line by line, the opening statement I would make on behalf of the 34-member Caucus delegation. And I had sent him a copy well in advance of the meeting; with the assurance not a syllable would be changed:

Irish National Caucus statement to Governor Jimmy Carter, Pittsburgh Hilton Hotel, Pittsburgh, Pennsylvania
October 27, 1976

Governor Carter,
On behalf of the Irish National Caucus, may we say that it is an honor to meet the next President of the United States.

The Irish National Caucus represents all the major Irish American organizations in the United States, and is their official voice on justice and peace in Ireland.

We are deeply saddened by the ongoing tragedy in Ireland; and as Irish-Americans we are deeply hurt by the stonewalling silence of the Nixon-Ford Administration. But we are greatly encouraged by the Irish plank in the Democratic Platform which states: 'The voice of the United States should be heard in Northern Ireland against violence and terror, against the discrimination, repression, and deprivation which brought about that civil strife and for the efforts of the parties towards a peaceful resolution of the future of Northern Ireland . . .

The United States should encourage the formation of a united Ireland, pertinent alliances such as NATO and international organizations such as the United Nations should be fully apprised of the interest of the United States with respect to the status of Ireland in the international community of nations.'

We are even more encouraged, Governor Carter, by your words in your recent address at the University of Notre Dame: 'We have watched passively as human rights are violated in Ireland. We should begin by having it understood that if any nation, whatever its political system, deprives its people of basic human rights, that fact will help shape our people's attitude towards that nation's government. If other nations want our friendship and support, they must understand that we want to see basic human rights respected.'

We welcome this, Governor Carter, as a reinforcement of the Democratic Party Platform which also states 'a primary object of American aid, both military and economic, is first of all to enhance the condition of freedom in the world. The United States should not provide aid to any government – anywhere in the world – which uses secret police detention without charges, and torture to enforce its power. Exceptions to this policy should be rare, and the aid provided should be limited to that which is absolutely necessary. The United States should be open and unashamed in its exercise of diplomatic efforts to encourage the observance of human rights in countries which receive American aid.'

Governor Carter, in a recent letter to the National President of the Ancient Order of Hibernians, you stated: 'I am sympathetic with those who seek to promote a stable and free Ireland with full civil and human rights for all citizens.'

'. . . A stable and free Ireland with full civil and human rights for all citizens', Governor Carter, is precisely what we in the Irish National Caucus stand for. We thank you for meeting with us and we look forward to meeting you again as President of the United States.

Not only did Stern have a copy in advance but he also suggested I would add the word 'stonewalling' before 'silence' in the third paragraph.

Then Jimmy Carter made his statement. And for the record, here it is, word for word:

President-Elect Jimmy Carter's Statement to Irish National Caucus in Pittsburgh, on Wednesday 27 October 1976.

It is a great honor to me to come here this afternoon to be with you who come to meet with me from a major part of this nation.

I don't disavow my own Irish heritage. As I said, in a speech earlier today, it does not matter when our ancestors came here, two years ago or twenty years ago or two hundred years ago or more . . . It is why we came here and what we do after we arrive to make our nation great.

It would be a mistake for all of us to forget that we have a dual commitment; first and foremost, of course, to our country, here, the United States. But then secondly, and very importantly, to the nations from which our families came.

When I was in Notre Dame two weeks ago last Sunday with Father Hesburg and just a few moments ago, as a matter of fact, with Cardinal Cooke in New York, we talked about the need for the establishment of a Commission on International Peace, to pursue in the multitude of places around the world, the concept of our country's standing firm in its commitment to human rights.

We see, or come on the evening television news and in the national headlines every now and then, specific instances where human rights are subjugated and where quite often our nation as was pointed out by Father [McManus], stands mute and doesn't speak.

The Democratic National Convention Platform Plank was written jointly, by my own staff and by Mayor Daley from Chicago, to be sure that the world knows that the Democratic Party understands the special problems in Ireland and that it is a mistake for our country's Government to stand quiet on the struggle of the Irish for peace for the respect of human rights and for unifying Ireland.

I would like to say that I almost feel like I am a member of the Ancient Order of Hibernians as well. For six years in a row I was honored to go to Savannah on Saint Patrick's Day, and if any of you have ever been to Savannah on Saint Patrick's Day, you know that it is one of the fine and wonderful events in the life of a human being, and those who come there from Boston and other major cities in the world say that they have never seen anything like it. Although Savannah is a fairly small city, we have two hundred and fifty thousand people participating in the parade and the beer is green, the grits are green, the streets are green, everything is painted green; in fact, one year we dyed the entire Savannah River green. So Georgia has an awful lot of Irish settlers including my own family. To some degree, I know the heartache that you feel to see the bloodshed and the disharmony and deprivation in Ireland. And I am very honored that you come to let me feel a part of a hope that will never be extinguished that we can have a redressing of grievances, and a realisation for hopes of our brave, unfortunate mankind in Ireland.

Needless to say, we were delighted by that statement. And needless to say, the British were not. The *Guardian*, supposed to be a moderate and reasonable paper, sniffed in an editorial: 'And now, a few days from what may be his elevation to the Presidency of the United States, along comes Jimmy Carter, sharing a platform with Seán Mac Stíofáin's confessor and pledging himself to a United Ireland'.[4]

Carter was roundly condemned by the British media and by British and Unionist politicians. Mr Roy Mason, the British Secretary of State for Northern Ireland told the House of Commons that Carter was, 'giving aid and succour to Ulster terrorists'. Nothing surprising there.

But what would surprise many Americans (but not this Fermanagh man) was the hysterical reaction of the obsequious Dublin government of that time. (*The Boston Globe* would later report: 'Irish embassy officials protested vehemently to Carter aides. Carter, under pressure, agreed to send a telegram of clarification . . . Carter, the next day, telegrammed Irish Foreign Minister FitzGerald': '. . . I have been informed that certain news reports concerning my meeting yesterday with Irish-American leaders have misrepresented both my position and my statements . . . I do not favor violence as part of a solution to the Irish question'.[5] No one, of course, had reported Carter had favoured violence. But this was classic Dublin government tactic – scare people from speaking out for justice in Northern Ireland lest they be accused of supporting violence. It was unconscionable to do that to Carter. Yet the media establishment in Ireland never objected to FitzGerald's inexcusable and disgraceful actions. Years later, when candidate Bill Clinton, on 5 April 1992 in New York City, made promises to a group of us (some who also had been at the Carter meeting in Pittsburgh), the huge difference was that Taoiseach Albert Reynolds welcomed Clinton's statement – and the rest is history. I am haunted by this thought: had FitzGerald welcomed Carter's statement, how much sooner the peace process could have started, how many lives might have been saved and how so much suffering could have been spared? And I am not alone in thinking this way. Well-known author and journalist Tim Pat Coogan says in his memoirs, 'During the 1974–7 coalition period the voice of the Dublin component of the Toffs' Brigade [pro-British elite] was particularly strong, powerful and continuous. I would blame Dublin's attitude in these years for helping to create a mindset that deepened the political vacuum and helped to prolong the Troubles'.[6]

But I had inadvertently given some of Carter's people an opportunity to make specious excuses. In my hurry to prepare my statement for the Carter meeting, I quoted the Irish plank in the Democratic Platform, as given by the *Guardian*. But that paper quoted a previous draft that had been changed. The phrase, 'The United States should encourage the formation of a united Ireland' was not, in fact, in the final version. It was a genuine mistake, which even the Carter people themselves missed, even though they had an advance copy and had approved every word.

Al Stern quite disingenuously went on to allege that I had tricked Carter into talking about 'unifying Ireland'. My response was if a simple man from Fermanagh could do that, what would the Soviets do to him, for goodness' sake. But Stern in the same *Globe* article was forced to admit that I had made an honest mistake: 'Stern said he telephoned Fr McManus after the flap and accused the priest of having tricked Carter into using the phrase [unifying Ireland]. The presidential aide subsequently accepted McManus's explanation that it had been an honest mistake based on an incorrect version of the platform as reported in the Manchester *Guardian* . . . But Stern added: "I have reason to believe he (McManus) was delighted".'[7] Stern could also have added that he himself did not catch the error even though he was intimately involved in the drafting of my statement, and was in possession of an advance copy, and had approved every word – even adding one. Stern also told the National Catholic News Service, that he was satisfied that what happened 'was not done deliberately or maliciously'.

But in fairness to Carter, he himself never withdrew his words, which were recorded. And it's his words that count, not my misquote.

But FitzGerald's apparatchiks at the Irish Embassy were instructed to continue the misinformation campaign so as to discredit the Caucus and make Carter back off. The *Jack Anderson Column* – then one of the largest syndicated columns in the United States – regurgitated the FitzGerald misinformation: 'At the height of the presidential campaign, Jimmy Carter inadvertently stirred up a tempest in Great Britain . . . He met in Pittsburgh with Irish-American leaders, many of them dogmatically anti-British. A militant priest read Carter what purported to be a copy of the Democratic platform on Ireland and asked whether he supported it . . . But the priest spiked the non-controversial platitudes with some language of his own . . . The unsuspecting Carter, groggy from the gruelling campaign, overlooked the inflammatory sentence.'[8]

Whitten, a writer for the *Anderson Column* had never contacted me and clearly allowed himself to be used to do a hatchet job. He came to realise that, and later he and the paper would do some fine pieces on British human rights violations in Northern Ireland.

Irish Americans were appalled by the unfairness of it all, so they took their grievance to the ultimate court of appeal – the intrepid Paul O'Dwyer, then President of New York City Council, who had the zeal for justice of an Old Testament Prophet. On 17 November 1976, Paul wrote to President-elect Carter: 'An article appearing in the Jack Anderson's syndicated column . . . has greatly disturbed members of the Irish-American community. It charges a most respectable clergyman with having played a vile trick on you . . . Leaders of the Irish-American community have requested me to make my own inquiry into the facts . . . I found the following to be the facts . . . The Carter campaign leadership in Atlanta, very properly, insisted that the leader spokesman of the delegation, long in advance of the meeting, present a written script which would contain the delegation's position. The delegation adhered to the rules with meticulous care . . . From the facts, and circumstances, I believe that the Anderson column is a garbled distortion carrying a scurrilous and unfounded accusation against a prestigious clergyman which has angered a whole community'.[9]

With that letter Paul O'Dwyer – in his own right, an important figure in the Democratic Party – was steadying President Carter and at the same time 'the Lion of Bohola', as I called him, was sending a message to the Irish government and Irish Embassy that he was on to them.

Despite the Irish Embassy's concentrated campaign to discredit me with the Carter White House, I was given about a dozen tickets to the Carter Inaugural Ball and continued to be invited to the White House – although the smear campaign against me did inevitably limit my access to Carter's policymakers.

Nonetheless, on 24 February 1977, I met for two hours with Marilyn Haft, Carter's Associate Director of Public Liaison, who specialised in advising the President on international human rights.

On 16 March 1977, Carter paid a visit to Clinton, a very Irish town in Massachusetts. Hours before, FitzGerald met with Carter and implored him not to refer to human rights in Northern Ireland, only to condemn IRA violence. Despite FitzGerald's plea,

'The President defended his policies on human rights, and said he would speak out on human rights in Northern Ireland, without saying why'.[10] Now you know 'why' . . . because FitzGerald tried to stop him, and Carter did not appreciate it .

Neither was the Irish Embassy able to stop my meeting with Andrew Young while he was US ambassador to the United Nations (1977–1979). It was just after the State Department had made Young apologise for saying that if England had not actually invented racism, she had institutionalised it around the world. Despite his forced apology, Young was in high good spirits, and with delight showed me some of the irate letters he had received from people in Britain. Andy had no doubt about who was the oppressed and who was the oppressor in Ireland.

And in face of the ongoing campaign by the Irish Embassy to blackball me, I was still invited to the Carter White House on two occasions. On Friday 11 April 1980, I was invited 'to join the President at a meeting for ethnic fraternal leaders'.[11] When I met the President for a handshake and photograph, I smilingly asked him if he remembered me from Pittsburgh. 'Oh, how could I forget?' he chuckled. I then said, 'Please don't forget human rights in Northern Ireland.' He replied, 'I shan't. I promise you'.[12]

But FitzGerald was obsessed by the success of the Caucus and was ridiculously concerned that the Caucus would be seen as having any influence with Carter. For example, he told *The New York Times* that '. . . the Irish Government had been anxious about American policy involving Ulster in the aftermath of widespread publicity in Ireland and Britain that the Irish National Caucus . . . had access to the White House. [The Caucus] has had a propaganda campaign suggesting that they had access to the White House, that they were influential.'

Apparently, according to FitzGerald, Americans should not have the right to free speech or the right to petition their government. But even FitzGerald cannot rewrite history. It was the Irish National Caucus that first got Carter speaking about the Troubles, and that nobody can deny. As Professor Paul Power says, 'The Irish National Caucus . . . achieved its first major mark in October 1977, when it obtained an "Irish justice" statement from candidate Jimmy Carter, providing the INC with a basis for claiming a seminal role in the later Carter statement on Northern Ireland'.[13]

The significance of that assessment is all the more apparent when it is realised that in the 1970s, Professor Power of the University of Cincinnati was 'the only American political science academic researching Northern Ireland affairs'.[14] 'The later Carter Statement' to which Power refers – also known as the Carter initiative – was made by the President on 30 August 1977.[15] Power states that it was 'the first, explicit comment on Irish political issues of any kind ever made by an incumbent President'. That is why it was so important to the Irish National Caucus – not so much for what it said, but that it was said at all.

But it did also contain the key points we had been pressing on the Carter White House. In fact, *The Sunday Press* (Dublin) on 4 September claimed that 'some hours before the long-expected Carter initiative was finally announced . . . the text of the statement was released word for word to an Irish newspaper [by the Irish National Caucus]'.[16]

The key part of the statement said: 'The United States wholeheartedly supports peaceful means for finding a just solution that involves both parts of the community of Northern Ireland and protects human rights and guarantees freedom from discrimination – a solution that the people of Northern Ireland, as well as the Governments of Great Britain and Ireland, can support. Violence cannot resolve Northern Ireland's problem: it only increases them and solves nothing.'

The Irish Times, the day after the Carter statement was released, carried the following headline: 'Irish Caucus cued Carter: McManus':

The Rev. Sean McManus, of the Irish National Caucus in the United States, said yesterday that it was the Caucus that first initiated President Carter's involvement in Ireland by making human rights, justice and peace in Ireland an issue in the Presidential election. In so doing, he said, the Caucus made such matters an international issue for which it was criticized by the British Government, and the previous Coalition Government, and leading SDLP members. Ultimately, Father McManus said in a statement, the real significance of the President's interest was that it would formally, and at the highest level, 'internationalize' British involvement in Ireland, thus making it clear to the world that Northern Ireland was not just a British internal matter.[17]

11

The Long Knives of the Dublin Government

The Dublin Government will fight Irish-Americans but not the Brits.[1]

In the previous chapter, I quoted the thank-you letter that Senator 'Scoop' Jackson had sent me, with his very respectful reference to Frank Stagg who had died for 'peace with justice in Ireland'.

There you have a non-Irish, non-Catholic decent 'Viking' paying deep respect to that young Irish martyr. What respect did the Irish government show this heroic young Mayo man? When his body was flown from England back to Ireland, the Irish government kidnapped the body, in a frightfully ugly fascist display, to stop Stagg being given a Republican burial, as he had requested. The Irish government, on 21 February 1976 had Stagg buried under six feet of concrete, in a grave 70 yards from the Republican Plot in Leigue Cemetery, Ballina, County Mayo. The grave was guarded twenty-four hours a day by armed Special Branch men to stop the Republican Movement from reinterring their martyred comrade. But on 6 November, the IRA succeeded in burying Stagg's remains in the Republican Plot.

Mrs Stagg, Frank's mother, had written me a beautiful letter to thank me for the Mass we celebrated for her son. I promised her I would visit his grave in Ballina and say a prayer there. In the summer of 1976, I went to his grave, not wearing my clerical collar. I started to take a photo, and was immediately surrounded by Special Branch men. 'Stop, that's not allowed,' they barked. 'What do you mean, it's not allowed. Has the Irish Constitution been changed to forbid photos?' Then in that bullying way that seems special to the Special Branch, they told me if I took photos they would confiscate my camera and place me under arrest. 'Am I allowed to say a prayer or is that, too, forbidden?' I snapped.

Can you imagine anything more guaranteed to recruit members for the IRA than the barbaric way the Dublin government treated the body of a dead hunger striker? Even the British did not do that to Bobby Sands and his nine comrades when they died in Long Kesh in 1981.

So you can imagine that when I returned to Boston, my condemnations of the Dublin government grew stronger. Then came the shameful sandbagging of Jimmy Carter by Garret FitzGerald and all my Fermanagh contempt for the Dublin government was mightily reinforced. There was simply no way of avoiding it: the Dublin government was collaborating with Britain in its dirty war in the North.

Now fast-forward again to March 1977. The St Patrick's Day statement of Senator Teddy Kennedy, Speaker Tip O'Neil, Senator Pat Moynihan and Governor Hugh Carey further indicated proof that FitzGerald had tried to muzzle President Carter from speaking about human rights in Northern Ireland. To explain what I mean, it is important here to give their statement in full:

> Joint St Patrick's Day Appeal for Peace in Northern Ireland
> For Release on Thursday a.m. 17 March 1977.
>
> The world has looked with increasing concern over the past eight years on the continuing tragedy that afflicts the people of Northern Ireland. Each of us has tried in the past to use our good offices to help see that the underlying injustices at the heart of the Northern Ireland tragedy are ended so that

a just and peaceful settlement may be secured.

It is evident to us, as it is to concerned people everywhere that continued violence cannot assist the achievement of such a settlement, but can only exacerbate the wounds that divide the people of Northern Ireland.

We, therefore, join together in this appeal, which we make in a spirit of compassion and concern for the suffering people in the troubled part of Ireland. We appeal to all those organizations engaged in violence to renounce their campaign of death and destruction and return to the path of life and peace. And we appeal as well to our fellow Americans to embrace this goal of peace, and to renounce any action that promotes the current violence or provides support or encouragement for organizations engaged in violence.

We make this appeal on St Patrick's Day 1977, a day on which Irish peoples of all traditions everywhere should feel proud to rejoice in our common heritage. And a year in which peace should come at last to Northern Ireland.

> Edward M. Kennedy
> Thomas P. O'Neill Jr.
> Daniel Patrick Moynihan
> Hugh L. Carey

Not a word about British violence, repressive legislation, and mistreatment of political prisoners. Not a whisper about how British security forces and the RUC were colluding with, arming and controlling Protestant murder gangs. Not a scintilla of mention about the deep-seated, all-pervasive, anti-Catholic sectarianism – the State religion of Northern Ireland. The 'Four Horsemen' (well versed in how the media, which had christened them thusly, operates) had to know how their statement would play. The headline in *The New York Times* makes my case: 'Four Top Democrats Urge Halt in Support for the IRA'.[2]

In fact, the statement did nothing to stop those who were supporting the IRA. I never met an Irish American who stopped supporting the IRA because of Tip O'Neill or Teddy Kennedy. The statement just gave the British carte blanche.

My collision course with the Dublin government was further escalated by a nasty development in Croke Park on Sunday 17 April 1977, before the Kerry–Dublin National Football League final. Before the game began, a group of human rights activists ran on to the pitch with banners protesting the treatment of hunger strikers in Portlaoise Prison. Two of the Dublin team – David Hickey, a medical doctor, and John McCarthy, a Dublin-based garda – attacked the protesters in an unseemly and unnecessary manner. My brother Frank, a most ardent attendee of all matches in Croke Park, alerted me to the outrage, pictures of which were prominently carried in all the papers. I was especially offended that a doctor and a garda were involved. I lobbied the two American GAA governing bodies, the New York GAA Board and the North American Board, urging them to ban the two offending Dublin players from playing in upcoming games in America. I knew most of the key members of both boards who were also members of the Irish National Caucus. In no time both boards authorised me to make the following statement, which was carried in all the Irish newspapers:

> These two players [Hickey and McCarthy] will not be allowed to play in any part of the US. They disgraced the uniform of the Dublin team and the spirit of the GAA by using Croke Park to violently express their political hostility to the hunger strikers. Hickey and McCarthy in the most sordid manner introduced politics into Croke Park. Therefore, the leadership of the GAA in the US is banning Hickey and McCarthy from playing with the Dublin team on their upcoming tour.[3]

Well, as they say, all hell broke out. I was told by an insider that Seán Ó Síocháin, GAA Director General, erupted wanting to know, 'When the f*** did Father McManus and the Provos gain control of the GAA in America?' There they go again . . . Any time a stand for justice is taken, it has to be the IRA!

Anyway, the hunger strike in Portlaoise Prison was settled and we called off the ban. Prominent GAA writer Paddy Downey reported: 'News that the ban had been lifted was announced by the Boston-based priest, the Rev. Sean McManus, after his brother, Mr Frank McManus, the former Westminster MP for Fermanagh and South Tyrone, had informed him that the Portlaoise prisoners had ended their hunger-strike . . . The North American Board of the GAA is now expected to follow the lead of the Caucus – as they had followed it originally when imposing the ban'.[4] But as I said, the GAA ban would speed up the Irish government campaign against me.

On 18 April 1977, *The Boston Globe* ran a front-page story on me, with photograph, 'Hub priest denies he backs IRA'[5], by top reporter David Nyhan. It told the story of how the Irish government, Irish Embassy in Washington and Irish Consulate in Boston were out to squash me. A month later, Nyhan had another front-page story on me, with a photograph of me without my clerical collar demonstrating at City Hall Plaza for political prisoners in Ireland, North and South: '"Ireland putting heat on me", says priest'.[6] It reported how the Irish Consul in Boston, Carmel Heaney, had approached the Chancellor of the Archdiocese, Bishop Thomas V. Dailey, to try and get him to silence me. And how, in turn, Bishop Dailey, called my Rector, Fr Jim Foley, to a meeting at the Chancery. Nyhan wrote: 'Heaney said, "I certainly have not made any approach of the kind described by Fr McManus. I really can't discuss what I may or may not do . . . Obviously, I have conversations with all kinds of people in the course of my job. In some cases they can be regarded as public, and in other cases as private."' Heaney's words give her away.

Nyhan's story continues: 'Last night Fr Foley said in an interview that Bishop Dailey had "mentioned his interest" in Fr McManus's activities . . . I told him what a wonderful priest Fr McManus is. We had absolutely nothing but the highest regard for him here. Asked if Bishop Dailey had told him of being approached by Heaney, Fr Foley replied, "I don't want to comment on the various details. It was a private conversation." Bishop Dailey was unavailable for comment.'

Naturally, many other US papers picked up the front-page story. The *Boston Herald American* ran with the headline, 'Hub priest charges Irish consul with "dirty trick"':

> A Mission Church priest yesterday accused Irish Consul Carmel Heaney here of 'running for cover behind a wall of equivocation and diplomatic immunity' after working her 'dirty trick' . . . In response to his latest criticism of her, she said, 'it would be counter-productive to get into a debate at second-hand or indirectly with Fr McManus' . . . The priest, who has been accused of terrorist activities by the Irish government in Dublin, said he learned of the 'dirty trick' from the Mission Church rector . . . Fr McManus said, 'I am opposed to violence, whether it be British or the IRA . . . I believe the fundamental violence in Ireland is institutionalized by the British government with its army, its enforced unemployment, its sectarianism and its discrimination'.[7]

The *Irish Post* in London – published by the late Brendan Mac Lua – went right to the source of the Heaney's dirty trick: 'A few weeks ago the Irish Minister for Foreign Affairs, Dr. Garret FitzGerald, singled [Fr McManus] out for special attention and condemned his activities in the U. S.'[8] The National Catholic News Service (the news wire service of the US Conference of Catholic Bishops) filed the following syndicated report:

> Boston priest will not be silenced on his Irish views, pastor says. 'There is no danger of Father McManus being silenced – either by the Archdiocese or the Redemptorist Order.' Father Foley told National Catholic News. 'I'm not going to report on the details of a very private and cordial conversation with Bishop Dailey . . . but I backed up Father McManus as a good priest and a good school prefect. As far

as his priestly work, he's tremendous. He has every right to talk out on human rights violations as long as he's doing it non-violently.'[9]

There was huge outpouring of support for me, not only in the parish but throughout Boston. The principal of the local public school, Charles H. Gibbons, Jr, wrote to *The Boston Globe*: 'I can personally attest to [Fr McManus'] commitment and humanitarian concern for the people of Mission Hill – black, White and Hispanic . . . Perhaps the Irish government would suggest someone else to help us in Mission Hill. If not, I would appreciate their concerning themselves with other affairs since the most impressive priest I have seen operating in Mission Hill is Fr Sean McManus . . .'[10]

A middle-aged black woman, not a Catholic, became a fierce defender. This lady was a social worker dealing with great deprivation in the area. She was a force of nature and as tough as nails. She phoned Carmel Heaney and bawled her out: 'You [expletive deleted], leave Fr McManus alone. How dare you say he's collecting guns for the IRA? In Mission Hill we keep our own damn guns.'

So there you have it. In Britain the government tried to have me silenced. In America, the Dublin government tried to have me silenced. And I am quite convinced that had it not been for David Nyhan, God rest him, and the other journalists, they might have got Bishop Dailey to move against me. Dailey never gave me any further trouble. He was scared of *The Boston Globe*.

But here's the rub, the moral, if you wish, of the story: the Irish Embassy and Consulates only really escalated their attacks on me after the Irish National Caucus formally adapted non-violence and wrote it into our constitution. Instead of welcoming this development, the Embassy and Consulates were frightened by it. Why?

I have mentioned that after Archbishop Benelli's plea to me at the Vatican, I knew we would have to formally adopt a policy of non-violence, even though I have been practising it since I decided at sixteen to become a priest. That did not mean that I could no longer understand what made the IRA fight. It meant that I personally could not join them in that struggle. It meant that I personally had to accept non-violence as a way of life. It did not mean I had to tell lies to cover up British injustice in Ireland, or to collaborate by my silence with that injustice. Non-violence does not mean doing nothing. It is short for 'non-violent resistance' to injustice and oppression.

In 1976, I went home for Christmas. *The Irish Press* interviewed me on my position on violence: 'In an exclusive interview with *The Irish Press*, Fr McManus said he was convinced that the only long-term solution to the problem was one of non-violence . . . [He] said he disagreed with many things the Provisional IRA had done."I disagree with the whole broad use of violence, but I must honestly say, I understand why they turned to these acts.""[11]

In 1977, I declared that the 'subtitle' of the Irish National Caucus would be: 'The non-violent pursuit of justice and peace for Ireland'. That appeared under our name in all our literature – and I should know, as I wrote all our position papers and announcements. 'The Irish National Caucus is totally opposed to the use of violence to achieve political objectives in Ireland. It is, therefore, logically and necessarily opposed in the very first place to British policy in Ireland because the British government historically and currently and par excellence, uses violence to achieve political objectives in Ireland. But the Caucus is opposed to all forms of violence, whether it is British or Irish, State or civilian. It is an exclusively American-based organization and does not support any party or organization in Ireland. It has no foreign principal and it does not, and never has, sent funds to any part of Ireland for any reason – least of all for violence.'

Could anything be more clear and unambiguous? Why did the Irish government not welcome that unequivocal non-violent declaration? Why were they not as happy as the IRA was unhappy about it?

But there would be no let-up in the Irish Embassy's campaign of character assassination. In 1977, Doubleday published a book,

The Power Peddlers, by Russell Warren Howe and Sarah Hays Trott. The book, about foreign-policy lobbies in Washington, had a section on the Irish National Caucus. On p. 391 it says, 'Father McManus's Irish Embassy file card bears the mention "homicidal tendencies".'

Paul O'Dwyer's law firm initiated a libel law suit on my behalf against Doubleday and the authors. My Provincial, the admirable Father Joe Kerins, totally backed my law suit and offered to sign on as a co-defendant. He also wrote to the then Irish Ambassador in Washington, John Molloy, expressing outrage and demanding an explanation. On 8 December 1978, an embassy counsellor replied for the Ambassador, denying that such a file card existed and that '. . . no representative of the Embassy has at any time suggested . . . that such a card existed or that Father McManus had such tendencies'.

Howe, a British subject, was ordered by a Federal judge to reveal his source in the Irish Embassy. He refused: 'He indicated,' said *The New York Times*, 'that the source could face retaliation by the Irish Republican Army because of the criticism of Father McManus'.[12] He was threatened with contempt, and the Embassy official (whom the Irish Ambassador denied existed) offered to appear before the judge in camera, so his identity could never be revealed, as he was allegedly scared the IRA would kill him and his family.

Anyway, the case was eventually dropped. Later Howe would write about the case in an article, 'Reveal the Name or go to Jail', in the *Washington Journalism Review*: 'During an interview in New York, an Irish diplomat read me the priest's address and telephone numbers from an Embassy file card. He chuckled and cited a cheeky comment that someone had written on the card: homicidal tendencies.'[13] Howe then continues: 'My source felt wretched about my case . . . He said his ambassador would not allow him to testify, in any case. He had considered bypassing me and "going public" on his own (although he feared IRA reprisals against his wife and children or his family in Ireland). However, his Ambassador had rejected that, saying waiving immunity would set a bad precedent. The source appealed to Irish foreign minister, Garret FitzGerald; although sympathetic, the minister decided against overruling his envoy . . . "The irony of it," said the source, "is that I'm sure they've guessed it's me, because the IRA knows I'm the Embassy member who keeps tabs on them here."'

But the Irish Embassy would have even more reason to be concerned by what *The New York Times*, in a front-page article, described was, up until that time, 'the Caucus' boldest success' – the formation of the Ad Hoc Congressional Committee for Irish Affairs.[14]

On Tuesday 27 September 1977, I chaired the press conference on Capitol Hill at which we appointed Congressman Mario Biaggi (D-NY) as chairman: "'Congressman Biaggi was selected by us," Fr McManus said, "because he has truly distinguished himself by his consistent and outspoken concern for my country. Although his ancestry is not from Cork, Kerry or Fermanagh, the Congressman has shown more compassion than some congressional leaders with Irish names. On behalf of the Irish National Caucus, the National President of the AOH and all Irish American organizations, it gives me great pleasure to appoint you, Congressman Biaggi, Chairman of the Ad Hoc Congressional Committee for Irish Affairs."'[15]

The one acid test that I had given Mario before we asked him to chair the committee was, 'Are you prepared to stand up to the Dublin government?' Mario had responded, 'Absolutely.' Is it not it pathetic that we had to have this concern? Is it not shameful that this highly decorated police hero, and proud son of Italy, had to not only take on the British government, but to watch his back with the Irish government as well? But that's the way it was. One could see Dublin's real policy towards the North far more clearly in America than in Ireland.

The Irish Embassy had been telling Members of Congress that Congress had no role to play in Northern Ireland – that it should be left to the British and Irish governments and to diplomats. In a very short time we had signed up over 100 Members – Republicans, Democrats, Liberals, Conservatives, Protestants, Jews, Catholics, etc.

On 28 September, the Religious News Service filed a report: 'In an interview [after the press conference] . . . Father McManus said, "We are disappointed with Sen. Edward Kennedy (D–MA) and Rep. Thomas P. O'Neill Jr (D–Ma) – the most powerful politicians in the United States, and both Roman Catholics. They condemn violence in Northern Ireland, but do not condemn British violence and torture . . . The American Catholic hierarchy has made several comments about violence in South Africa, Rhodesia and Chile, and quite rightly so. But they are silent about British violence in Ireland – with only one honorable exception, Bishop Thomas J. Drury of Corpus Christi, Texas."'[16]

In February 1978, I was tipped off that the Irish Embassy was planning something big against us for St Patrick's Day. My informant heard one of the Irish Embassy staff boast: 'Come St Patrick's Day, only McManus and Biaggi will be left standing.' So we braced ourselves for the gathering storm, and it came on 17 February 1978. On that date, Taoiseach Jack Lynch wrote to Congressman Mario Biaggi, denouncing him and the Irish National Caucus. But before sending it to Biaggi, Lynch made it public to *The New York Times*, *The Washington Post* and all the major American media. The intention was clear: to put the Ad Hoc Congressional Committee for Irish Affairs and the Irish National Caucus out of business. The Irish Embassy genuinely thought the Members of Congress we had signed up for the Committee would resign en masse. When Lynch made his attack, we had 93 Members of Congress signed up for the Committee for Irish Affairs. Only two resigned, and we went on to recruit a total of 133 Members of Congress.

The conflict with the Irish Embassy would be carried across the Atlantic to Killarney when the AOH held its annual convention there from 27 to 29 June 1978. The Irish Embassy had engineered Division 36 of the AOH in Shrewsbury, Massachusetts, to submit a resolution to the convention: '. . . that the Convention record itself as in favor of the goals and directions of the government of the Republic of Ireland, and further, that the Convention repudiate all groups advocating violence in Northern Ireland.'

The Irish Embassy had simultaneously arranged for Teddy Kennedy to send a telegram to the convention supporting the resolution. Well, one did not need a degree in political science to know what was going on here. I made a statement to the convention that if Senator Kennedy and Division 36 would amend the resolution to include British violence – the violence of the British government, British army, RUC, etc. – I would support it. No such amendment was offered.

The chairman of the Resolutions Committee felt the pressure would be too much for him, so he called in sick and asked me to act as chairman. When the resolution came up, I ruled it out of order on the grounds that the AOH had no 'foreign principal' and therefore could not support a foreign government. All hell broke loose and the establishment media went crazy.

The Irish Times screamed, 'AOH refuses to back government'.[17] I thought one journalist was going to assault me. 'How the f**k is the Irish Government a foreign government?' he snarled at me. (And he was a 'religious' reporter.) I patiently explained, 'Any government outside the USA is a foreign government to an American organisation.' Then I really set him off by adding, 'Besides it is not the government of Ireland, only of twenty-six counties.' He would later write that there were angry scenes between Jack Keane (AOH president) and me, when, in fact, he was the one causing the angry scene. Jack only got angry because the reporter had used the F-word to a priest.

One of the most disappointing things for me about the Irish media was how they allowed themselves to be co-opted, with some honourable exceptions, by the Dublin and British governments. They were scared stiff of deviating from the party line on the North. Oh yes, they could take on the governments on all sorts of issues, but on the North they were docile.

The convention would go on to pass resolutions calling for 'the absolute independence of Ireland and urged the US government to work for the re-unification of Ireland'. It also passed resolutions endorsing the Ad Hoc Committee and the Irish National Caucus and our initiative for the Ad Hoc Committee to host an Irish

Peace Forum in Washington, to which 'all parties could come without preconditions or compromise'.

During the convention, I went to a private location for a meeting with Ruairí Ó Brádaigh, Dave O'Connell and Joe Cahill. They were clearly concerned about my emphasis on non-violence and expressed great concern about Fred O'Brien (of whose affiliations they were suspicious). Each of them asked me a series of questions, and played a recording of an interview I had given to RTÉ radio on why I had ruled out of order the resolution calling for support of the Dublin government. At the end of the meeting, Ó Brádaigh very formally asked O'Connell and Cahill if they were satisfied with my answers and both said they were. Then he, again very formally, summed up the discussion and pronounced that he too was satisfied. Later, he told me I had been 'in a Sinn Féin court'.

After the convention, Fred O'Brien, Bob Bateman and I travelled up to the North to sound out all the groups and parties on the Irish Peace Forum. We checked into a hotel in a strong Loyalist part of East Belfast for three nights. The UDA put a guard outside our door so that no freelancer would 'shoot the priest' – at least, while I was under safe passage. In one amusing incident, when a UVF man came into our room, he challenged me very aggressively about the armed guard. But he calmed down when I told him it was UDA, as he had suspected it was IRA.

One of the first things one of the Loyalists said to me was, 'I've always wanted to see you, Sean – down the barrel of a gun.'

'Isn't much nicer this way, at least from my point of view,' I replied.

We met with all the Loyalist paramilitary groups – UDA, UVF, Red Hand Commandos, etc.

John McKeague, leader of the Red Hand Commandos, told me that he could always tell when Rev. Ian Paisley was going to tell a lie: he would remove his collar. He sent one of his top commandos to meet me so that 'I could see his men were of better mettle than either the UDA or UVF'. After I talked to that young man, he started to cry as he said goodbye. He said I was the first priest he had ever met, and that maybe he had been told lies about priests. I don't remember his name and I often wonder what became of him.

The late Paddy Reynolds, Northern Editor of *The Irish Press*, came to see me in a panic: 'Fr Sean, the only way you are going to get out of this hotel alive is if I call RTÉ to come over and cover your exit with their cameras.' I appreciated his concern but told him I was in no danger. Years later, I tended to think he may have had good reason for his concern.

All the Loyalists were in favour of the Peace Forum and so was the Republican Movement, at first. They later turned against the idea because the British would not attend. The Dublin government, as expected, was totally opposed to the idea of giving 'terrorists a platform'.

However, although the forum did not happen, I believe it helped to further our concept that Washington held the key to unlocking the stalemate in the North. It also made nonsense out of the Dublin government's allegation that the Caucus was supporting violence when we were trying to organise a Peace Forum in Washington.

Back in Boston, I concentrated on making preparations for my move to Washington. But, before that, a couple of things should be mentioned. I began to finalise the naturalisation process of becoming a US citizen. When I went for my final interview, the official had a copy of *Trinity* by Leon Uris sitting on his desk. He was an Irish Catholic, and proud of it. He conducted all the questioning, and I got all the answers right – until he came to the part about me being prepared to bear arms in defence of the United States. 'Catholic priests do not bear arms,' I responded. He sat up in the chair and with obvious relish said, 'So, Father, tell me where in the US Constitution does it exempt Catholic priests from bearing arms?' I told him I had a problem with that. Then he told me that I would have to help him out because if I did not give the right answer I would be denied citizenship. So he said, 'Father. I'm going to ask you that question again, and I can only ask it once. I am going to make it easy for you and ask, "If the communists invaded Boston would you bear arms to defend Boston?" I asked him not to say that but instead to ask me if the British invaded. He did, and I said yes.

When the interview was over, he confided that my file was the largest he had ever seen, indicating with his hands that it was about 3 feet tall. And me in the Land of the Free only five years! I became a US citizen on 8 May 1979.

But back to the Peace Forum: if the forum was going to work, then Irish Republicans would have to be allowed to enter the United States, from which they had been banned for a number of years. Opposing the visa double standard had been one of our main campaigns: Loyalist paramilitaries were given visas to enter the US, Irish Republicans were not. I had asked my good friend Congressman Hamilton Fish (R–NY) to take the lead on the visa issue. He was the ranking Republican on the Subcommittee on Immigration, Citizenship and International Law (which came under the full Judiciary Committee). The Chairman of the Subcommittee was Joshua Eilberg (D–PA), also a good supporter of the Irish cause. Both of them got the Judiciary Committee Chairman, Peter Rodino (D–NJ) – famous for chairing the impeachment proceedings against Richard Nixon – to commission them to investigate the issue. He directed them thus: 'Respected members of the Irish-American community [i.e. the Irish National Caucus] have indicated that US consular officers at posts in London, Belfast and Dublin have recently been more reluctant to issue non-immigrant visas . . . I believe the interests of the Committee on the Judiciary would be well served if you would . . . interview . . . the officials . . . to determine whether their decisions are arbitrary . . .'[18]

Congressman Fish was really insistent that I travel with them, but I could not, so I sent Fred O'Brien instead. Their visit to Ireland and London took place from 28 August to 1 September 1978. It was a major coup for the Irish National Caucus, and their report of 675 pages totally exposed the double standard of the visa policy: 'The delegation feels that the Department of State may have acted unfairly . . . the delegation failed to understand the rationale of labeling only the individuals in the Provisional IRA as terrorists and exonerating individuals in Loyalist paramilitary organizations . . .'[19]

The London and Dublin governments were furious at the report and, of course, they blamed me and the Irish National Caucus.

And how did the Republican Movement show their gratitude to me for orchestrating this major indictment of the visa policy that excluded them from the US? On 27 September 1978, the IRA made a most unusual statement: 'The Irish Republican Army would like to put on record that Dr Fred Burns O'Brien is persona non grata. Signed, P. O'Neill.'[20]

Because they had given me no advance notice, which would have been the decent thing to do, I knew the statement was a way of getting at me, and not really about attacking Fred. And sure enough, when I later met with Ruairí Ó Brádaigh, Dave O'Connell and Joe Cahill in the Sinn Féin office in Dublin in December 1979, I asked them if the statement was meant as much for me as for Fred. 'About sixty:forty,' said Ó Brádaigh, sternly. 'Who's the sixty and who's the forty?' I asked. 'You're the sixty, Fr Sean,' said O'Connell in his great Cork accent, but no twinkle in his eye this time.

They obviously thought Fred was much more important to the workings of the Caucus than he really was, and that without him I would be handicapped. In truth, Fred did very little actual work for the Caucus, and was mostly only seen in my company. The ironic thing was that since they were trying to 'crack the big whip and keep me in line' there was no way I could be seen to accept that. As a consequence, I kept Fred on much longer than I would have otherwise done.

I made a public statement that, 'My response is to simply point out that it is irrelevant what group or party in Ireland finds Fred O'Brien acceptable or unacceptable'.[21]

Gerry Adams was also supposed to be at that meeting in the Sinn Féin office. The other three leaders were noticeably concerned that he did not show. And I realised something was wrong – my first glimpse of the brewing problem between Ó Brádaigh and Adams.

Later in the Caucus office on Capitol Hill, a BBC correspondent from Belfast told me that a Republican spokesman was able to tell him that the IRA could not be seen to be attacking a brother of Patrick McManus, so instead they had a slap at Fred O'Brien, to bring me into line. But that, too, would change – soon the IRA would have no scruples about attacking me.

12

Move to Washington

*Thus McManus became Britain's nemesis in America, the driving
force that would eventually erode Britain's influence within the
US government.*

Joseph E. Thompson[1]

I mentioned previously that while at the Vatican I felt I was being
drawn to the ineluctable conclusion that if we were going to
get the job done (whatever that might eventually be), I knew I
would probably have to 'go full time'.

When we had finished our business at the Vatican, Bishop
Drury and I broke away from the rest of the delegation to pray in
St Peter's. When we finished praying, I told the Bishop I wanted
to talk to him in confidence. We sat in the pews and I told him
about a recurring dream I was having: 'I am rushing back from
some Irish activity to the Redemptorist rectory to check the
assignment board only to discover I'm late for some assigned duty.
I wake up in a panic.'

Bishop Drury listened very sympathetically. And, of course,
one didn't have to be a dream interpreter to see what was going
on. 'You shouldn't have to feel so torn,' he said. 'I must see how I
can help.'

With that I knelt down and asked for his blessing. When I

The author's parents, Celia and Patrick, 1929.

Patrick McManus, the author's eldest brother, who died in 1958 when an IRA bomb he was transporting exploded prematurely.

Six brothers pictured here in 1984. Back (l-r): Myles, Terence and Frankie; front (l-r): the author, Thomas and Jim.

The author with Seán MacBride, 1976.

In 1974, the author with Tip O'Neill, then Majority Leader of the US House of Representatives.

Tip O'Neill at the hearing regarding the International Fund for Ireland in March 1986. The author (left) and Congressman Mario Biaggi (centre) keep a close eye on him.

The author with Presidential candidate Jimmy Carter, 1976.

The author with Senator Edward Kennedy, 1980.

Demonstrating at the British Embassy in 1988, the
author meets Congressmen Joe Kennedy (centre)
and John Lewis (right), hero of the US Civil Rights
Movement.

The author with Congressman Ben Gilman, 1989. Gilman would later chair the House Committee on Foreign Affairs.

The author with actors Richard Harris and Anne Turkel, 1976

The author with Presidential candidate Bill Clinton, 1992.

The author with First Lady Hillary Clinton, St Patrick's Day, 2009.

In 1987, the author (centre) with Mario Biaggi (right), Chairman of the Ad Hoc Congressional Committee for Irish Affairs, and Biaggi's Chief of Staff, Bob Blancato (left).

The author with Raymond McCord (left) in Washington, 2008.

The author with Speaker Nancy Pelosi, 2008.

The author (far right) with his family at Kinnoull in Perth, Scotland, in 2007. (L-r): Myles, Frankie, Celia, Jim, Mary Kate, Alice.

With the Ballymurphy Massacre Committee at Capitol Hill in December 2010, seeking a Congressional hearing on the British Army Massacre, 1971. (L-r): Alice Harper, the author, Briege Foyle and John Taggart.

got up, it was as if a huge weight had been lifted off my shoulders. Bishop Drury was seen in his Diocese of Corpus Christi as a very conservative man. And he certainly would have eschewed all talk about charismatic blessings or healings. But something happened to me when he blessed me there in St Peter's. I was confirmed in the peace of Christ – I don't know how else to put it. And man, would I need that peace as the attacks from all sides would keep escalating: from the British, the Irish government, SDLP and finally from the IRA and Sinn Féin – almost as if directed by the same hand.

Over the next two years the Bishop and I talked about how I could be less 'torn'. He then made the remarkably generous offer that if the Redemptorists would agree, I could come under his jurisdiction and he would appoint me to a Special Ministry of Justice and Peace for Ireland. What a courageous gesture from a conservative Bishop! And here is where praxis trumps theory every time: the Bishop was born in 1902. His experience of the Black and Tans was real. And he had not forgotten.

With Vatican II, the Catholic Church had begun to recognise the validity and importance of the 'Special Ministry'. And with the new stress that 'action on behalf of justice was a constitutive dimension of the preaching of the Gospel' (*Justice in the World*), why should there not be a Special Ministry for that? Bishop Drury was not scared of the British government. And so in December 1978 he appointed me to a full time Special Ministry of Justice and Peace for Ireland.

Before I left, I met with the Archbishop of Boston, Cardinal Medeiros, to ask for his blessing on my new Special Ministry. He provided me with a warm letter of introduction to Cardinal Baum of Washington, so despite the efforts of the Irish Consul in Boston to get me silenced, the Cardinal was giving me his blessings. Indeed, I am firmly convinced – and so was Bishop Drury – that one of the main reasons why the Irish Consul escalated her attacks so strongly was to sabotage my appointment to the Special Ministry. The word had somehow leaked out, leading the Bishop to wonder, 'Sean, do you think the buzzards have our phones tapped?' 'Buzzard' was the strongest word I ever heard him use for the British government.

In a press release announcing my appointment, dated 11 December 1978, Bishop Drury said: 'I have been deeply impressed by [Fr McManus'] dedication to human rights, justice and peace in Ireland. The Catholic Church teaches that certain priests are given special charisms, or "gifts" for special work. I recognize that Father McManus has been given by God a "charism" for this work. He has truly distinguished himself by his total commitment to peace in his country. Anyone who has met Father McManus or has heard him speak must have been deeply impressed by his determination and zeal. He is uniquely suited for this Special Ministry. For the past several years, in the face of disappointments and frustration, he has worked with true Christian Charity. Father McManus is committed to non-violence, reconciliation and freedom in Ireland. I ask people to pray hard that his work will be blessed.'

On 10 December (International Human Rights Day) 1978 the Irish National Caucus opened its National Office on Capitol Hill, marking the first time in Irish American history that the Irish had an office on Capitol Hill to lobby for justice and peace in Ireland. (The Friends of Irish Freedom opened an office in 1919, not on Capitol Hill but downtown. It lasted only a few years.)

I had moved down to Washington without a red cent to my name. But I had called a dear old friend, Howard Smith (not the Howard K. Smith, whose broadcast I had interrupted) and he gave me $5,000 for the first month's and last month's rent of the office on Capitol Hill.

Now we were perfectly positioned to increase our influence on Capitol Hill. The Washington Bureau of *The Boston Globe* predicted that, 'with the arrival of McManus here, one thing is certain, [Tip] O'Neill will probably feel at least two thorns on that issue'. The other 'thorn' was Congressman Biaggi.

Now that I had moved to Capitol Hill to lobby full time, the roles of Bernadette O'Reilly-McAuliffe and Fred O'Brien petered out. Rita Mullan, who had arrived in the US from Belfast in May 1977, became Executive Director. She did a lot of fine work until she became ill in 1983.

I immediately went to work on an eighteen-hour daily schedule. I knocked on the door of virtually every Member of Congress, building up goodwill for the Irish cause, signing them up as members of the Ad Hoc Committee for Irish Affairs, putting pressure where needed, but always politely and respectfully. I made sure I would never mislead the Members or give them wrong information. I immediately levelled with them that the Irish government was bitterly opposed to me, not to mention the British. I acknowledged that I had in the past, as a private individual, expressed support for the IRA but that the Irish National Caucus was non-violent, and that we would never compromise them – that we would only seek to get Members of Congress to support non-violent projects. I also emphasised that we would not seek any special favours for Ireland, only for America to apply a single, not a double, standard in its policy of promoting international human rights; that the 'hands off Northern Ireland lest we offend the Brits policy' had to end; that left to the triangle of Belfast, Dublin and London, no solution could emerge; that an outside catalyst was needed and that it was only possible and proper for America to be that catalyst.

Knowing that we could not depend on Senator Kennedy and Speaker O'Neill, whom the Irish Embassy, working in cahoots with the British Embassy, had scared off, I concentrated on non-Irish and non-Catholic Members of Congress. And to further broaden and 'mainstream' the Irish issue I made a point of enlisting the support of Republican Members of Congress. The Washington correspondent for *The Irish Times*, Sean Cronin, would write, 'The "Irish question" was almost exclusively a Democratic Party matter up to recently when the Irish National Caucus . . . began to make inroads in Republican ranks'.[2]

As we began to make impact on Capitol Hill, the media in Northern Ireland sent reporters to check us out. The well-known journalist David McKittrick would describe our approach thus: 'The Caucus has done some effective lobbying in the past few years, achieving its propaganda successes simply by doing it the American way – playing the lobbying game according to Washington's rules, making contacts and friends in Congress, presenting the human rights case convincingly. It has become the Madison Avenue of Irish Republicanism . . .'[3] And another equally well-known journalist, Barry White of the *Belfast Telegraph*, wrote, 'from there [the Caucus office] Fr McManus is just two and a half minutes from the Capitol building, where he is becoming one of the best known faces among the lobbyists . . . the way the British and Irish Embassies react to what they see as the twin menace of the Caucus and the Ad Hoc Committee of Congressman Biaggi demonstrate its potential'.[4]

One of the first signs that we were beginning to have an impact was – according to a senior *Boston Globe* writer – the change in tone of Teddy Kennedy and Tip O'Neill.

On 15 March 1979, *Boston Globe* journalist Ken Harnett telephoned me and told me he had no hesitation in believing the Caucus was responsible for the change in the upcoming St Patrick's Day statement critical of the British. I immediately told him that I never even had a meeting with Kennedy. Harnett persisted, explaining he had checked it out and because of the pressure the Caucus was putting on Congress, Tipp and Kennedy had been forced to move to 'cover their asses'.

Two days later, Harnett would write:

> The leader of the Irish National Caucus listened as the long statement from the 'Big Four' – Senators Kennedy and Moynihan, Speaker O'Neill and Gov. Carey – was read to him over the telephone, and for a moment, Fr Sean McManus was almost at a loss for words. 'I'm a little inarticulate right now,' said the Ulster-born priest. 'God, I'm elated. I welcome that statement enormously.' . . . The conventional wisdom, as reflected in the 'Big Four's' earlier statements, was to stress the responsibility of the Irish Republican Army for the violence in the North, and to warn Irish-Americans against giving either financial or psychological support . . . [McManus] felt

frustrated trying to get across the idea of British culpability for the violence and stalemate in the North . . . But suddenly, this year, someone listened . . . It was not that McManus had changed, or the IRA, or the perception of the IRA . . . Rather, it was a variety of changes in the Irish situation itself, not the least of which was the growth in the awareness of the human-rights violations . . .

And so, the annual St Patrick's Day proclamation had its obligatory condemnation of sectarian violence again this year but it had much more. It had a scolding of the British government, not just for its political lassitude but for its acquiescence in 'official brutality and violation of human rights'. The pressure on the British was being raised by several degrees and Sean McManus couldn't hide his great enjoyment. 'Everyone was saying we were terrorists last year for saying these things. Now it's the popular respectable thing.'[5]

But not everyone would be pleased with our success, as my first St Patrick's Day Parade in Washington would show.

The late Matt Hannon, an ardent Irishman and very active member of the Irish National Caucus, was the Chairman of the Parade. Matt insisted that I would lead the Caucus contingent seated in a fancy limousine, with the name Irish National Caucus emblazoned on both sides. When the limousine arrived at the reviewing stand, Matt announced me with great theatricality and with aplomb escorted me up on the reviewing stand. I was seated next to a local bishop, so naturally I stood and shook his hand. Then I realised that Sean Donlon, Irish Ambassador to Washington (1978–1981) was seated next to the bishop. I knew he was hostile to me, but I did the well-mannered thing, held out my hand and said: 'Happy St Patrick's Day, Mr Ambassador.' With the entire reviewing stand looking on, Donlon burrowed himself deeper in his chair and refused to shake my hand. I kept my hand extended for a long while, until everyone could plainly see what was happening.

Donlon was a protégé of Garret FitzGerald. FitzGerald claims he had got Taoiseach Jack Lynch to appoint Donlon as Ambassador to Washington.[6]

Donlon would go on to be a bitter and hysterical opponent. The ever-colourful Con Howard, at that time an official of the Irish Embassy, recounted this story to me: Donlon was speaking to him in the Irish Embassy, giving out about us. 'In six weeks I will have stomped out the Irish National Caucus,' he said as he stomped the floor with his foot.

Mind you, the same Con Howard did not hesitate to attack us when so directed. On the night of that same St Patrick's Day, I was in his home for a party. He hoisted a glass of champagne, drank it down and then with great flourish smashed it into the giant fireplace, vowing with patriotic fervour never to say a bad word about the Caucus, no matter who ordered him. A few days later, he had a letter in *The Washington Post* charging the Caucus with supporting violence. That evening I ran into him at an event in the Library of Congress and I said, 'Con, what happened to your dramatic vow never to attack us?' He replied with a sheepish smile, 'Orders from the Captain.' I was never sure who he meant.

The strange thing about Donlon is that years earlier, while I was still in Boston, and he was head of the Anglo-Irish Division of the Department of Foreign Affairs, he called me from the home of a mutual friend in New York City. He told me there was no interest in a united Ireland by anyone in the Irish government. And that if 'Ó Brádaigh and O'Connell were to take over in the morning', he would be working for them (Ó Brádaigh was then President of Sinn Féin and O'Connell the most visible IRA leader in Ireland).

As Ambassador, Donlon disgusted Irish Americans by his silence about British violence and human rights violations. He seemed only concerned about IRA violence, and he had a particular animus for me. One former member of an important Fianna Fáil national organisation amazed me by suggesting that one of Donlon's problems with me could be explained by the 'spoiled priest' syndrome, i.e. that Donlon had been studying for the priesthood but left the seminary. Therefore, according to the former Fianna Fáil apparatchik, when Donlon arrived in Washington, he was really incensed to find a priest (me) saying, 'Don't listen to the Irish Embassy, listen to the Irish National Caucus instead.'

But whatever explained Donlon's problems, he seemed to be obsessed with destroying the Irish National Caucus. So much so that we launched a campaign to have him recalled as Ambassador, and it almost worked, too. This is how it came about.

The veteran Donegal politician, Neil Blaney, TD and MEP, was on a speaking tour for the Irish National Caucus. He was in our office on 7 December 1979 when Charlie Haughey called him with the dramatic news that he, Haughey, had just been elected Taoiseach. Before hanging up the phone, Blaney said, 'Fr Sean McManus is right beside me. Why don't you say hello?' There was silence. I knew very well Haughey would not speak to me. Then Blaney hung up, and said Haughey could not speak then, but that he said he would call back. 'Yeah, right,' I sceptically thought to myself.

But, nonetheless, it did represent the possibility of an improvement. Taoiseach Jack Lynch was gone. Blaney was now in a position to influence Haughey, at least to some degree. Maybe he could convince Haughey to issue a new policy directive to the Irish Embassy, like stating that British injustice was the enemy not Irish Americans.

Blaney became convinced Donlon had to go after we told him about how Donlon had sabotaged an effort to free the Birmingham Six.

A month earlier, November 1979, the Caucus had brought Fr Raymond Murray from Armagh to Washington to help promote our campaign to free the Birmingham Six. We brought him along to meet our dear friend, the late Congressman Hamilton Fish (R-NY) whom I held in great affection and esteem. Ham, as he was known, was the great grandson of US Secretary of State Hamilton Fish who, having slapped the Fenians on the wrists for one of their invasions of Canada, urged that they be released. On 16 August

1870, Secretary Fish wrote to President Grant: 'I always supposed that you would deem it wise to release the prisoners convicted of participation in the Fenian raid. Purely political prisoners are the worst kind of birds to keep caged.'[7] I always kidded Congressman Fish that the reason he was so good on the Irish issue was that he had to do penance for his great grandfather locking up the Fenians in the first place.

Anyway, one of the results of bringing Fr Murray to meet Ham Fish was that the Congressman promised to try and get the law faculty of some prestigious university to examine the entire case of the miscarriage of justice that the Birmingham Six represented. Fish, an officer in the American Consulate in Dublin in the 1950s, being a very diplomatic man, met with Donlon at the Irish Embassy to inform him of his plans. Donlon went berserk. Fish told me that he had never been talked to in such a disrespectful fashion. Donlon followed up the meeting with a letter on 6 November 1979:

> Dear Mr Fish,
> In view of our recent conversations and correspondence I thought it might be useful to let you have the attached recent reports from *The Irish Times*.
> The report dated 27 October describes a recent interest of yours in the Birmingham bombings case as 'the fruit of the work of Fr Raymond Murray of Armagh . . .' In the report of 22 October, Fr Murray is criticized by the leading elected representatives of both sections of the divided Northern Ireland community. . .'[8]

The two 'elected representatives' were Gerry Fitt and Martin Smyth, the head of the Orange Order, who was not then an MP.

So here was the Irish Ambassador in Washington using the head of the Orange Order to discredit a Catholic priest of the calibre of Fr Murray, all with a view to stopping the campaign to free the Birmingham Six! Neil Blaney was outraged and embarrassed that, in his name and in the name of the Irish people, Donlon would dare pull that stuff. He began to privately urge the new Haughey government to replace Donlon. Haughey agreed but Donlon rallied Tip O'Neill, Teddy Kennedy and other important Americans to intervene on his behalf (not what one would expect from an ambassador). Haughey backed off. *The Washington Post* reported that 'Irish Prime Minister Charles Haughey decided today to keep Sean Donlon as Ireland's ambassador in Washington after being warned that replacing him would harm relations between Haughey's seven-month-old government and leading Irish American politicians. Haughey was told that he would upset Sens. Edward M. Kennedy (D-MA) and Patrick Moynihan (D-NY), House Speaker Thomas P. O'Neill (D-MA) and New York Gov. Hugh Carey if he removed Donlon in response to complaints about him from the Washington-based militant Irish nationalist lobby, the Irish National Caucus, and its ally in congress, Rep. Mario Biaggi (D-NY), according to well-informed sources.'[9]

Later Brian Lenihan, Minister for Foreign Affairs, told us on the phone, 'maybe we will have another stab at Donlon and send him to Tehran' (which was then in the midst of the American hostages crisis).

But even when Donlon was eventually replaced in 1981, it did not really change the bad attitude of the Irish Embassy. That only changed with the beginning of the Irish peace process and the IRA ceasefire of 31 August 1994.

In November 1985, Donlon's opposition to the campaign to free the Birmingham Six resurfaced in the Irish newspapers. *The Irish Press* reported: 'In yesterday's *Sunday Press*, Mr. Donlon said any action he had taken had been on the instructions of the Irish Government. But last night, the then Foreign Minister, Mr O'Kennedy, to whom the diplomat was answerable, rejected the claim ... Mr O'Kennedy said ... he did not give Mr Donlon any authority to write such a letter.'[10]

As I had expected, Haughey himself would go on to condemn the Irish National Caucus on 27 July 1980. But he did so under threat from FitzGerald: 'A threat to end the bipartisan policy on Northern Ireland is contained in a letter which will be sent from the Fine Gael leader, Dr Garret FitzGerald, to the Taoiseach today calling on Mr Haughey to spell out his attitude to IRA front organizations in the United States.'[11] And FitzGerald, eager to claim the credit for the condemnation, released a copy of the letter he had sent to Haughey on 21 July, demanding such condemnation:

> You will have seen that John Hume, Frank Cluskey and myself speaking independently . . . urged on the 9th July, that you clarify at once your Government's position with respect specifically to Congressman Biaggi, and to organizations such as Northern Aid and Irish National Caucus . . . Failure to re-state in unambiguous terms the position of three successive governments on this matter can only confuse the issue in the United States, as may be seen by the statement on RTÉ news programme last week by the Rev. Sean McManus, speaking on behalf of the Irish National Caucus, that he presumed that they were 'right in thinking that there is a difference between the policies of Mr Haughey and Mr Lynch – it is our general impression and hope that Mr Haughey's policies will be quite different . . .'[12]

In his autobiography, FitzGerald crows: 'My letter achieved its purpose . . . the Taoiseach provided belatedly the necessary clear repudiation . . . The Caucus' leader, Sean McManus, responded that the Taoiseach's statement was a response to "threats and blackmail from me", and that I had "once again dictated policy to Mr. Haughey" – a statement that I did not feel it necessary to deny.'[13]

But here it must be noted, as FitzGerald makes clear, that John Hume was in full collusion with the Irish government's policy of marginalisation of any group that wanted the British embarrassed and pressured. John would later go on to do great work on the peace process, but for too long, he, in effect, gave the British a pass, as will be seen when I give the history of the MacBride Principles.

Donlon was the first person who ever refused to shake my hand. The second and only other person ever to do so, was Donlon's master, Garret FitzGerald. It happened this way: on 2 August 1979, the State Department announced it had suspended the sale of US weapons to the RUC. (This was one of our greatest victories and I will explain it in a moment.) I was back in Belfast at the time so naturally the media was very interested in what I had to say about the arms ban. As a consequence, I was constantly in the news. When my press work was over, I noticed that Garret FitzGerald, now no longer in government, was due to give a lecture at the Corrymeela Reconciliation Centre on the north Antrim coast. I decided to attend. And so did, it appeared, the entire Supreme Council of the UDA, including Andy Tyrie, Glenn Barr, etc. FitzGerald spoke eloquently about the need for both parts of Ireland to come together (albeit not in a united Ireland) in mutual understanding and forgiveness. During the question-and-answer period, he warmly addressed the UDA leaders by their first names, clearly making great play for the UDA. Now remember, at that very time, the UDA, with the cooperation of the British government and security forces, were slaughtering hundreds of innocent Catholics. After the speech, FitzGerald, his wife and a core group went into a private room. The Rev. Ray Davey, founder of the Centre, then came and invited me to join the 'inner circle'.

When I entered the room, the group was sitting in a semi-circle, facing the entrance, with FitzGerald and his wife sitting in the middle. The Rev. Davey announced, 'This is Fr Sean McManus, president of the Irish National Caucus.' Of course, all of them knew me anyway, even though I was not in my clerical collar but in a suit and tie. As I approached the semi-circle to the right, they started to stand and I shook their hands. Out of the corner of my eye I noticed FitzGerald was still sitting down with his eyes resolutely fixed on the floor. 'This is going to be interesting,' I thought, suspecting what was going to happen. I pleasantly shook the hands of all the polite Ulster folk, as I approached FitzGerald. When in front of him, I held out my hand and said, 'I enjoyed your lecture, Dr FitzGerald.' Like a clocking hen he fluttered in his seat. I kept my hand extended, it seemed forever. He finally hissed, 'Please go away, you are creating a disturbance.' I calmly responded that the Rev. Davey had invited me. Davey was standing by my side and he nodded in assent.

I finally moved on, skipping over Mrs FitzGerald, to shake the hand of Glenn Barr who was sitting next to her. With a smile, I expansively said, 'Maybe you guys are right, after all, Glenn, that there are two nations in Ireland.' He laughed loudly. (The UDA at the time were advocating an independent Northern Ireland based on the alleged premise that Northerners and Southerners were two distinct peoples.)

So there you have it. That's the Blue Shirt's version of reconciliation in Ireland. I had shaken the hands of ex-Black and Tans, B Specials, RUC, British soldiers, and leaders of every Protestant paramilitary group in Northern Ireland. But FitzGerald, in best Blue Shirt tradition, refused my hand, after waxing eloquently about reconciliation.

Of course, FitzGerald, apart from his long antipathy for me, was seething in particular about our success in stopping the sale of US weapons to the RUC, and about all the publicity the media was giving me. Because, you see, the obvious issue it raised was why did the Caucus have to do it? Why had the Dublin government not done it?

But it was not just the likes of FitzGerald who resented the Caucus victory. *The Irish Times* clearly had a problem with it. I spoke to a young male and female reporter in the Belfast office of *The Irish Times*. The male reporter, whom I had never met before, could barely hide his hostility. He pompously told me that his sources in Washington told him that the Caucus had nothing to do with the ban.

Months later, *US News and World Report* would write: 'high among the concern of the Irish National Caucus is human rights in Northern Ireland. When members protested the issuance of a license to ship machine guns and magnum pistols to the Ulster police, the shipment ceased'.[14] And on 28 May 1980, *The New*

York Times ran an editorial, 'What's a Boycott Between Friends?' Referring to the RUC ban, it said: 'What should have been a routine transaction aroused the opposition of the Irish National Caucus, whose leader, the Rev. Sean McManus, has been an open supporter – and occasional critic – of the Provisional wing of the Irish Republican Army. The Caucus has its ardent partisans in Congress, and House Speaker O'Neill was moved to oppose granting an export license for guns . . .'[15]

I duly sent both articles to the male *Irish Times* reporter in Belfast with a letter suggesting that he might want to reconsider his position. I also sent copies to Douglas Gageby, then Editor of *The Irish Times*, and to Sean Cronin, the Washington correspondent. I never heard back from the reporter in Belfast. Cronin emphatically denied that he was that reporter's alleged 'source'. Later a well-established reporter from another newspaper told me that *The Irish Times* liked to indulge in the conceit that it was not only the paper of record, but that it also shaped and influenced national events – and that it had to give its stamp of approval before a person was considered a 'player'.

The Washington Post would also refute the pompous young man from *The Irish Times* when it wrote: 'British officials believe the Caucus and Biaggi's ad hoc committee are responsible for influencing the Carter administration to hold up the sale of American-made guns to the police in Northern Ireland . . .'[16]

But the Rev. Paisley had no doubt who was responsible. He said it was an insult, but said that clearly it was seen as a triumph for the Irish National Caucus in America and the Ad Hoc Congressional Committee for Irish Affairs, led by Congressman Mario Biaggi.[17]

Notice in that *New York Times* editorial it says, Speaker O'Neill was 'moved'. It uses more parliamentary language than Ken Harnett of *The Boston Globe*, but it amounts to the same thing: O'Neill was bounced into taking that position because we made the pressure irresistible. Tipp did not want to take that position, but he had to. Why do I say that? Because O'Neill, and indeed Teddy Kennedy, only took anti-British positions when forced to because the Dublin government had pressured them into silence: criticise the British, and you will seen to be pro-IRA and anti-Irish government.

Perfect proof that the Irish government did not want the RUC to be blacklisted by the Unites States is that when we got dozens of Members of Congress to co-sign Congressman Mario Biaggi's letter of protest to the State Department, Matthew Nimetz, Counselor, replied in a letter, defending the weapons sale to the RUC: 'The Royal Ulster Constabulary is the legally constituted police force in Northern Ireland . . .' He then plays his trump card: 'In this connection I would note that Irish Foreign Minister O'Kennedy, in a 31 May foreign policy speech to the Dail, pledged the continued cooperation of the Irish police and army with the Royal Ulster Constabulary in the fight against violence in Northern Ireland'.[18]

Congressman Biaggi responded to that *New York Times* editorial as follows:

> It was my amendment to the fiscal 1980 Department of State appropriations bill which led to the decision by the State Department to suspend further sales or shipments of United States arms to the RUC pending a full review of our policy.
>
> My initial reason for raising this issue in congress was the incomparability of the sale of arms to the RUC and our foreign policy philosophy – respect for human rights. Section 502 (b) of the Foreign Assistance Act of 1961 bars the sale or export of any U.S. arms to nations or organizations that engage in persistent patterns of human rights violations . . . Finally, the leadership provided by the Irish National Caucus on the issue of suspending arms shipments is fully consistent with their role as the leading Irish-American organization working for peace, justice and human rights for Ireland'.[19]

It was clear to all by now that the Irish National Caucus was beginning to have significant influence in changing American foreign policy on Northern Ireland – despite the opposition of both the British and Irish Embassies.

The secret of our success was in hammering away on the theme of the single standard: America must apply a single standard, not a double standard, to human rights in Northern Ireland. I zeroed in like a laser beam on all double standards. For example, we had long opposed the policy of refusing visas to Irish Republicans who wanted to come to the United States to denounce British policy in Northern Ireland, yet the Rev. Ian Paisley was allowed into America. Because he was an MP, I knew it would be all the more difficult to frame the double-standard issue. But when the State Department refused a visa to Owen Carron MP, a Fermanagh neighbour of mine, who was elected to fill the seat of martyred Bobby Sands, I struck like lightning. Now I knew we could have Paisley's visa revoked, and we did, on 21 December 1981.

I will let the late David Nyhan of *The Boston Globe* tell the story: 'The State Department yesterday revoked the visa of militant Northern Ireland Protestant leader Rev. Ian Paisley, who had planned a visit to the United States next month, because of the "divisive tone" of his recent speeches . . . The campaign to revoke Paisley's visa was launched Dec. 2 by the Irish National Caucus . . . [which] devised a strategy of asking conservative Republicans to lead the fight in congress, instead of the Irish-Catholic Democrats . . .'[20]

We got 125 Members of the House and 22 Senators (including Senator Joe Biden, now US Vice President) to co-sign a letter by Congressman Bill Carney (R-NY) and Senator Al D'Amato (R-NY) to Secretary of State Alexander Haig demanding that Paisley be refused entry. And that number did not include Tip O'Neill and Teddy Kennedy who again were forced to take action. When they saw that the two arch-fundamentalists, Senator Strom Thurmond (R-SC) and Senator Jess Helms (R-NC), had signed on, they simply had to get on board. In a previous article Nyhan pointed out that, when O'Neill and Kennedy finally wrote to the Secretary of State, 'the letter from the two Massachusetts

Democrats followed by several hours a speech on the floor by Rep. William Carney . . .'[21]

In the lead-up to the visa denial, Paisley kept saying that 'priest McManus would never stop me going to America'. When he was stopped, he then started blaming Prime Minister Margaret Thatcher and President Ronald Reagan. Of course, it was not lost on him that US Secretary of State Al Haig was Catholic, with a Jesuit brother. Paisley's benefactor, Bob Jones III, attacked Haig as 'a monster in human flesh'and publicly prayed that God would 'smite him hip and thigh, bone and marrow, heart and lungs'.[22]

The year 1981, of course, was the year of the Irish hunger strike. We had been trying to move heaven and earth to get America to put pressure on Margaret Thatcher to grant the hunger strikers' demands. I had asked Congressman Hamilton Fish (R-NY) to work on his good friend Vice President George H. Bush. When Fish called me to tell me that Bush had got back to him with a final decision that President Reagan would not intercede, I knew Bobby Sands was going to die. Twelve days before his death I embarked on my own hunger strike right outside the British Embassy. Because I did not hold any poster, and because I was by myself, I did not have to remain at the mandatory distance of 500 yards. Prince Charles was staying at the Embassy and each time he left in the car, he had to drive right past me. I could see him peering out of the darkened car windows – not without empathy, or so I thought. Certainly he was not glaring with hostility. I stayed on hunger strike for twelve days, only drinking water, losing 25 lb. When Bobby died I came off the hunger strike, knowing I had to continue the work.

But I felt disgusted that although two of the most powerful men in the world, President Reagan and Speaker O'Neill, had Irish roots, they did not lift a finger to save Bobby Sands and his nine fellow-patriots who went on to die, 'hungering for justice'. I could never think the same way again about Reagan and O'Neill.

On 12 May Francis Hughes (twenty-four) was the second Irish martyr to die on the 1981 Hunger Strike. Francis is commonly regarded as being one of the most fearless soldiers the IRA ever produced. On 30 May, the Irish National Caucus brought his brother, Oliver, from Bellaghy, County Derry, to Washington. Oliver – one of the most dynamic and charismatic speakers I have ever heard – declared in that unique Bellaghy accent: 'I came to the United States to give a simple message. My brother, Francis, was not a criminal. He was an Irish patriot.'[23] Later we would bring out Mrs McElwee, the mother of Oliver's first cousin Tom, who would also die on the hunger strike. I marvelled at the fortitude of this woman as she went around Capitol Hill speaking to politicians and the media, trying to save the life of her son. I would later attend Tom's funeral, and have my heart broken at the sight of his eight beautiful sisters carrying his coffin. I would also attend the funerals of hunger strikers Ciaran Doherty and Kevin Lynch.

13

The Old Sow that Eats Its Own Farrow

Loyalty is the sister of Justice
Horace[1]

James Joyce, through his alter ego, Stephen Dedalus, famously quipped, 'Ireland is the old sow that eats her farrow'.[2] That, of course, could be said of any institution. But maybe it can apply to the IRA with particular force.

The *Sunday World* carried the headline, with a photograph of President Carter and me, 'Provos Fall Out With Caucus Priest' (21 March 1982). The unsigned article described me as having been 'long a painful thorn in the flesh of British Embassy officials in Washington' and reported on the increased attacks by the Republican Movement and Irish Northern Aid on the Caucus: 'changed times indeed, when it's realized that Father McManus probably did more than any single individual to publicize the provisionals' political aims among influential people in the United States.' Its conclusion was that '. . . the present fall-out between the Provisionals and McManus is probably due to the fact that, having built up a powerful Irish–American support lobby in the U.S., McManus doesn't want it sabotaged by heavy-handed interference . . .'[3]

That certainly, in part, explained my attitude, but what were the Provisionals' reasons? I always put it down to the age-old fear of Irish leaders (whether Parnell, de Valera, IRA, Dublin government, SDLP, whoever) of the 'tail wagging the dog' – that Irish Americans would end up dictating to Ireland. It was a fear I was always sensitive to. I knew from my study of the history of Irish American nationalism that the 'home group' only fully trusted the Irish American group to the degree it totally controlled them. But as the years have passed, and as revelations of British infiltration of the Republican Movement continues to mount, I now begin to wonder who really was behind the attacks on the Irish National Caucus. Now nothing is as simple as it once seemed.

Gerry Adams, then Vice-President of Sinn Féin, was the first to launch a personal attack on me. In a question-and-answer interview in *Hibernia Review,* he said: 'The [Irish] National Caucus and especially people like Fr McManus have been using Republicanism as a justification for what they've been involved in. They started off by calling for a United Ireland and now they're into human rights . . . I think to a large extent Fr Sean McManus is an opportunist.'[4]

It was Sean Cronin, Washington correspondent for *The Irish Times*, who first alerted me to this article. 'If you were an opportunist, you have picked a funny way to opportune,' he laughed. Then he went on to point out that the IRA always accused priests for not speaking out because they were scared of the British and that it would damage their career, and now there was I being accused by Adams of speaking out to advance my career!

I had never met Adams, nor spoken with him, but I was struck by the unfairness of his attack. I recognised that it was the beginning of a calculated plan to put the Caucus out of business – just as the British and Irish Embassies were committed to doing. But I could not miss the irony of Adams thinking there was a contradiction between human rights and national self-determination. It was so reminiscent of de Valera's infamous dismissal of labour and social concerns in 1918, when he said 'labour must wait'.[5]

Adams' charge was all the more patently false since we had made our paraphrase of the Pledge of Allegiance quite famous all across America: 'The Irish National Caucus believes that Ireland, too, has the right to be one ntion under God, indivisible, with liberty and justice for all.' The injustice of Adams' attack was unworthy of a man who was supposed to be fighting for a just cause. Justice can never be served by injustice.

Then like clockwork, attacks followed from Irish Northern Aid Committee (Noraid) and their paper, the *Irish People*, which once lionised me. In October 1980, the *Irish People* published an editorial, dictated by the Republican Movement, which declared, '. . . the Caucus is an anathema to the Republican Movement in Ireland'.[6] Notice the exact same term as Jack Lynch used – 'anathema'. It was as if the attacks were written by the same hand.

But I can honestly say the attacks did not really upset me too much. Because I had a clear vision of the absolute need for an Irish lobby on Capitol Hill long before others realised it, I was not going to let anything deter me from my mission – not the British or Irish Embassies, not the IRA or Gerry Adams. Years later, the *Sunday World* would reflect on this: 'political observers in America say he was light years ahead of his time when he set up the Irish National Caucus to fight for justice and rights for nationalists back home in Northern Ireland'.[7]

Gerry Adams went on to order a spokesman for Irish Northern Aid and editor of the *Irish People* never to mention me or the Irish National Caucus in the *Irish People*, except to condemn me. In one absurd incident, the New York City Comptroller ran an election campaign advertisement in the *Irish People* that mentioned the Caucus, and the editor deleted the name of the Caucus. When the Comptroller's office called to demand by what right he had censored a paid advertisement, the editor plaintively pleaded he had no choice as he was under strict orders from Adams.

Many Irish Northern Aid members were privately disgusted by the attacks and would secretly call me to assure me they did not approve. They would admit to me that the IRA had sent orders that Irish Northern Aid were to infiltrate, disrupt and destroy Caucus chapters throughout the country – just as the British and Irish Embassies were trying to do.

The head of Irish Northern Aid, Michael Flannery, was especially resentful of the Irish National Caucus. Because he was an old IRA man, and because he lived to be a great age, Flannery had a certain credibility. And he let everyone know he went to Mass every morning. But he could be a mendacious old knave. He put me in mind of Cardinal Spellman of New York (4 May 1889 – 2 December 1967), of whom it was said that he would tell any lie for the good of the Church. But in Flannery's case, he would tell any lie for the good of the IRA, only as long as the IRA agreed with him. He would tell members of Irish Northern Aid, and even journalists, that I had built 'a mansion on the shores of Lough Erne with all the money I collected that should have gone to Irish Northern Aid'. I sent a message to him that if he wanted to know when my parents' humble home had been 'roofed' (that is, changed from a thatched house to a slated one), all he had to do was ask the chairman and vice-chairman of Sinn Féin in Fermanagh, who were both neighbours of ours and they would tell him it was in the 1960s, long before I came to America.

Flannery would also tell people that I had to be a front for the CIA because our office on Capitol Hill was so big. Many Noraid leaders would tell me that they had received specific instructions from the Republican Movement to oppose and obstruct the Caucus in every way possible. One Irish-born woman told me in 2010 that, much to her regret, she had believed the lies the Republican Movement/Noraid had spread about me. One absolute whopper of a lie was that I 'owned a yacht'. That was told to her by a 'person in authority, and one that was respected'.[8]

It was all rather ridiculous, yet sad. I always feel there is something tragic about a person who is supposed to be working for a just cause but who does not hesitate to tell malicious and malevolent lies. What does that say about his commitment to justice?

To some of the Noraiders I would give 'a fool's pardon'. Many of them were the salt of the earth – fine, decent Irish Americans with an admirable dedication to Irish justice. But they naively thought that if the IRA wanted the Caucus out of business, they had a patriotic duty to oppose us. Later on, of course, they would come to be deeply embarrassed. Over the years, I have had dozens of calls or conversations that began with, 'Now, Fr Sean, I am very embarrassed I opposed the Caucus . . .'

However, I was not willing to give a fool's pardon to those who were trying to sabotage us on behalf of the Irish, British or American governments.

Professor Joseph Thompson would later reveal in his book that, '. . . the U.S. government singled out the INC for special surveillance'.[9] I was fully aware there was a multilayered campaign to put us out of business. And it was often difficult to know which entity was behind it – though it made no difference to me since they all had the same goal: to destroy the Caucus.

For example, there was a very determined effort to infiltrate the Washington local chapter of the Irish National Caucus, and to use it to oppose the National Office. I moved rapidly and disaffiliated the chapter. The leader of the attempted coup then disappeared like snow off a ditch – clear proof that he was up to no good. If he had been committed to working for Irish justice, why did he not continue working in some other capacity? Clearly, his only function was to disrupt the Caucus. When he was thwarted in that, he had no longer any interest in working for the cause of Ireland. That, for me, is always a dead giveaway.

In another part of the United States, I had taken an Irish-born man 'in from the cold' and put him in a leadership position in a local chapter. (This was before Noraid had started to oppose us.) He had been previously isolated in that city, and a local priest and Noraid leaders warned me he could not be trusted. Indeed, Tyrone-born Eoin McNamee, IRA Chief of Staff in 1942, called me in Boston from Chicago and urged me to get rid of him because he was too close to the Dublin government. I refused, but I should have listened to Eoin.

Many years later that individual let it slip that an official from the Irish Consulate for that region had visited him with the proposal that the Irish government would back the Irish National Caucus 'if they dumped McManus'. The same individual was involved with a new Irish grouping in the 1980s. A representative of this new grouping came to see me in my office. He said he would offer the Caucus $200,000 a year if we came under his umbrella. I asked him what I would have to do for such kindness. 'Do as I tell you,' was his arrogant response. I told him that he had not the slightest idea of who I was, and what I was about if he thought he could silence me with money: 'All sorts of people in Church and State have been trying to silence me for years. Do you really think you can?' Then, when I discovered that he had been driven to the Caucus office by the Irish Embassy's car (which was parked around the block with the driver waiting), I knew I had to keep him at a firm distance.

Years later, my old friend, the late Matt Hannon, would reveal something that would validate all my suspicions. For a while Matt and I had become alienated because the Irish Embassy had told him all sorts of lies about me. Later on, when he realised he had been deceived by the Embassy and by the IRA and its supporters, he sought to be reconciled with me. I gladly welcomed him back. He then proceeded to tell me that shortly after the visitor to my office attempted to buy me off, a top Irish Embassy official telephoned him, urging him go to a very important meeting in Chicago, which that same visitor was organising. 'Why is it so important?' asked Matt. The official responded that the meeting was going to get rid of McManus, and the new grouping was going to take over from the Caucus, and would be backed by the Dublin government.

Before the Chicago conference, there had been a lot of pressure on me to attend. I had a lot of calls from individuals who had no real history of involvement in the Irish cause, all stressing how important it was for me to attend. I knew something was up, so I had stayed away. Again, my Kinawley instincts had served me well. Also, at the actual conference, the Irish-born man told people from Boston (not realising they were friends of mine) that, 'the Irish National Caucus would be out of business in six weeks'.

I never went public with any of this at the time because there are only so many fronts one can fight on at once. But I also knew that if all these people were going to defeat me, they would have to rise very early indeed and be prepared to fight for a very long time. I also knew that the rank and file of the new grouping had no idea what was going on, and that over time the Irish Embassy could not control them. So I just got on with my work, all the more convinced I was on the right tracks as so many were trying to sabotage me.

There is the peculiar case of an Irish American, who has kept up a thirty-year campaign against me. He once urged a journalist for a top British newspaper to contact my Provincial in London and demand to know why he was allowing me 'to be involved in politics on Capitol Hill'. He would go to absurd lengths. In 2001, a Florida State Senator introduced a Bill that would repeal the MacBride Principles legislation, which was passed in 1988. I branded the Bill as anti-Catholic, wrote to all the Florida State Senators and effectively raised the issue in the Florida media. We killed the Bill almost immediately. State Senators, Protestants and Catholic, telephoned me to assure me urgently that they were no way associated with the 'anti-Catholic Bill'. Meanwhile, the individual – who was prominent in the AOH but who kept hopping from one Irish organisation to another – was lobbying members of the AOH to dissociate themselves from my campaign.

In another example, he went to see Seán MacBride in Dublin to get him to change the MacBride Principles to accommodate the Ford Motor Company, against whom the Caucus had a very effective boycott for their refusal to sign MacBride. I telephoned Seán MacBride to warn him about the impending visit and he replied, 'Do not worry, good Father. People like that have been coming to see me all my life to get me to change my principles and they never succeeded.'[10]

And then there the case of another prominent former AOH leader. In 1989, the Irish National Caucus was leading a very strong campaign in the State of Pennsylvania to get the MacBride Principles passed by the State Legislature. The INC leader in Scranton, the late John Breheny, had done magnificent work. He had got the local Scranton bishop and the Governor of Pennsylvania to support the Principles. The Chairman of the Senate Finance

Committee, State Senator Gibson Armstrong (R–Lancaster) had bottled up the MacBride Bill in his Committee, and we were having a hard time getting it out. Lancaster was heavily Amish, very conservative, with hardly any Irish connections. John and I went to see his staffers and convinced them to hold a hearing on the MacBride Bill.

Shortly after our meeting, I had a call in my office from one of the staffers expressing alarm because he had had visitors who demanded I should be taken off the Witness List, i.e. the list of people who were scheduled to testify at the hearing. I told him he should not be surprised as I had told him up front that both the British and Irish Embassies were very hostile to me. 'But Fr McManus,' this non–Catholic staffer said, 'it was not the Embassies but someone we thought supported the Irish cause.' And he named the former prominent AOH leader. I almost fell off my chair. Anyway, on 19 September 1989, the hearing on the MacBride Bill took place in Harrisburg, the State Capital. When I had finished my testimony, the entire hearing room broke into applause even though Chairman Armstrong had opened the hearing by stressing that there should be none. When the applause ended, Chairman Armstrong said, 'Fr Mc Manus, your church must always be full. I'm glad I don't have to run against you in an election.'[11]

The AOH in Pennsylvania went on to eloquently repudiate the rogue AOH member by electing me Grand Marshal of the Harrisburg St Patrick's Day Parade for March 1990. Neil McGinley, prominent AOH leader and General Chairman of the Parade, said: 'We chose Fr McManus to acknowledge the leadership of the Irish National Caucus on the MacBride Principles nationally and specifically in the State of Pennsylvania . . . Having him Grand Marshal will effectively demonstrate that we want the MacBride Principles passed in Pennsylvania, to which end, we have dedicated the Parade.'[12] And so it came to pass. The MacBride Principles were passed and signed into law by Governor Robert Casey (D–PA).

However, the rogue AOH member would just not quit. On 10 March 1993, there was a public hearing on the MacBride Principles Bill before the Baltimore City Council. The Bill had mistakenly been crafted as a disinvestment Bill but we had lined up the complete support of the City Council to have it changed and brought into conformity with our national MacBride campaign. Bill Hughes was my key ally. A fervent Irishman and an all-round justice campaigner, Bill was one of the first Irishmen I met when I had arrived in Baltimore in 1972. And by a very nice coincidence the person who introduced the Bill, Council Member Perry Sfikas, represented my old parish of Sacred Heart of Jesus. The President of the City Council, Mary Pat Clarke, would write to me: 'It is our family's honor to be counted among your Irish-American supporters. Best wishes for a Brit-free Ireland.'[13]

Anyway, at the hearing the rogue AOH member was the very last witness and the first words out of his mouth were, 'I am here to oppose Fr McManus.' Then in an incoherent rant he proceeded to say that the MacBride Principles had failed, there was no point in getting American companies to sign the Principles and the only effective thing was to get American companies out of Northern Ireland. I quickly squashed his nonsense. Maryland Attorney General, Joe Curran, backed me up, as did his son-in-law City Council Member Martin O'Malley, future Governor of Maryland – a most ardent Irishman, and a possible future US president.

This AOH member's outburst played right into the hands of the British government – intentionally or otherwise. But he was routed and the day was saved for MacBride.

But enough of informers, agents and 'useful idiots' (those being used by the British without even knowing it). For every scoundrel, there were thousands upon thousands of honest, decent, patriotic Irish Americans. Those were the people who made my work possible. And despite all the attacks on me, from the right and the left – from Garret FitzGerald to Gerry Adams – the *Times* of London had to concede: 'The most influential group of all is the Irish National Caucus . . . From an office on Capitol Hill in Washington, a few yards from the heart of the US government, Father Sean McManus, leader of the Caucus, can sit at his computer terminal and summon up the names of 50,000 supporters.'[14]

14

Capitol Hill Struggle

If there is no struggle, there is no progress.
Frederick Douglass[1]

As indicated previously, our presence on Capitol Hill really rocked the boat. However, there is no doubt that without that presence, the issue would have been horribly neglected. Noted journalist and commentator Vincent Browne, in August 1979, stated in the Irish media, 'The growing U.S. interest in the Northern Ireland issue is traceable almost entirely to the efforts of the Irish National Caucus'.[2]

Our job was to get the US Congress involved in Northern Ireland – the aim of the British and Irish Embassies was, in effect, to block that involvement. I know Irish Embassy officials at the time would publicly deny that. Indeed, Sean Donlon would later claim that he was responsible for creating Congressional pressure on the British. And I know the Irish government (like the Vatican) can pull out a document to prove it always supported or opposed something.

Sean Donlon and Irish Embassy officials had tried to persuade Members of Congress that there was no role for Congress in Northern Ireland. In his authoritative book *American Policy and Northern Ireland: A Saga of Peacebuilding,* Professor Joseph E. Thompson, states it well: 'The British Government and the congressional leadership stopped laughing . . . when the Ad Hoc Congressional Committee membership went over the 100-member mark.[3] Thompson further explains: 'Despite being ignored by the leadership . . . the Ad Hoc Congressional Committee joined with the INC to successfully make the Northern Irish question a public issue'.[4] And then, very revealingly, he states what I always knew but which the Irish media would never acknowledge: 'To counterbalance the growing impact of the Ad Hoc congressional committee, Michael Lillis of the Irish Embassy masterminded Tip O'Neill's trip to Ireland in April 1979. This visit was to muster the Irish American leaders behind the John Hume–Sean Donlon–Michael Lillis approach toward moderate nationalism.'[5]

I would add this, however, so that the perspective is not lost: it is not as if the Irish National Caucus was advocating 'immoderate' nationalism. And this is where Professor Thompson tends to fall prey to Irish Embassy propaganda. We never asked the Congress to support the IRA or anything radical or revolutionary. Indeed, the reason we were so effective was because our demands were reasonable: ending torture, human rights violations, unfair trials, anti-Catholic discrimination, unfair visa policy towards Irish Republicans, etc. – everything the American Constitution stood for. And we had an official policy of non-violence to which we adhered totally.

So why did the Irish Embassy oppose us so bitterly? Because they did not want the British exposed, which in turn would expose the shameless, cowardly record and policy of the Dublin government on Northern Ireland.

Throughout his book, Professor Thompson refers to us as, the 'republican Irish National Caucus'. Well, we are certainly not monarchist, but I have never said the INC is republican. Indeed, I have always refused to use labels like that, and I've always stressed that the Irish National Caucus has no foreign principal – that is, it does not support any group or party in Ireland, North or South, nor do we take orders from there.

So when Thompson says the Irish Embassy was for 'moderate nationalism' and we were 'republican', he is echoing the Irish Embassy spin – unconsciously, I'm sure, as he is a professionally objective political scientist.

Again, let me stress, there was not one thing the Caucus was lobbying for that the Irish Embassy should have properly and legitimately opposed. I fully understand that governments and people in power have to be diplomatic and do a lot of stuff in private. And that's okay. But why attack others who are publicly speaking out? The role of the Irish Embassy ought to have been totally different from that of Irish Americans.

Irish Americans, like all Americans, have a right, even a duty, to demand that the United States apply a single, not a double, standard in its foreign policy. And why should Irish Americans not have demanded that their Congress denounce British violations of human rights in Northern Ireland? Why should the Irish Embassy seek to muzzle Irish Americans and the US Congress?

I know the Irish Embassy – remember here we are speaking of the 1970s and 1980s – welcomed American pressure, discreet and private, if it enhanced their own status (and the status quo), but just as surely they did not want a Catholic priest from County Fermanagh kicking the hell (non-violently, of course) out of the British government all over Capitol Hill and across the United States. Seriously, could anybody in Ireland at that time dispute this?

Again, Professor Thompson provides suitable context: 'As the republican INC and the Ad Hoc Congressional Committee grew in strength, so too did Dublin's commitment to lobby in support of Irish constitutional nationalism and Irish-American leaders in Congress.'[6]

However, by this time, it was clear to the Irish Embassy that it could not make us disappear. Furthermore, their sterile policy of telling Members of Congress that they had no role to play was clearly in shambles. We now had 130 Members signed up. Taoiseach Jack Lynch's frontal attack on the Ad Hoc Congressional Committee had spectacularly failed, as previously explained.

What could the Irish Embassy do to save face, and also

take the heat off the British that we were so very effectively applying? . . . Drum roll, please . . . Enter the Friends of Ireland! Yes, indeed, the Irish National Caucus not only initiated the Ad Hoc Congressional Committee for Irish Affairs – the Friends of Ireland came into existence as a direct reaction to our forming the Ad Hoc Committee.

The Friends of Ireland was launched on St Patrick's Day, 1981 by Tip O'Neill, Teddy Kennedy, Senator Patrick Moynihan, etc. As my good friend Congressman Gilman told me at the time, 'It was a place for Tip to hang his hat.' Desmond Rush would write in the *Irish Independent* that Speaker O'Neill's office had told him that its purpose was to put the Ad Hoc Committee out of business, and it would happen in six weeks. 'That's what Jack Lynch thought,' I told Rush. I then called Kirk O'Donnell, one of O'Neill's top people. O'Donnell would not deny Rush's story.

Former British MP, Kevin McNamara, in his book, *The MacBride Principles: Irish America Strikes Back* (more of which later), says: 'The Ad Hoc Congressional Committee was proving so successful that the SDLP supporters . . . encouraged by the Irish Embassy established the Friends of Ireland . . . The Embassy was alarmed by the activities and influence of the Ad Hoc Committee on the Hill and its closeness to the INC.'[7] And even more tellingly, McNamara goes on to say that Werner Brandt, a key aide to future Speaker Tom Foley, would later authoritatively state that 'The Friends of Ireland was formed to prevent Northern Ireland becoming "an irritant" in Anglo-Irish-US relations'.[8] And there you have it, folks: the less than noble origins of the Friends of Ireland. However, I was careful not to condemn them, feeling that in time they could do good. Our aim was to have a strong Irish presence on Capitol Hill. And now there were two Congressional committees, where a short time ago there was none.

Congressmen Mario Biaggi, Ben Gilman and Hamilton Fish asked me to come over to meet with them regarding the formation of the Friends of Ireland. I urged them to immediately join and told them we would be urging all members of the Ad Hoc Congressional Committee to join. I knew that although Tip

and Teddy would toe the safe Dublin line, there was no way large
numbers of Congressmen would be content with a 'do-nothing'
policy. They were being pressured by their constituents to speak
out against British violations of human rights, and there would be
no use in their just saying 'we can't do anything but Tip and Teddy
are engaging in private diplomacy with the Dublin government'.
That was no platform to run on. So many of them became just
as outspoken as the members of the Ad Hoc Congressional
Committee.

In time our strategy would bear great fruit. When the
Democrats lost power and the Republicans took over in 1995,
Congressman Jimmy Walsh from Syracuse, NY, took over as
chairman of the Friends of Ireland. He was an ardent Fenian, a
good friend, and a strong member of the Ad Hoc Congressional
Committee. He would go on, in effect, to merge the two
Committees together – making the Friends of Ireland just as
strong on the issue. (And by this time, the Irish Embassy had eased
off from trying to demonise me.) When the Democrats came back
into power in 2007, Congressman Ritchie Neal (D–MA) became
the chairman – a most dedicated Irishman who had long been a
member of the Ad Hoc Congressional Committee, and whom
we listed on our letterhead as a Congressional Friend, as we did
Congressman Walsh until he retired from Congress in 2009.

I should explain here that in 1982 we began the practice
of listing on our letterhead the names of the Senators and
Representatives who had become 'Friends of the Irish National
Caucus' – those who sent us a signed written statement confirming
their support of our 'non-violent work for justice and peace
in Ireland'. The list had to be updated every two years because
of the elections for the House of Representatives. And the list
got so long we had to put the names on both the front and the
back of our stationery. Democrats, Republicans, Conservatives
and Liberals wanted their names to be proudly displayed – from
Congressman Barney Frank (D–MA), commonly seen as the most
liberal, to Senator Strom Thurmond (R–SC), commonly seen as
the most conservative (which made the Irish Embassy look a bit

daft in trying to brand us as radical revolutionaries with old Strom on board!).

I should add a note of interest here about the development of the Friends of Ireland. Congressman Brian Donnelly (1979–1993) was elected with the help of many of our supporters in Boston and pledged to them that I would be one of the first people he would meet with when he came to Washington. He kept his promise. I went to see him in his office, and the very first words out of his mouth were, 'Father, I want to be briefed by you before I hear the bullshit from the Irish Embassy' – exactly his words. Brian would go on to attend our functions in Boston. He would, however, become a protégé of the future Speaker Foley, and one of the first chairmen of the Friends of Ireland. He always remained friendly, and did good work on increasing the number of Irish visas.[9] However, when Joe Kennedy came to Congress (1987–1999), the first thing he told me when I met with him was that I 'should keep him involved with the issues with an edge, as Brian Donnelly had all the soft issues'. And I knew I could count on this eldest son of the revered Bobby Kennedy to do the 'heavy lifting'. I was sorry Joe left Congress as I felt in time he could have become President. He had guts and charisma in abundance.

One of the mandatory ways for a human rights lobby to frame its issue on Capitol Hill is through Congressional hearings. Nothing happens in Congress without the appropriate committee (Appropriations, Judiciary, Foreign Affairs, etc). Obviously, the committee for our concerns was Foreign Affairs. And the way to get real action by a committee is to have it hold a hearing, at which experts and concerned citizens are called to testify – like the hearing we arranged back in 1973 at which my brother Frank testified.

So with crusading zeal we set out to have another hearing on human rights in Northern Ireland. But this time it would not be so easy. In 1973, we had snuck in under the radar, so to speak. We had pulled off the hearing before our opponents (all those who did not want the British embarrassed) could block it. After that, I knew there would be all-out opposition to further hearings.

On Ash Wednesday 1979, I was concelebrating Mass in St Peter's, which is on the same side of Capitol Hill as the House of Representatives. Hence, Catholic Congressmen/women tend to go there (whereas Catholic Senators tend to go to St Joseph's, on the Senate side of Capitol Hill). I 'gave the ashes' to Tip: dipping my thumb into previously blessed ashes, I made the sign of the cross on his forehead, saying, 'Remember, man, thou art dust, and to dust thou shalt return'. I did the same for Congressman Clement J. Zablocki (D-WI), the Polish-American Chairman of the House Foreign Affairs Committee from 1977 to 1983. After the Mass, I cornered Chairman Zablocki on the steps of St Peter's. 'You've got to do the right thing, Mr Chairman. You should not block our hearings on Northern Ireland,' I said. He grasped me by the arm – looked over his shoulder to make sure Tip was out of hearing range – and pleadingly said, 'Fr Sean, I want to, but Tip won't let me.' He then assured me that as a good Catholic he was deeply sympathetic to the plight of Catholics in Northern Ireland. 'But Tip won't let me,' he said again, ever so plaintively. I was sure he was telling me the truth.

I went back into the empty church and knelt for a long time to compose myself, and to pray for the grace to forgive Tip. (My head was pounding: here was a Polish American willing to hold hearings, and an Irish American was blocking him.) But while I was prepared to forgive Tip, I was not prepared to give up my struggle for justice. I had come to adopt a motto as my spiritual compass: 'fight like hell for justice, but always forgive like Heaven.' As I knelt there, my mind went back to kneeling in the other St Peter's in Rome when Bishop Drury blessed me. And, again, I experienced the same tranquility – and the same determination to fight on.

There had to be something about Ash Wednesday and my relationship with Tip. The previous time I had a meeting with him was on Ash Wednesday the year before, 1978. I was still in Boston at the time, and I had been trying for a long time to arrange a meeting with him. He had become Speaker in January 1977, and, understandably, it was difficult to get a meeting. I had got to know the wonderful John McCormack of Boston who was Speaker from 1962 to 1971. By then he was a very old man, having been born in December 1891. He used to take me to the famous Jimmy's Harborside Restaurant for dinner at 4.30 p.m. And he used to love it when I had him invited to Mission Church to join the other priests for dinner. Speaker McCormack had taken Tip under his wing when he came to Congress and Tip felt very indebted to him. Anyway, I told Speaker McCormack I was having difficulty in getting a meeting with Tip. He took care of it right away, and on Ash Wednesday, 8 February 1978, I brought a group of INC leaders into Tip's office. Tip greeted me with great charm and friendliness. As I introduced each of the others, Tip very openly refused to shake the hands of one, a judge from Pittsburgh (I later found out it was because Tip considered the judge to have been part of a group that had had sent him thirty pieces of silver – Judas' price for selling out).

Tip immediately began the meeting from behind his very imposing desk: 'Fr Sean, what is all this spying about?' he asked most sternly. I was dumbstruck and said I had no idea what he was referring to. He said, 'Before this meeting the Irish Embassy called me to express concern and was able to tell me the names of the entire delegation. Did you give them the names of these people?' I told him I certainly had not. 'That's what I mean about spying,' he said.

I briefed Tip on the situation and urged him to speak out; nobody expected him to support the IRA, but his silence could give the impression that he was condoning British oppression. He shot back, 'There's a long history of anti-English bigotry in my family.' Tip then told me that Desmond O'Malley TD, of Fianna Fáil, had been in to see him recently and had told him that both main parties in the Irish Republic, Fine Gael and Fianna Fáil, supported the Sunningdale Agreement.[10] I just happened to have in my briefcase a copy of an article by Vincent Browne in the *Sunday Independent* that said the exact opposite: 'The Government would not reiterate the Sunningdale declaration on the status of Northern Ireland, according to the Minister for Foreign Affairs,

Michael O'Kennedy . . . "That declaration is merely part of the negative British guarantee to help the Unionists . . ."[11] As I read out the article, Tip got visibly angry at what he was hearing. He said he would demand an explanation of the Irish Embassy.

He then told me that the Irish Embassy kept insisting I was a front for terrorism. I told him exactly where I stood. Then he demanded: 'I want you to write a letter to me, in your own hand, stating that you are not involved in violence, and I will keep it here in my drawer [and he pulled out the top drawer on the right of his desk to demonstrate], and when anyone tells me you are a terrorist, I will show them it.' I promised him I would, and as we were leaving he said, 'Don't forget your ashes, Father.' Two days later, on 10 February I wrote him a three-page letter – not in my own hand, as he wouldn't be able to read it! But I spelled out exactly where I stood.

Sometime later, I went to see Ari Weiss in the Speaker's office. Ari was Tip's top policy adviser, and then only twenty-five. Kirk O'Donnell, then thirty-two, was the general counsel and chief political strategist. Ari was considered one of the most brilliant people on The Hill, and I had great regard for him. He was a straight shooter: 'A strict orthodox Jew who won't ride in a car on Saturday [he] walked 22 miles in a torrential downpour to attend the Speaker's son's wedding.'[12] I always felt I would get total directness from Ari, whereas not from Kirk who would dance and weave. He tended towards the elitist approach on Ireland. Furthermore, because he was Irish American he was more susceptible to pressure from the Irish Embassy. Ari told me that Tip was very impressed with the honesty and openness of my letter and that he completely believed me. Ari himself tried to get to the bottom of the Irish Embassy's accusations and he called well-known journalist Jimmy Breslin to ask his opinion. Breslin told him that 'there was likely more truth on the priest's side'. But then Ari added that for as long as the Irish Embassy was insisting I was an IRA agent, the Speaker felt he could not continue to meet me – even if John McCormack called him again.

Now back again to Ash Wednesday 1979, and to what

Chairman Zablocki had told me about Tip not letting him hold hearings.

Of course, I was already well aware of Tip's conniving with the British and Irish governments. We had got the famed Jack Anderson Column – nationally syndicated and carried in nearly 1,000 papers – to expose it three times within one year, 1977/1978.

(1) 'Speaker Thomas (Tip) O'Neill, the big beloved boss of the House, is as Irish as anyone who ever kissed the Blarney stone. But he quietly squashed a congressional hearing on alleged British outrages against the Irish . . . To dig up atrocities, the speaker pleaded, would only inflame the already emotional issue. It would be an 'inappropriate' time to stir up trouble over Irish rights, he said'.[13]

(2) 'Under pressure from two foreign governments, President Carter is betraying a campaign promise to speak out against human rights violation committed by British authorities in Northern Ireland. He made the pledge to . . . [the Irish National Caucus] in Pittsburgh six days before the 1976 election, in exchange for their endorsement. Shortly after Carter took office . . . [the Irish National Caucus] supplied the White House with 10 documented cases of alleged torture perpetrated by British security forces against suspected IRA members or sympathizers . . . A move to air the charges on Capitol Hill is being thwarted by House Speaker Tip O'Neill at the behest of the Irish government . . . An aide told us that the Speaker, a Carter confidant, was told by prominent members of the Irish government that an investigation would be counterproductive. In Dublin's view, the Irish National Caucus is pro-I.R.A., and a congressional hearing would signal U.S. support of the terrorist IRA gunmen'.[14]

(3) 'Human rights violations, reported to us by a number of reliable sources, have put Northern Ireland on an unenviable

par with some of the most barbarous regimes of communist commissars or tinhorn Latin American dictators. The British are trampling on the rights of Irish citizens in a manner reminiscent of Oliver Cromwell's iron-fisted rule more than three centuries ago ... An Ad Hoc Committee of 119 members has been formed in congress. But the committee's attempts to publicize the outrages being committed in Northern Ireland, along with the efforts of the Irish National Caucus, have been blocked by House Speaker Tip O'Neill and other congressional leaders who are reluctant to offend our British ally'.[15]

What's wrong with that picture? A Mormon journalist, of Swedish–Danish descent, forced to outrage at an Irish-Catholic Speaker of the House covering up British atrocities against Catholics in Northern Ireland! How profoundly sad is that? Jack Anderson was considered one of the fathers of modern investigative journalism.

Despite all this, the Dublin government was not too eager, at the time, to admit its role. However, Professor Thompson in his previously mentioned book (published in 2001) tells us that 'the Irish and British ambassadors to the United States, John Molloy and Sir Peter Ramsbotham, respectively, made a joint request to Speaker Albert [1971–1977] not to hold any official hearings on Northern Ireland'. Professor Thompson explains he elicited this information in a personal interview with Garret FitzGerald in 1999. Thompson then says: 'Speaker Albert did not hold any official hearings on Northern Ireland, but to combat the growing influence of the INC in congress, he followed Congressman O'Neill and Senator Kennedy's advice and requested that the Congressional Research Service (CRS) of the Library of Congress produce the report Developments in Northern Ireland 1968–1976.' Professor Thompson continues with keen observation:

The introduction to the 1976 CRS report spread the blame for Northern Ireland's increased violence among several parties. The Nixon and Ford administrations were admonished for not offering to facilitate a solution to the crisis. The administrations were accused of hiding behind the pernicious policy of realism, which allowed the party inflicting the injury to decide if an outside party should come in and expose the injured party's grievances. Kissinger knew that Britain would never ask the United States to assist in U.K. domestic affairs . . . The same excuse for inaction in Northern Ireland was used by the United Nations (U.N.) when it was confronted by the INC request for an investigation into British violations of Irish human rights. U.N. Secretary General, U Thant, said that he was waiting for the United Kingdom to ask for U.N. assistance, implying that this request would publicize Britain's ineptitude to control its domestic violence.[16]

As I write this, and as I go back over the record, I must confess to feeling that old righteous Kinawley anger stirring up within me. The cover-up was cynical, calculated, and cowardly. And the ever-compliant establishment media went along with it (with a few honourable exceptions). Shame, shame, shame on all responsible.

In an October 1986 interview with Niall O'Dowd, a well-known commentator on Northern Ireland, Tip said, referring to Irish activity in Congress: 'it all started with Father McManus. When he came over here we were all sympathetic to him. Then he started to bring over some of the terrorists from Ireland and we didn't agree with their philosophy and basically their means to the end, which we didn't like. So we broke away and started our own group, a more stable one.'[17]

The British and Irish Embassy had done their job well. O'Neill would trot out the old nonsense that the reason he opposed a Congressional hearing on Northern Ireland was because it would provide a platform for the IRA. Yet he knew perfectly well that for years the IRA and members of Sinn Féin were denied visas to enter the US. Furthermore, even if they had been able to enter, they just could not turn up and testify, because Tip had the power to veto the witness list. So his excuses were dishonest. Tip and the

Irish government were not scared of the IRA – they were scared of the truth.

My problem with Tip was that he was not just opposed to Congressional hearings on Northern Ireland. After he had been 're-educated' by the British and Irish Embassies, he refused to show any interest in individual human rights violations – the Birmingham Six, Guildford Four, etc. (The same, sadly, can be said about Teddy Kennedy. This is particularly ironic in the case of the Guildford Four, as one of them, Paul Hill, would eventually marry one of Bobby Kennedy's daughters, Courtney.)

Tip turned a blind eye to torture, and showed no interest in combating anti-Catholic discrimination. It is as if the little people did not count – the victims of London's oppression and Dublin's negligence – despite Tip's image as champion of the working class. Nothing seemed to matter but 'the big picture', whatever that is. All that mattered was that Tip would, to use that famous phrase of Werner Brandt, 'prevent Northern Ireland becoming "an irritant" in Anglo-Irish-US relations'. Of course he would occasionally raise a question about British practice, and in private he might nudge them, but always within the Brandt parameters. It is the typical elitist approach – again, despite Tip's image to the contrary. He may have been a working class guy from Boston, but like so many Irish before him, when it came to Her Majesty's government, Tip would doff his hat and become ever so 'respectable and diplomatic'. And, in the meantime, Irish Americans were supposed to sit down and shut up. Oh, sure, let them talk about every issue under the sun, except their own homeland – that had to be left to the quiet diplomacy of himself, Teddy Kennedy, and the Dublin government. I recognise Teddy went on to do very important work in the Irish Peace Process, and I salute him for that.

Tip and I would also clash over US contributions to International Fund for Ireland (IFI), which was formed to support the Anglo-Irish Agreement of 1985.[18]

Like many, I had my problems with that Agreement, which gave the Dublin government a semi-formal institutional role –

a right to have an opinion, so to speak – on the North. But it also obliged Dublin to accept that there could be no change in the constitutional position of Northern Ireland unless a majority there agreed. Because FitzGerald had such a hopeless record on the North, Nationalists/Republicans were very suspicious of the deal. To make matters worse, Garret FitzGerald had marketed it as the way to marginalise Irish republicans in the North, not to end British injustice and anti-Catholic discrimination. The words of T. S. Elliott immediately come to mind here: 'The last temptation is the greatest treason: to do the right deed for the wrong reason.'[19]

Anyway, we were determined that any US money for the IFI would have conditions attached. On 14 January 1986, I wrote to every member of the House Foreign Affairs Committee (twenty-four Democrats and thirteen Republicans), saying: 'The Irish-American community is deeply concerned that US Foreign Aid to support the Anglo-Irish Agreement could in effect serve to bolster up British oppression and injustice in Northern Ireland or subsidize anti-Catholic discrimination. That is why we urge: (1) Foreign Aid should not be used by the British Government for military or security purposes or for the gathering of intelligence; (2) Foreign Aid should be tied to the MacBride Principles; (3) Foreign Aid should be tied to the human rights provisions of the Foreign Assistance.'

Tip was furious – several sources informed me.

When the Foreign Affairs Subcommittee on Europe and the Middle East held its hearing on Wednesday 5 March 1986, Tip made a point of testifying in person. Although he did shake my hand, his look said, 'I am going to blow you out of the water.' And he certainly tried. 'I believe,' he thundered, 'that Congress should make the aid subject to standard conditions for assistance and not make it contingent on a long list of political conditions. We need to express our unqualified support for the Accord [Agreement], not our doubts about it.'

However, we won the day. I had lobbied the Subcommittee so thoroughly that they were prepared to stand up to the Speaker. Congressman Lee Hamilton (D-ID) actually held up my letter, read out our conditions, one by one, and – looking directly at me – said all of them had been met and that should satisfy those who had concerns. It was a remarkable achievement, and of course the British and Irish media played it down. However, an excellent reporter for the *Union Leader* newspaper, Manchester, New Hampshire, Tom Gorey would report: 'The House Foreign Affairs Committee approved Reagan's aid proposal on Thursday, after attaching certain conditions that McManus had lobbied for and were inserted by U.S. Rep. Ben Gilman (R-NY). Gilman's provisions restate an existing ban on the use of U.S. economic aid for military or security purposes, and insist that the aid be distributed "according to the principles of equality of opportunity" and that it promote "human rights".' (As we shall see later, Gilman and I would finally succeed in getting the actual MacBride Principles tied to the International Fund for Ireland in 1998, when the Principles became part of US law.)

Gorey's article then continues:

> McManus said O'Neill 'wanted to come in and personally crush the campaign to add conditions. And yet we won this one . . . We took him on – toe to toe – and we won. McManus branded O'Neill's testimony to the subcommittee as 'vintage British propaganda'. His presentation was exactly how the British Government presents the Northern Ireland problem. Namely, that the British government is not at fault for maintaining an unjust, sectarian, oppressive system (in Ulster) in which violence is inevitable. But that the problem in Northern Ireland is the inability of two tribes – Catholic and Protestant – to get along with each other. There wasn't one condemnation of anti-Catholic discrimination, of repressive legislation, of mistreatment of persons. There wasn't one condemnation of British violence – military or institutional. There was only a condemnation of IRA violence.[20]

That is fine journalism by Tom Gorey. He captured the story

perfectly, and accurately reported my long-standing grievance with typical elitist misrepresentation of the Northern Ireland problem.

By this stage, I'd had it with Tip. I was always fond of him – he was a hard man not to like – but I could no longer excuse his actions. And it was not a matter of his being totally controlled by the Dublin Government because when it suited him, he could take a strong line. Remember in Chapter 12, when Tip thought Taoiseach Charlie Haughey was going to take a stronger anti-British line and remove Sean Donlon as ambassador, Tip very 'undiplomatically' and, some have argued, very improperly intervened and made Haughey back off. Garret FitzGerald would claim that by removing Donlon, Haughey was siding with IRA supporters in America. Nonsense. Who would expect the Irish Embassy, for goodness sake, to be pro-IRA? Haughey did not want the Embassy to be pro-British, but apparently Tip did.

In celebrating that his protégé, Donlon, had been spared, Garett FitzGerald would write: 'Our American policy was back on course . . . thanks to the intervention of Tip O'Neil.'[21] That policy being, of course, that the Irish Embassy would continue to shield the British government from really serious Washington pressure. No self-respecting country should have tolerated the Lynch, Cosgrave or FitzGerald governments. Their spineless policy ensured that Catholics in the North would continue to suffer needlessly, and that, in fact, the IRA would thereby increase, not decrease.

Finally, regarding Tip's public record on Northern Ireland, he may have argued that he was doing all sorts of good things privately but one cannot judge a public figure by his private, secret negotiations. Furthermore, what politician runs on a platform of secret negotiations? What politician can get away with saying, 'You don't know what I'm doing, and I can't tell you, but trust me anyway'? That certainly was not his policy on all the other issues he felt strongly about. On those – South Africa, El Salvador, etc. – he was vehemently outspoken, But on Northern Ireland, he had to be 'diplomatic' and ever so careful in criticising Her Majesty's government. Unqualified condemnations were only for the IRA. That was the double standard and dishonesty that drove me up the wall. I just could not take it, and never could. It is what forced me to get involved in the first place back in England, and it has kept me going all these years.

Now I recognise that Tip occasionally did apply some pressure, and the British reacted out of all proportion. One could argue that showed the British felt the pressure. Or one could argue that the British disproportionate reaction was their way of making sure that Tip would back off and not apply real pressure. I favour the latter argument.

Nobody wanted Tip and President Reagan to 'nuke' London, send in the marines, or apply sanctions. But can you imagine what real pressure could have accomplished? Sadly, the two most powerful Irish Americans in the world did not have the guts to do it – and the Irish governments at the time did not want them to do it. So we had to wait for President Bill Clinton, God bless his southern Baptist heart.

The International Fund for Ireland (IFI) would also be the arena for another joust with one of Tip's successors, Congressman Tom Foley (6 June 1989 to 3 January 1995) from the State of Washington. (Tip was Speaker from 4 January 1977 to 3 January 1987 and Jim Wright from Texas replaced him from 6 June 1987 to 6 June 1989.)

By this time there was growing concern about the performance of the IFI. Most of the funds were simply adhering to the systematic pattern of discrimination in Northern Ireland – going to the Unionist/Protestant areas. The Second Annual Report on the IFI revealed, for example, that West and North Belfast and Derry received less than 6 per cent of the 1988 budget: '. . . the bulk of the money went to a variety of projects which had had no relation to northern violence: funding for hotels, tourist amenities, a skydiving club, golf courses and a $1.9 million gift of a fishing vessel to the British government . . .'[22]

I had been inundating the Foreign Affairs Committee with documentation, and creating a lot of noise. I convinced Chairman

Lee Hamilton that my concerns should be aired at a hearing, and that he should allow other Irish American groups to testify, too. Gerry Coleman, an Irish American from New Jersey, would represent eight Irish American organisations, including Irish Northern Aid. I would speak for the Irish National Caucus.

On 26 April 1989, the Subcommittee for Europe and the Middle East held its hearing. In strode Tom Foley (Speaker-in-waiting) who proceeded to launch an attack, which clearly took the Subcommittee members by surprise: 'We don't usually ask criminal organizations to come before the committee and recommend how to improve the law'.[23] Sean Cronin of *The Irish Times* recorded that when asked to whom he was referring, Foley said, 'Mr. Coleman has chosen to appear before you for Irish Northern Aid, the registered agent for the IRA . . . Mr. Coleman . . . looked startled'[24]

Then I would be given a blast but I wasn't a bit startled as I was well used to holding my own with Members of Congress. Significantly, Foley did not claim I was IRA. The worst he could come up with was that I 'was on record of opposing the Anglo Irish Agreement'. Then, clearly thinking he had the knock-out punch, pronounced: 'Father McManus has referred to Tip O'Neill, President Reagan, Pat Moynihan and Teddy Kennedy as lapsed Irishmen. Well, if that's a lapsed Irishman, I want to be included,' Come on Foley, I thought, is that all you've got? My good friend Congressman Gary Ackerman (D-NY), a Jewish American, asked Foley what it meant to be a 'lapsed Irishman'. 'It means that you do not agree with Father McManus,' was his reply.[25] First time I knew Foley had a sense of humour.

Another major battle we fought on Capitol Hill, this time in the Senate, was against the Supplemental Extradition Treaty agreed between the British and the State Department in the summer of 1985. It proposed to remove the historic and venerable 'political exception' to extradition – giving Britain the privilege of being the only country in the world without a political exception clause in its treaty with the United States, which meant that no Irish person who was wanted for a violent crime – and had escaped to America

– could plead in a US court that his or her offence was political. The British had hoped the Treaty would go through quietly, especially because of a recent Beirut hijacking. British Prime Minister Margaret Thatcher would also link to the Treaty her support for President Reagan's bombing of Libya on 15 April 1986.

However, the Treaty had to be ratified by two-thirds of the Senate. And I was determined to battle it for all my worth. I formulated three basic arguments, which became the accepted platform of all opposed to the Treaty: (1) it legitimised British rule in Northern Ireland; (2) it took away authority from the US courts, which historically and properly adjudicated such cases; and (3) it surrendered an Irish person to a corrupt system of British law.

Although this Treaty was a terrible development, I pointed out to Irish Americans all across the country that it provided us with the chance to bring our cause right into the US Senate – an opportunity that rarely arises. We had to make the most of it. I extensively briefed the Minority Staff, i.e. the staff that worked for the Senate Democrats, whose ranking member was Joe Biden (who became Vice President in January 2009). We put out a press release saying:

> It was a delight to hear Senator Biden right in the middle of the most prestigious committee state: 'But I think this Extradition Treaty is an opportunity to do what we have been unable to do so far. There is an incredible reluctance on the part of this government to criticize one of our closest allies for what I believe to be an absolutely outrageous position which they have continued to maintain with regard to Northern Ireland, and an unwillingness on the part of the present government to do anything constructive about it, that is, the British government. So I want to make clear to you that I am going to do all that I can do to hold this up as long as I can to make the case.'[26]

You know you have done your job when you hear your own words being repeated back virtually word for word in a Congressional hearing. The press gave our struggle considerable coverage. Even the British press was relatively fair with us this time. 'Britain and Irish in battle on Capitol Hill', said the *Observer*, while displaying a photograph of the British Ambassador to Washington, Sir Oliver Wright, with whom I had clashed many times. The reporter, the well-respected Simon Hoggart, explained: 'The British Government and the powerful Irish republican lobby are squaring up this week for their greatest fight . . . Father Sean McManus is an affable and persuasive man who operates from an elegant office a few hundred yards from the Capitol . . . [He] has sent a direct mail package to 250,000 people. The [outside] envelope says urgently: "The British are coming, the British are coming" – so cunningly associating their cause with the American Revolution'.[27]

The Washington Post, national weekly edition, not usually a fan of those opposing Jolly Old England, was so taken with my direct mail package that it published a photograph of the outside envelope, with its entire graphics. In an lengthy article it proceeded to explain: 'Inside the direct mail package the letter began: "The British are indeed coming, this time into the United States Senate, and it's here we must meet and beat them".'[28]

Even the brilliant curmudgeon Christopher Hitchens – who would go on to say bad things about God and Mother Teresa – did not bad-mouth me:

> The master of these revels, in publicity terms, is Father Sean McManus, a burly, plausible charmer whose Irish National Caucus has taken center stage. In the years since the Redemptorist order found him too much of a handful to retain in Britain, the good Father has made himself expert in congressional lobbying techniques . . . I spent a long and, to be perfectly frank, rather enjoyable afternoon with Father McManus in his Capitol Hill office. He knew that I wanted him to come clean about the Provisionals, and it became clear that he hadn't been raised as a clerical apologist for nothing . . . Did he regard the Irish government (which through its embassy is lobbying for the extradition treaty)

as the legitimate government of Ireland? A knowing smile: 'Do the Dublin government recognize Sir Oliver Wright as the legitimate representative and envoy of Fermanagh and West Belfast? If they do, they admit they represent only part of the Irish people'.[29]

I knew I had a massive task but I was committed. *The Sunday Times* revealed just how committed: 'The powerful Irish lobby is . . . working hard to kill the treaty. For example, Father Sean McManus . . . has even cancelled his annual summer holiday in Ireland'.[30] Now that's commitment – giving up a chance to go back to Kinawley!

Our first task was to block speedy ratification, which we did. *The Boston Globe* reported, 'The committee originally intended to hold one hearing last July 25. But opposition quickly developed chiefly under the auspices of the Irish National Caucus'.[31] 'Caucus blocks anti-IRA move: Irish group's pressure works on U.S. Senate', was how Niall O'Dowd's article in *The Sunday Press* heralded the story. 'The U. S. Senate has baulked at quick ratification of the proposed new extradition treaty . . . following a major lobbying effort by Irish-American groups headed by the Irish National Caucus . . . According to a spokesman for Sen. Richard Lugar, head of the Senate Foreign Relations Committee, pressure from Irish and concerned civil rights groups played a major role in the postponement'.[32] Margaret Thatcher lashed out: 'The British Prime Minister, Mrs. Thatcher, yesterday criticized the delays, through "a very effective Irish lobby" in the U.S. Congress, that have prevented the introduction of extradition for people accused of IRA activities.'[33]

But despite our gallant effort, we did not win this one – but we were not beaten either. Although the 'political exception' was rescinded, we, nonetheless, succeeded in getting some important conditions attached. Noted journalist Karen Tumulty – who covered Congress for the *Los Angeles Times* for fourteen years and would later join *Time* Magazine – assessed it this way:

a compromise . . . essentially allowed both sides to declare victory. Included in the compromise is a provision that permits a judge to deny extradition if he determines the accused could not get a fair trial because of 'race, religion, nationality, or political opinions'. Additional language in the accompanying report, not part of the treaty itself, would allow U.S. judges handling extradition cases to consider whether the British court system is fair. The language was added to answer criticism of the non-jury, single-judge courts, called Diplock courts, that are used to try IRA defendants.

As I said, we were not beaten either. And I think it may have been a pyrrhic victory for the British. An indication of this is that the British did not try to extradite Joe Doherty – who had been in prison for years in New York – under the terms of the new treaty. He was deported but not extradited.

I should note here that we not only briefed the Democrats on the Senate Foreign Relations Committee, but also the Republicans, as was always our bipartisan approach. Senator Orrin Hatch, a Mormon from Utah, whom we got to know quite well, became a strong opponent of the treaty. This deeply conservative man became an ardent supporter of Irish justice. Indeed, at that time, he was very critical of Teddy Kennedy's weak response. We proudly listed him on our letterhead as a Congressional Friend of the Irish National Caucus for many years. But in 1991, I sent out a very large, direct-mail package in an attempt to stop Margaret Thatcher from getting the Presidential Medal of Freedom, and from being invited to speak at the Republican National Convention in 1992. As you can imagine, I told the truth about Thatcher's racist and anti-Irish Catholic record. Senator Hatch wrote demanding I take his name off our letterhead because of the '. . . offensive and intolerable language that was directed at Mrs. Thatcher . . .' I responded in kind. 'You shall, indeed, be removed because anyone who is prepared to condone and cover-up Margaret Thatcher's record of anti-Catholic bigotry and oppression in Northern Ireland has no right to be on our stationery'.[34]

It was the end of a beautiful relationship. I never met with him again. But, still, he was a fine man, and I will always be grateful for what he did to oppose British violations of human rights – when some Irish American Congressional leaders were too scared to take a stand.

I must not neglect to mention one other campaign, which like so many others had not been attempted until the Caucus came along: repealing the anti-Catholic sections in The Act of Settlement 1701.

The Act of Settlement is an integral part of the unwritten and uncodified British Constitution. It determines succession to the Crown of England, and is, therefore, a fundamental constitutional statute, indeed, the very foundation stone of the Royal family. It contains provisions that decree a Catholic cannot succeed to the British throne and that if the Monarch becomes a Catholic, or marries a Catholic, he/she forfeits the throne and 'the people are absolved from their allegiance'.

Imagine had there been a provision in the US Constitution forbidding an African American becoming President, or forbidding the President to marry a black person – think how that would have stoked the flames of racism and white supremacy.

While this statute may mean little to the average British man in the street, it has always been of the utmost importance to Protestant/Unionist/Orange extremists in Northern Ireland. It provides the ideological and philosophical underpinnings for their bigotry and sectarianism. For, you see, the spurious but deadly logic goes, if a Catholic by law can't get the top job, then Catholics are inferior to Protestants, and therefore it's okay to discriminate against them.

But don't first blame extreme Orangemen – they did not create the Act of Settlement. Put the blame where it belongs: on the British monarchy and parliament – and on the Church of England and British Establishment for going along with this inherently sectarian Constitution. (The Constitution is also sexist and discriminates against women: if there is no direct male heir, a royal princess can succeed to the throne, but a younger brother takes precedence over an elder sister.)

It was a source of satisfaction to me that at long last the sectarian, anti-Catholic and undemocratic Act of Settlement 1701 was getting a public airing. For thirty years I had been 'a voice crying in the wilderness' when I raised this issue. It astonished me that some Irish Americans and indeed many Catholics in Northern Ireland failed to see that there was a causal connection between an anti-Catholic Constitution and anti-Catholic behaviour by those extreme Orangemen who saw themselves as loyal upholders of the British constitution.

But now, in great measure due to the consciousness-raising done by the Irish National Caucus, there is a growing awareness in Britain and Ireland that those bigoted and sectarian provisions must be repealed.

The MacBride Principles: Genesis and History

An Army of Principles Will Penetrate Where an Army of Soldiers Cannot
Thomas Paine[1]

I want to set out here for the historical record how the Irish National Caucus initiated, proposed, and launched the MacBride Principles. This is all the more important since there have been some attempts at revisionism. I will have to give an abundance of quotes from the press and other sources to document the clear and incontestable role of the Irish National Caucus. And the issue here is not the drafting of individual Principles, which are not particularly unique but generally modelled on the Sullivan Principles[2] and other such principles.

But first a statement of what the Principles are: the MacBride Principles − consisting of nine fair employment principles − are a corporate code of conduct for US companies doing business in Northern Ireland and have become the Congressional standard for all US aid to, or economic dealings with, Northern Ireland.

The Principles do not call for quotas, reverse discrimination, divestment (the withdrawal of US companies from Northern Ireland) or disinvestment (the withdrawal of funds now invested in firms with operations in Northern Ireland). The Caucus positively encourages non-discriminatory US investment in Northern Ireland. The MacBride campaign is conducted on a three-fold level:

(1) Federal: the MacBride Principles became the law of the US in October 1998. The US House and Senate passed the MacBride Principles – as part of the Omnibus Appropriations Act for Fiscal Year 1999 – and President Clinton signed them into law. The MacBride law mandates that recipients of US contributions to the International Fund for Ireland (IFI) must be in compliance with the MacBride Principles. (The US has been contributing about $19.6 million per year since 1986 to the IFI.)

(2) State and cities: millions of dollars in State and city pension and retirement funds are invested in American corporations doing business in Northern Ireland. The MacBride campaign lobbies to have legislation passed to direct these funds to be invested, in the future, only in companies that endorse the Principles (again, note, not divestment or disinvestment). This is the first step. The second step – once the MacBride Principles investment law has been passed – is to get a contract compliance law passed.

(3) Shareholder Resolutions: the Campaign works to have shareholders pass resolutions endorsing the Principles.

The MacBride Principles did not suddenly appear from the sky like the Ten Commandments. They were the result of many years of hard and unrelenting work by the Irish National Caucus. The Principles were 'conceived' in August 1979; 'born' in June 1983; and 'christened' in November 1984.

One of the first objectives of the newly opened office of the Irish National Caucus was to 'stop United States dollars subsidising anti-Catholic discrimination in Northern Ireland'. To have impact on foreign policy you have to find the foreign policy nexus – that which connects Northern Ireland and the United States. The obvious 'nexus' was the United States companies doing business in Northern Ireland. These companies could also be the 'fulcrum' through which we could exercise leverage to oppose discrimination in Northern Ireland.

So these companies had to be held accountable to American legislators and investors. In July 1979, Congressman Ben Gilman (R–NY), a member of the House Committee on Foreign Affairs, and a member of the Subcommittee on International Economic Policy and Trade, commissioned the Irish National Caucus to conduct an investigation of the US companies in Northern Ireland. We travelled to Northern Ireland at the end of July 1979 and the *Sunday News* announced our mission:

Caucus in Jobs Blacklist Move: Americans probe workers' religions.

American firms with production plants in Ulster are to be asked for a religious breakdown of local workers in a move to tighten up on United States equal opportunity laws. And some companies located in 'sensitive' areas of the Province which do not have balanced Protestant–Catholic worker ratios could have a black mark against them in a report to an influential congressman in Washington.

Later this week leading members of the Irish National Caucus from the federal capital will be touring Northern Ireland, knocking on the doors of American firms for details of their employment registers.

The most significant of the credentials the team will present is a letter from New York Republican Congressman Ben Gilman, who sits on an international trade subcommittee with powerful controls on US corporations operating overseas.

Fr Sean McManus said the letter from Congressman Gilman gave their visit to American firms in the North a semi-official status. He added that the INC delegation would almost certainly be visiting the Ford-owned Autolite components factory at Finaghy and the management of the new DeLorean car assembly plant.[3]

The Irish Times said:

> While in Northern Ireland the members of the Caucus will visit some American-owned companies to ascertain whether any discriminatory employment practices operate. The investigation is being carried out at the request of Congressman Benjamin Gilman, who is a member of the House Committee on Foreign Affairs and the Subcommittee on International Economic Policy and Trade. US corporations which are found not to reflect American respect for and protection of equal opportunities for all could face withdrawal of tax concessions and trading licences.
>
> One of the Caucus's recent achievements concerns the suspension of US arms sales to the RUC, pending an investigation into the human rights situation in the north. They are also speaking of their determination to make Ireland an issue in the coming Presidential campaign'.[4]

The Irish Press carried the story this way:

> [Leaders of the Caucus] are in Ireland at present to investigate the behaviour of American firms in the North. They are undertaking this mission on behalf of Congressman Benjamin A. Gilman, who is a member of the Congress Committee on Foreign Affairs and the Subcommittee on International Economic Policy and Trade.
>
> This committee controls overseas aid and if American firms locating outside the country are found to be discriminating against anyone on the basis of race, creed or colour, their US tax concessions may be cut off.[5]

The *Belfast Telegraph* said:

> The Irish National Caucus is investigating alleged
> discrimination at Goodyear's Craigavon factory. The Caucus
> has asked for a breakdown of religious affiliations of the
> 1,400 people employed at the Silverwood plant.
>
> Goodyear was one of many firms which signed the Fair
> Employment Declaration . . . Prominent members of the
> Caucus are involved in the investigation – including Fr Sean
> McManus.[6]

We made contact with most of the US companies and asked them
to submit a detailed breakdown of the religious composition of
their workforce (in doing so we were years ahead of the British
government's Fair Employment Laws, which did not make this
demand until 1989).

But the launching of the investigation into US companies
in Northern Ireland was not the only important initiative the
Caucus took on its August mission to Ireland. There was another
equally important initiative that would be full of significance and
symbolism for the MacBride Principles later on. The Caucus
established, in Dublin, the Irish National Caucus Liaison Group,
chaired by Dr Seán MacBride himself. The inaugural meeting was
held in Seán's home, Roebuck House. *The Irish Times* reported:

> Mr Seán MacBride, the Nobel Prize and Lenin Peace Prize
> winner, has become chairman of a new group in Ireland
> which aims to put forward the views of the Irish National
> Caucus, a United-States-based organization.
>
> Mr Michael Mullen, general secretary of the Irish
> Transport and General Workers' Union, is another member
> of the new group.
>
> The Rev. Sean McManus, a leader of the Irish National
> Caucus, said last night in Dublin that the new group in
> Dublin would be called Irish National Caucus Associates. It
> would be based in the Republic and, besides Mr MacBride,

it would include Mr Mullen and Mr Kevin Boland, a former Fianna Fáil Minister.

The initial meeting, which was attended by 20 people, was held on Thursday, and another one would be held later this month.[7]

Back in the US, the *Irish World* told Irish Americans of this initiative in the following way:

Sean MacBride, recipient of both the Nobel Peace Prize and Lenin Peace Prize, has announced his agreement to act as chairman of a new organization in the Republic of Ireland which aims to act as a liaison between the U.S.- based Irish National Caucus and the people of Ireland . . . 'The idea of our organization,' MacBride said, 'is to get across to the Irish public the truth about the United States organization and to emphasize the significance of the Irish American dimension. The success of the Irish National Caucus was seen in the U.S. State Department policy review on supplying arms to the RUC.' MacBride added that, in his opinion, the work of the I.N.C. had been somewhat misrepresented by a number of individuals in Ireland and that it is his hope that the work of the new organization will present a clearer picture of Caucus activities. 'The Irish National Caucus is not a "front" for any group in Ireland. It is undoubtedly the most effective and widely-respected Irish American Organization in the States and we hope to contribute to its goal of a just and lasting peace in the North of Ireland.'[8]

It should be obvious to all that in these two Caucus initiatives (investigation of US companies in Northern Ireland and Seán MacBride becoming Chairman of our Liaison Group in the Republic of Ireland) were sown the seeds of the MacBride Principles. Since he had left the Dáil in 1958, Seán MacBride had established a policy of not belonging to any party or group dealing specifically with Northern Ireland. But he broke this policy to identify with the Irish National Caucus. He was attracted to the Irish National Caucus for the following reasons:

(1) It is non-violent.
(2) It has no foreign principal – that is, it is neither controlled nor directed by any organisation, party, or government in Ireland.
(3) It did not send funds to Ireland.

Seán MacBride particularly admired the Caucus' focus on stopping US dollars subsidising anti-Catholic discrimination in Northern Ireland. Paddy Harte, TD for Donegal, launched an appalling personal attack in the press on MacBride, calling him senile and other abusive things. (Harte never apologised for his attack.) The other Donegal TD, the late Neil Blaney, congratulated MacBride, joined the Liaison Group, and announced he was going to the US to speak for the Irish National Caucus. Neil had a life-long record of concern for the North of Ireland. Paddy Harte would later become the founder of Irish American Partnership that was launched by Taoiseach Garret FitzGerald in 1984.

We decided that a good way to 'frame the issue' of US dollars subsidising anti-Catholic discrimination in Northern Ireland would be to have the Ad Hoc Committee for Irish Affairs, which we had initiated, hold a hearing and bring Fr Brian Brady over from Belfast to testify about the hiring practices of US companies in Northern Ireland. The hearing took place on 22 July 1981. It was the first time ever that discrimination by US companies in Northern Ireland was raised in the United States Congress.

After the Ad Hoc Congressional Hearing, the Irish National Caucus planned to have our principle, that United States dollars should not subsidise anti-Catholic discrimination in Northern Ireland, enshrined into law. We worked assiduously on this. In 1983, we succeeded at last in having a Bill introduced into Congress, HR 3465: 'Requiring United States persons who conduct business or control enterprises in Northern Ireland to comply with certain fair employment principles.' It was modelled on the Sullivan Principles and became known as the 'Ottinger Bill', after its chief sponsor, Congressman Dick Ottinger (D-NY). Although the Bill did not pass, it was of singular importance because it perfectly framed our issue. We now had in place all the essential elements of what we would later call the MacBride Principles:

1) The ongoing investigation of the United States companies in Northern Ireland.
2) The high-profile involvement of Seán MacBride in our campaign.
3) A set of fair employment principles for those companies to serve as a corporate code of conduct.

The very first lobbyists against the Ottinger Bill were the Irish Embassy in Washington, DC, and John Hume. I issued the following press release:

Irish Embassy Cover-up on Anti-Catholic Discrimination
Washington, D.C., November 4, 1983

The Irish National Caucus has reacted with anger to attempts by the Irish Embassy to sabotage legislation in Congress that would outlaw discrimination by American companies in Northern Ireland.

The Caucus claims that it has been told by a number of Congressional offices that the Irish Embassy is advising them not to sponsor the Bill of Congressman Richard L. Ottinger (D-NY). One office reported in amazement to the Caucus that the Irish Embassy is saying that the Ottinger Bill would actually increase unemployment in Northern Ireland.

Fr Sean McManus, National Director, said: 'The Irish Embassy is quite simply conspiring with the British Embassy to cover up anti-Catholic Discrimination in Northern Ireland. I call upon the Opposition Parties and

Independents in the Dail to demand that this disgraceful sellout of the Catholics in Northern Ireland cease.'

When Congressman Ottinger first introduced the Bill, Irish Embassy officials told him that they approved of it. Then John Hume and [the Rev. Ian] Paisley came to Washington. John Hume was quoted in the *Washington Times*, September 20, 1983, as saying, 'There are 27 U.S. plants in N.I., and I have not heard one complaint about discrimination practices. We have a fair employment bill that makes discrimination illegal.' That is an extraordinary thing for John Hume to say.

Paisley has leaned on John Hume, and the British Government has leaned on the Irish Government to oppose the Ottinger legislation. How can Garret FitzGerald possibly explain to the people of Ireland that it would be bad for the U.S. Congress to make it illegal for U.S. companies in N.I. to discriminate?

The greatest weapon the British have for oppressing Catholics in Northern Ireland is the Irish Embassy in Washington.

Whenever the Irish National Caucus succeeds in raising the Irish issue, the British always make the Irish Embassy jump to defend British interests,' concluded Fr McManus.[9]

Niall O'Dowd – who would later become the publisher of the *Irish Voice* newspaper and *Irish America* magazine in New York – would report from San Francisco:

The revelation that the Irish Embassy was actively campaigning against the Bill came yesterday from the offices of Congresswoman Barbara Boxer (D–CA) who confirmed that in separate meetings representatives from both the Irish and British governments had asked her to oppose the Bill . . . In response to Fr McManus's criticism, Michael Collins [later the Irish Ambassador in Washington], the Irish Government's press and information officer in the

United States, stated that the embassy had 'taken a long and detailed look at all aspects of the Ottinger Bill and that they foresee problems with it. We believe that this Bill could have a counter-productive effect'.[10]

The Ottinger Bill contained in essence the principles we would later call the MacBride Principles. That is why we say that the MacBride Principles were born in 1983. To promote the Ottinger Bill, the Irish National Caucus sponsored a visit to Northern Ireland by Congressman Ottinger in 1983. We hosted the Congressman's appearances at meetings and Press Conferences in Belfast. The visit received considerable press coverage in the Irish and British media. Bob Blancato, the Staff Director of the Ad Hoc Congressional Committee for Irish Affairs, was also part of the delegation, representing the Chairman of the Committee, Congressman Mario Biaggi (D-NY).

We could tell we were on to something very important by the way the press reacted. The *Daily Telegraph*, under the heading 'Americans in Ulster Maelstrom', said:

> Mr Ottinger's mission is regarded with far more suspicion in the Protestant camp. At the moment, he is steering legislation through Congress to force American companies investing in Northern Ireland to employ more Roman Catholics.
>
> In June, he introduced a Bill called the Northern Ireland Fair Employment Practices Act, which would require American firms with branches or other enterprises in Ulster to desegregate employees of different religions and eliminate religious discrimination in jobs.
>
> The spotlight is being put on Short Brothers, the Belfast plane-makers, who are bidding to sell aircraft to the United States Air Force. The contract would mean an extra 600 jobs ...
>
> Advising the Congressman, and helping him in the talks, was Fr Sean McManus, the Washington-based Redemptorist priest ordained in England and now a scourge of the British Government. The lime-and-soda-drinking cleric is not

liked by British diplomats in the American capital, where he leads the Irish National Caucus, a lobbying group aimed at influencing American foreign policy with the target of Irish unity, freedom and peace'.[11]

The *News Letter* screamed the headline, 'Anti-British to the Hilt', and said:

> The leading light in the delegation, Fr Sean McManus, is a well-known republican sympathizer who rarely disguises his anti-British stance . . . this fiery advocate of Irish republicanism did his utmost to embarrass British diplomats in Washington with a brief hunger strike outside the Embassy in support of Bobby Sands' death fast.
>
> He was instrumental in persuading the Carter administration to impose an embargo on American gun sales to the RUC in Belfast. And his latest campaign aimed at undermining the attempt by Shorts to secure a multi-million pound order to sell its SD-330 Sherpa freighters to the United States Air Force.
>
> It was back in 1979 that Fr McManus told reporters: 'The British thought they were getting rid of me in 1972, when they had me packed off to America. Little did they know I would be far more vocal on Capitol Hill'.[12]

The *Daily Express*, 18 August 1983, however, really outdid itself. It devoted an editorial to our visit:

> Sean McManus, a rancid bigot loosely described as a 'priest', is campaigning to stop a £33 million order from the United States Air Force going to Shorts, the Belfast plane-makers.
>
> McManus – born in Northern Ireland but now in Washington heading an anti-British pressure group – alleges there is discrimination against Catholics at Shorts: though the firm denies it.
>
> Doubtless he is delirious at the calls from other pip-

squeak Irish-American politicians urging President Reagan to appoint a special envoy to Northern Ireland.

Indeed, he probably has a hand in the setting up of the 'Irish-American Presidential Committee' to push the issue of a unified Ireland into the 1984 presidential campaign'.[13]

While in Belfast, we took the occasion to pursue the other very hot issue – the question of the United States Air Force doing business with Short Brothers (Shorts had a notorious record of anti-Catholic discrimination). The Caucus had been raising this issue for quite some time. This was really one of our pivotal campaigns because it dramatically raised the whole issue of US dollars subsidising anti-Catholic discrimination in Northern Ireland. We met with Short's executives at the office of the Fair Employment Agency. Again, this meeting received considerable press coverage. Our Shorts campaign would eventually lead to Congressman Joe Kennedy (D-MA) getting an Amendment passed (1988, 1989 and 1990) in Congress to the US Defense Bill. The Amendment required Shorts to submit an annual statistical report to the Defense Department on its subcontracting and recruiting practices.

At the meeting, I remember the Shorts' spokesman – with barely concealed hostility – telling me, 'Shorts does not have to give any explanations to the Irish National Caucus or anybody in America'. How their tune has changed. That same spokesperson would later have to go, cap in hand, to meet with the then Comptroller of New York City, Elizabeth Holtzman, to assure her that Shorts was making attempts to hire more Catholics.

Just before one main press conference was due to take place, Fr Brian Brady called and told us that a high-ranking Catholic Church official in Belfast had asked him to ask us to meet with someone who had a special interest in the Shorts issue. We agreed.

The person arrived and asked to meet with us behind a big curtain in the room where the press conference would take place, in the Europa Hotel in Belfast. He did not want to be seen by the press. His name was James Eccles, a former Head of the Knights of Columbanus (a lay Catholic organisation in Ireland. It is quite powerful and very 'respectable'). Eccles' pitch was that the Knights had done a lot of investigation into anti-Catholic discrimination in Northern Ireland. We asked him to provide us with the results of the alleged investigation. He was completely taken aback. We knew the guy had an angle, to say the least. He said he agreed that Shorts was guilty of very bad discrimination, but . . . 'But,' I cut in, 'you still think they should get the contract with the US Air Force?' Eccles said yes. He then promised if Shorts got the contract, the Knights would put pressure on them to end discrimination. We politely told him that we would keep up the pressure on Shorts, and showed him the door (or rather, the curtain).

While he was giving us this unbelievably disingenuous pitch, I couldn't help remembering that it was the Catholic Bishop of Belfast, Cahal Daly, who was among the very first to voice public opposition to our campaign against Shorts. There is a morning radio programme in Northern Ireland called *Thought for the Day* on BBC Ulster. Bishop Daly instructed Fr Gerry Patton – the media person for the diocese – to use the programme to attack our campaign. Patton deplored the fact that there was a campaign in the US to oppose Shorts getting an Air Force contract and wanted to make sure the people realised that the priest (myself) who was leading it had no connection with the Diocese of Down and Connor.

Mr Eccles, about a year later, sent us an unsigned note identifying himself as the person who had met with us prior to the press conference and he wanted us to know that we had been right about Shorts – that they had only made promises to get the contract with the US Air Force, and then it was business as usual.

The same Mr Eccles would surface again in the US as the main lobbyist against the MacBride Principles – assuring legislators that discrimination was a thing of the past, that the MacBride Principles would only hurt Catholics, etc. Eccles travelled all across the US with the same message.

At one MacBride Hearing in Nebraska, on 13 March 1989, one of Eccles' prize statements was: 'I was knighted by the Pope, and

I'm very close to the workings of the Catholic Church in Ireland.'
I hung my head in shame and thought to myself, 'Once again the
Catholic Church is being used for British interests in Ireland.'

I had many reports that while lobbying in the US against
the MacBride Principles, Mr Eccles allegedly gave the impression
that he was doing so with the blessing of the late Cardinal
Tomás Ó Fiaich, Archbishop of Armagh and Catholic Primate
of Ireland. I made a statement in *The Irish Times* that I would
be very surprised and deeply disappointed if Cardinal Ó Fiaich
was allowing his name to be used by the British government's
anti-MacBride campaign in the US. The next day, I received a
mailgram stating, 'No one authorized to use my name in any way
to oppose MacBride Principles. Northern Catholic Bishops have
never made any statement on the MacBride Principles.'[14] It was
signed: Cardinal Ó Fiaich, Ara Coeli, Armagh.

Mr Eccles would later spread the word in the *Sunday News*
that he was not paid for his anti-MacBride work: '. . . Mr. Eccles'
son Jim said: "My father does speak out against the MacBride
Principles because he firmly believes that they will do more harm
than good. But he has never received money for it, not even
traveling expenses . . . He visits America frequently. While he is
there, he makes his views known on the MacBride Principles . . .
He sees it as an extension of the charity work he has been heavily
engaged in for nearly 30 years."'[15]

But former British MP Kevin McNamara in his book on the
MacBride Principles would reveal – having had access to British
government documents – that Eccles, 'was expensive. He was
employed for a maximum of 60 days a year at £220 per day plus
expenses, and was in receipt of an annual retainer'.[16] Mr Eccles
was also a member of the board of the Fair Employment Agency
(FEA) from 1985 to the autumn of 1989, when the Agency was
replaced by the Fair Employment Commission (FEC). In May
1990, the FEC issued a report charging that the motor trade in
which Mr Eccles worked had a very serious imbalance – that
Catholics were seriously under-represented. Indeed, the FEC said
that the actual company for which Eccles worked – A. S. Baird

Ltd – was only 18 per cent Catholic. The FEC 1991 figures are 67 Protestants (73.6 per cent); 24 Catholics (26.4 per cent); 34 'unknowns'; in all, a total of 125 employees.

What did Mr Eccles say in response to this very embarrassing exposure? He alleged he 'had not come across any pattern of discrimination during his years in the trade. I was too busy trying to earn an honest pound.'[17] Indeed.

By the way, the other very interesting 'champion' that sprang to the defence of Shorts was Aer Lingus. One of our members had written to them complaining that they were using Shorts 330 aircraft. The Chief Executive Officer of Aer Lingus, David M. Kennedy, wrote back on 23 June 1983, saying, 'We are satisfied there is no religious discrimination in recruitment or employment practices of Shorts.' At that time, Short's percentage of Catholics was less than 5 per cent out of a workforce of 6,300.[18]

I was outraged and issued the following press statement: 'I simply cannot believe that any responsible spokesperson for Aer Lingus – not to mention the chief executive – would make such an extraordinary statement. There is simply no other way to put it: This is a blatant cover-up. Whenever the British Government is in trouble, it seems it can always get some gombeen man to do its dirty work. Mr Kennedy is but the latest example in this dismal tradition.'

Aer Lingus is semi-state-owned and it is unlikely Mr Kennedy would have made that statement without the explicit approval of the Irish government. Garret FitzGerald was Taoiseach at the time.

On 3 May 1983, I sent a letter to all 535 Members of the United States House of Representatives and Senate, outlining the case against Shorts. The following week (10 May 1983), the British Ambassador, Oliver Wright, sent letters to all the same people – with a glossy brochure, specifically written by Shorts to refute our charges of discrimination. Two black-and-white photos were enclosed with the brochure: one of Garret FitzGerald standing beside a Shorts' aircraft, and one of the head of Aer Lingus receiving a Shorts' aircraft.

But the plot thickens. In 1983, James Shannon was a

Democratic Congressman from Massachusetts. He was very close to the Irish Embassy in Washington, DC, and would not make a move on the Irish issue without the blessing of the Embassy. One of our members – a constituent of his – wrote to the Congressman asking him to support the Caucus' campaign of opposing Shorts getting a US Air Force contract. This was his response:

> The Irish Government recently reviewed the situation at Short Brothers in Belfast. It noted historical patterns of clear discrimination, and also noted recent efforts to correct that situation, including: the appointment of a Catholic personnel director, active recruitment in Catholic schools and in the Catholic press, and agreeing with the Fair Employment Agency to set up an affirmative action program. It also noted that the prevailing opinion in both communities in the North was that the proper approach is to eliminate discriminatory hiring practices, and then to promote foreign investment and employment. The Irish Government recently contracted with Short Brothers for the production of aircraft for the national airline, Aer Lingus. This is the best evidence that progress is being made in correcting historical patterns of injustice'.[19]

So there you have it. The first opponents of our campaign to stop the US subsidising anti-Catholic discrimination were John Hume, the Catholic Bishop of Belfast, the Knights of Columbanus, Aer Lingus and the Irish government. And you thought the British government ruled only through the Protestants of Northern Ireland! It would seem that the Irish Embassy was a wholly owned subsidiary of the British government. The architects of the Embassy's policy were Garret FitzGerald, Sean Donlon, Michael Lillis – and John Hume.

It is also interesting to note here that on our visit to Ireland in 1979, we met with the late Paddy Devlin, former Social Democratic and Labour Party (SDLP) leader. He was very excited about our idea of making an impact on discrimination through the leverage of American companies. He kept saying he could not believe that he himself had not thought of this idea, and that nobody in the North even knew which were the American companies.

The next time I saw Paddy Devlin was in the US at a hearing testifying against the Principles. He became one of the team of Catholics the British government (through its Department of Economic Development) recruited. Devlin would write later in his column in the *Sunday World*: 'My personal view of the principles is that they will undermine our efforts to eliminate discrimination, deflect US investment away and cause the withdrawal of US companies by putting them into conflict with our labour laws'.[20] The following year he said, 'The MacBride Principles are a sham. It is time we identified the primary issue of the hidden agenda that is the disestablishment of Northern Ireland society'.[21]

The Caucus/Ottinger visit to Northern Ireland served as a watershed in our campaign. After this, a number of elected officials contacted us, wishing to become associated with our campaign. Chief among these were: New York City Comptroller Harrison J. Goldin, Council Member Sal Albanese of the New York City Council, New York State Assemblyman John Dearie, New York State Senator John Flynn and Massachusetts State Senate President Bill Bulger.

The Caucus saw the need not only to involve United States legislators, but also institutional investors in our campaign. As New York City Comptroller, Mr Goldin was one of the custodians of millions of dollars of New York City funds invested in a number of United States companies doing business in Northern Ireland. We eagerly welcomed him into our campaign. We worked with his office on issuing a new set of principles. For me, there could be no question as to the person after whom we should name these principles: Seán MacBride.

But let me go back a bit. I first met Seán MacBride in New York City in the spring of 1976 when he was the guest speaker at an AOH function. At the time I was the Deputy National Chaplain of the AOH, and as such, I was seated at the head table, next to Seán. I was amazed and humbled he took such an interest in me and the work of the Irish National Caucus. I was used to the 'great and the good' in Ireland not wanting to know me, which I took as a badge of honour.

The next time I saw Seán was at the previously mentioned AOH Convention in Killarney, 27–29 June 1978. When he spoke, he went out of his way to commend me and the work of the Irish National Caucus. A journalist commented to me that it was significant that he had done so, given the open hostility of the Dublin government to me. I kept in touch with Seán, and as explained earlier, in July 1979, I asked him to head up the INC Liaison Group in Dublin.

Then I invited Seán to be the guest speaker at the Fifth Annual Testimonial Dinner Dance of the Irish National Caucus on 10 December 1982 in New York City, attended by close to 1,000 guests. The following morning I picked him up at his hotel to bring him to speak to the Caucus chapter in Huntington, New York. 'Did it [the dinner dance] end peaceably?', he smilingly inquired in his still partial-French accent. I asked him why he put the question. 'Well, in my day, Irish American events sometimes ended in a fight,' he replied.

Later on I dropped him off at the airport. As we sat for a moment, before he left the car, I was deeply conscious of the history he represented and felt in some inchoate way that I needed to do something to honour his family history. In truth, he was the only person in whose presence I felt overawed, indeed, a bit intimidated. I asked him if we ever came up with something – a document, proclamation, something – if he would lend his name to it. Without hesitation he consented.

So when the time came, I talked to Seán MacBride on the phone a number of times about naming the Principles after him. On 18 October 1984, I formally wrote him, proposing and enclosing, the Principles.

On Monday 5 November 1984, the Irish National Caucus announced the launching of the MacBride Principles. Thus the Principles were 'christened'.

Our press release carried the heading, 'Caucus's New Plan to Combat Discrimination' and went on to say: 'The Irish National Caucus today announced a major new initiative to combat employment discrimination in Northern Ireland . . . The Caucus has endorsed a set of Equal Opportunity Affirmative Action Principles for Northern Ireland that have been sponsored by Seán MacBride . . . "This approach," said Fr Sean McManus, ". . . is the way for Americans to deal with anti-Catholic discrimination."'

The Irish Echo (New York) captured the historic moment accurately with the headline: 'Caucus Proposes New Initiative to Stop Discrimination in Northern Ireland'.[22] The *Sunday Tribune* reported: 'The nine-point employment code, which was drawn up by the Washington-based Irish National Caucus (I.N.C.) is sponsored by Seán MacBride S.C., leading Northern Ireland trade unionist Inez McCormack and Northern surgeon Senator John Robb and Father Brian Brady.'[23] That was the very first occasion the MacBride Principles were mentioned by name in the Irish or American media.

Thus, a historic initiative was conceived, born, and christened.

We wanted to mention Comptroller Goldin's name in our announcement, but at that stage he was not prepared to associate his name with the Principles. In fact, he backed out at the last moment, after I had told Seán MacBride that he would join us in the announcement. The first New York politician, in fact, to publicly associate himself with the MacBride Principles was City Councilmember Sal Albanese (D-Bay Ridge). I had been advising Goldin to associate himself publicly with the MacBride Principles, otherwise other New York politicians would beat him to the punch. But he thought it was just a tactic to stampede him into supporting the Principles earlier than he wanted to.

The moment Councilmember Albanese read *The Irish Echo*'s report on the launching of the MacBride Principles, he contacted the Irish National Caucus with a view to introducing a Bill in the New York City Council. He and the Caucus worked on the drafting, and on 19 December 1984, a Bill was introduced: #878. This was to be the very first MacBride Bill in the US.

And so, the MacBride campaign had formally begun. The *New York Daily News* reported: 'City Councilman Sal Albanese (D–Bay Ridge) will appear at City Hall tomorrow in a rally with Rev. Sean McManus, National Director of the Irish National Caucus, to seek support for the bill.'[24] *The Irish Echo* announced: 'Fr Sean McManus, national director of the Irish National Caucus, will hold a press conference with Councilman Albanese at City Hall on Jan. 3 at 10:30 am calling on Irish groups to support Intro. No. 878.'[25] The *Chief Leader* said: 'The Irish National Caucus has chosen New York City to be the first where pension fund investments will be used to increase pressure for equal rights for Catholics in Northern Ireland . . .'[26] The *Catholic New York* newspaper said: 'Father McManus was present at City Hall recently to speak in favor of the [Albanese] legislation . . . Father McManus said that proposed legislation is "eminently reasonable . . . One of the most effective ways for us to combat the situation is to get the investors involved and make them aware they are supporting anti-Catholic discrimination," he told *Catholic New York*'.[27]

The Sunday Times: 'The [MacBride] campaign is being run by the Irish National Caucus . . . The move, inspired by Father Sean McManus, who has been consistently opposed to British policy, is particularly well timed. For even if the law is never passed, it provides an opportunity to link, however, tenuously, the issues of South Africa and Northern Ireland. The MacBride Principles also call for the same kind of affirmative action programs for Catholics which American companies already use in the employment of women and Blacks in the U.S.A'.[28] This was the very first mention of the Principles in the British press.

In an interview with Niall O'Dowd in *The Irish Press* Comptroller Goldin said: 'Moreover, having reviewed the MacBride Principles, I endorse this initiative'.[29] (Notice: he speaks about 'having reviewed', not having originated the Principles. It was only later that people associated with the Comptroller made the retroactive claim that he had developed the Principles.)

But in New York papers, Comptroller Goldin, unfortunately, came out very publicly against the Bill. The *New York Daily News,* under the headline 'Koch & Goldin Oppose Ulster Investment Ban', said:

> Mayor Koch and City Controller Harrison Goldin expressed opposition yesterday to a City bill that would prohibit city Pension fund investments in the U.S. owned businesses that discriminate against Northern Ireland. Their reaction came after the Rev. Sean McManus, National Director of the Irish National Caucus Inc., a Northern Irish Catholic lobbying group based in Washington, appeared at City Hall to urge passage of the bill. The measure, sponsored by Councilman Sal Albanese (D–Brooklyn) [*sic*], is awaiting a hearing in the Council's economic development committee . . . Goldin said the Council Bill was premature.[30]

A leading column in *The Irish Echo* stated:

> Mayor Koch and City Comptroller Harrison Goldin are opposed to such tough measures on the grounds that the British have an official policy that is against discrimination, and the situation in Belfast is very different from South Africa where the government has an official policy of discrimination.
>
> The 'unofficial' nature of discrimination in Northern Ireland notwithstanding, it is still a fact that Catholics do not have equal opportunity in the North, and that New York City officials have every right to be concerned about it . . .
>
> It is for this reason Councilman Albanese should be encouraged . . . and that Mr. Koch and Mr. Goldin – who I am sure are acting in good faith – should be asked to take another look at their position. Mr. Koch has the strong support of the majority of the Irish community in New York and I am sure he would like to maintain that support.[31]

The New York Times reported: 'The Council measure is opposed by Mayor Koch, who sits on the boards of the four largest pension funds for city workers, and City Comptroller Harrison J. Goldin, the custodian for all five funds in the system and a trustee of the four largest funds'.[32]

At this stage – and for a good while later – Goldin was opposed to legislation on the Principles. He felt that shareholder resolutions would have sufficient leverage and his office did not want anything to overshadow his role. His office fought Albanese's office on this, so much so that Albanese and I had to call a meeting in New York City to push the need for legislation. About 400 Irish Americans attended the meeting. I spoke very forcefully about the need for legislation – not just shareholder resolutions. Even at that meeting, Goldin's office opposed the idea of legislation. But the mood of the meeting was clearly in our favour, and soon afterwards Goldin's office withdrew their opposition to legislation. That meeting was a key building block in the long construction of the MacBride campaign. At the meeting, Pat Doherty, Goldin's aide, was visibly shaken by the anger towards Goldin. Time and time again, I witnessed people say to him, 'There has to be a law. There has to be a law,' the adopted refrain of the Albanese–Caucus supporters. Indeed, I had to run interference several times to ask them to leave Pat alone. Goldin soon realised, however, that he had made a terrible mistake. The train was leaving the station, and he was not on board! He was in a position to play a key role in our campaign, but his public opposition to the New York City legislation had hurt him badly.

Comptroller Goldin had lost the high ground. How could he reclaim it? The Caucus wanted Goldin to be prominently involved because as the custodian of millions of dollars, he represented the vitally important role of investors in the MacBride campaign.

There is a well-known technique whereby American politicians stake claim to an interest in Irish issues – the highly publicised visit to Ireland. There is nothing wrong with this. Presidents Kennedy and Reagan did it; why shouldn't a non-Irish American also do it? So Comptroller Goldin needed to visit Ireland. But how to go about it? Who would sponsor the visit? Who would set it up? And very importantly, who would have the resources to pay for it? The answer – the Irish National Caucus. That the Caucus attached great importance to the role Goldin could play is seen in the fact that it was prepared to spend so much money on the trip.

Furthermore, the Caucus had already 'covered' the legislative dimension of the MacBride Principles – we now needed to 'cover' the investment dimension. The *New York Daily News* would give the Caucus–Goldin visit prominent coverage: 'A. U.S. based Irish lobbying group paid up to $12,000 so City Comptroller Harrison Goldin could visit Ireland – with his family and aide – to look into complaints of economic discrimination against Catholics in Northern Ireland . . . A spokesman for the controller said it was official city business.'[33]

The aide was Pat Doherty, who would go on to feature prominently in the MacBride campaign, and become a good friend.

Some Irish American groups shortsightedly criticised the Irish National Caucus for 'wasting money'. But when they finally understood the significance of the Caucus strategy, they were very eager to associate themselves with the MacBride campaign. The Goldin visit received heavy coverage in the British and Irish media, thereby helping to establish the MacBride Principles firmly in the public mind. It was on this trip that Goldin met Seán MacBride for the first time – eight months after the Irish National Caucus had launched the MacBride Principles.

The Caucus arranged meetings with Charlie Haughey, the Fair Employment Agency, John Hume and various US companies. It was ironic that the British government attempted to make great play out of the fact that Sinn Féin was the only political party in Northern Ireland to support the MacBride Principles. However, when Sinn Féin met with the Goldin group in Belfast, they expressed strong opposition to the Principles, saying they were not radical enough. But the real reason for their opposition was because the Principles were launched by the Irish National Caucus. (Sinn Féin opposed the Irish National Caucus because it is non-violent, and because the Caucus does not allow itself to be controlled from Ireland.) But later, when Sinn Féin saw that the Principles were driving the British government up the wall, they reversed their position and began to express public support for them.

In the United States, the trip was also given considerable press coverage. *The New York Times*, the *New York Daily News* and the *New York Post* all devoted editorials to it. For example, the *New York Daily News* editorial said: 'How did Goldin get involved with the so-called MacBride Principles? Although named for an aging Irish Nobel laureate Seán MacBride, they were actually drawn up in the U.S. by the Irish National Caucus. The Caucus organized and paid for Goldin's trip – at a cost of about $12,000.'[34]

The New York Times editorial said: 'A lofty but misguided proposition for opposing discrimination against Catholics in Northern Ireland has reared its head in Congress, three state legislatures and the New York City Council. Based on what are called the "MacBride Principles" . . . The principal sponsor is the Irish National Caucus, a Washington lobby intent on getting Americans to pressure Britain to withdraw from Northern Ireland . . . Comptroller Harrison Goldin, just back from Northern Ireland, is pressuring pension funds to act on their own.'[35]

A *New York Post* editorial said: 'City Controller Harrison Goldin says he recently visited Northern Ireland as a trustee of the city's $28 billion-plus pension fund. He wanted to see if employment discrimination exists, with an eye toward using the fund's considerable muscle to end it. It was official business, says Goldin. The Irish National Caucus – a private organization which lobbies politicians on behalf of Ireland – paid. It wasn't cheap, either. The Caucus estimates it cost upwards of $12,000.'[36]

In a short time, the Irish National Caucus campaign would be featured in *The Wall Street Journal*, the *Philadelphia Inquirer*, *The Boston Globe*, and many other major newspapers.

At our urging, our good friend State Senator Billy Bulger used his influence to have Massachusetts become the first State to pass the MacBride Principles. I launched the Massachusetts Campaign in Springfield with a speech before the John Boyle O'Reilly Club – a very appropriate place – in February 1985.

The Sunday Republican reported: 'U.S. dollars mustn't subsidize anti-Catholic discrimination in Northern Ireland . . . the Caucus is asking American firms to adopt the MacBride Principles . . . "American businesses can have a profound effect," [Fr McManus] said. "You're talking about millions of dollars . . . We're not calling for disinvestment. We are not trying to end American investment in Northern Ireland," he said'.[37]

We worked closely with State Representative Tom Gallagher (D-18th Suffolk District). On 1 October 1985, he wrote to me: 'I expect the Massachusetts House will shortly take up legislation applying the MacBride Principles to state pension fund investment. I believe the measure will reach the Governor's desk this session, and will make Massachusetts the first state to apply MacBride to its investments. I look forward to working with you in the future.'[38]

The Massachusetts MacBride Bill was signed into law by Governor Michael Dukakis on 21 November 1985. It was the first MacBride law in America. Dukakis still supported the MacBride Principles as a presidential candidate in 1988 (despite the strong lobbying of John Hume). While I was still based in Boston, Governor Dukakis invited me to his office on St Patrick's Day 1978, to present me with a proclamation he was issuing at our request, 'Human Rights for Ireland Day'. (That, of course, caused Irish Consul Carmel Heaney further fury.)

New York Assemblyman John Dearie and New York State Senator John Flynn initiated Bills on the MacBride Principles.

Soon afterwards, in May 1986, New York became the second State to pass the MacBride Principles. In 1992, New York State became the first State to pass a MacBride Principles Contract Compliance Bill.

The Irish National Caucus then initiated Congressional legislation on the MacBride Principles (the Fish–D'Amato Bill, introduced on 1 October 1986), just as we had done on the seminal Ottinger Bill in 1983. And, as they say, the rest is history. Virtually all Irish American organisations, the AFL-CIO, many religious groups (Catholics and Protestants) rallied behind the

MacBride Principles, making them the most powerful American campaign on Northern Ireland since its creation in 1920.

After Seán MacBride's death on 15 January 1988, his son Tiernan – with typical MacBride generosity – wrote to me: On behalf of the late Seán MacBride I would like to thank you most sincerely for travelling to Dublin to attend his funeral. He will never be forgotten while the Principles drawn up by the Irish National Caucus are named after him.[39]

And on 28 June 1993, Caitriona Lawlor in Dublin wrote the following letter to Ken Bertsch, Investor Responsibility Research Center:

> I understand that you are preparing an updated version of 'The MacBride Principles and US companies in Northern Ireland' . . . During the years 1976 to 1988, I worked as Personal Assistant to Seán MacBride and witnessed the attention he paid to the causes in which he believed, in days when such causes were neither popular nor profitable. It amused me, therefore, to see the reference contained on p. 60 of the current edition, 'Doherty and McManus dispute exactly who should take credit for the idea of a fair employment code for recruiting Seán MacBride as Sponsor.' My understanding always was that the fair employment initiative for Northern Ireland lay squarely with Father Sean McManus and the Irish National Caucus in Washington, and it was to great advantage when the Comptroller of New York City, Harrison Goldin, and his office took up the cudgels. Indeed, Father McManus was adamant even in the initial stages of preparation, that MacBride should be involved and should lend his name to the Principles, based loosely on the Sullivan Principles for South Africa.
>
> This is a very slight correction, but I feel in the interests of historical accuracy, due credit for initiating the code and recruiting Seán MacBride, should be given to Father McManus and the Irish National Caucus, and I hope you will feel able to do so . . .'[40]

In 2009, former British MP Kevin McNamara released his book, *The MacBride Principles: Irish America Fights Back*. In it he makes the remarkable statement about me: 'What is not comprehensible is why he [McManus] should seek to exclude the important role played by Comptroller Goldin's office in the run-up to the launch, particularly as he takes great pains to credit him for his support once he came on board in 1985.'[41] Of course, McNamara partly refutes his own accusation by pointing out that Goldin only came on board in 1985, whereas we had launched the Principles in November 1984. However, it is patently absurd to claim I tried to exclude Goldin when I went to great pains, and expense, to dig him out of the hole he had dug for himself.

Things admittedly became messy when Pat Doherty improperly made an issue of the drafting of the MacBride Principles. That was not expected, as staffers are not supposed to claim pride of authorship when assigned a project. And I have never known one to do so except for Pat. These were the MacBride Principles, not anybody else's. Just as, 'Ask not what your country can do for you . . .' is JFK's speech, not anybody else's.

That is also why I found it extraordinary when McNamara criticised me for saying the drafting of the Principles never concerned me too much: 'This was a surprising statement to make'.[42] There was nothing surprising about it. I was never too concerned about the drafting of the principles contained in the Ottinger Bill, the Fish–D'Amato Bill, or the Gilman legislation that became Federal Law in 1998. Nor did their staff make an issue of it.

But what had really forced me go public and set the record straight was Doherty's bizarre version of events as reported by the iconic journalist, Mary Holland in *The Irish Times* in 1987: 'Mr. Doherty researched the problem and drew up a set of guidelines for American companies . . . Through Irish American contacts, he then approached Seán MacBride and asked him to sponsor them.'[43] Now that's chutzpah for you! Pat did not even really know who Seán MacBride was until I named the Principles after him – as Pat himself admitted to me at the time. Mary Holland was very upset when she realised she had got the story wrong. She apologised profoundly, writing in a personal letter to me: 'I am really sorry that . . . I misrepresented the genesis of the MacBride Principles . . . I'm sure you'll understand that I was told the story as I recounted it.'[44]

The historical reality is that the Principles only became the powerful force they did when they became the MacBride Principles. And the Principles would never have got off the ground with such a bang had they not been launched by the Irish National Caucus, which did all the initial publicity – framing the issue, briefing the media, educating the public, and lining up political support. As McNamara states, Goldin only 'came on board in 1985'.[45]

However, apart from the corrections forced on me here, I am the first to acknowledge the vital importance of Pat's contribution. In 2008, *The Irish Echo* asked me to rate his work. This is what I said: 'Pat has played a key role in the campaign to stop U.S. dollars subsidizing anti-Catholic discrimination in Northern Ireland . . . He is one of the most effective Irish-American campaigners since the time of the Fenians in 1858.'[46] Pat just needs to be reminded occasionally that it was the Irish National Caucus that took him and Goldin to Ireland – not the other way around; and that we dug them out of the hole they had dug for themselves politically, launching Pat onto an excellent Irish American adventure.

16

Anti-MacBride Campaign

*The Irish National Caucus have never seemed to us to have the
interests of the people of Northern Ireland genuinely at heart.*
British Embassy, Washington[1]

The Irish National Caucus launched the campaign for the
MacBride Principles. The British government launched the
campaign against the MacBride Principles. The battle lines were
as clearly drawn as that. For Irish Americans, the moral clarity of
the campaign could not be more luminous.

The extraordinarily arrogant quote above is from N. E.
Sheinwald, First Secretary of the British Embassy, and current
British Ambassador to Washington. He wrote it in a letter in
March 1985 to my good friend Tom Donahue, then Secretary
Treasurer of the giant labour organisation, AFL–CIO. It strikingly
personifies the imperial attitude. He is concerned about the
people of the North and I, a Fermanaghman, am not! He then
goes on to lecture Donahue: 'As always with this sort of thing,
it is important to look not only at the words used, but at the
people and the organizations promoting the initiative and the
commentary they themselves provide on the text. It is, in my view,
instructive that the Irish National Caucus is playing a prominent
part in promulgating the MacBride Principles.'

But then, in the best imperial fashion and in the favourite British technique, Mr Sheinwald conscripts the Dublin government by stressing: 'The leader of the Irish Labour Party and Deputy Prime Minister, Dick Spring, said in January that the INC campaign may be designed at depriving the people of Northern Ireland of much needed investment rather than any concern about discrimination.'

Well, thank you, Mr Sheinwald and Mr Spring: your opposition made us all the more determined to win – all across the United States and in the US Congress, making the MacBride campaign one of the most successful Irish American initiatives ever. Had those gentlemen supported me, I would have been examining my conscience.

Of course, neither Sheinwald nor Spring was calling the shots. That was the job of the Secretary of State for Northern Ireland, Douglas Hurd. On 11 February 1985 he laid down the marching orders: 'We continue to brief US companies and US opinion to oppose the INC campaign . . .'[2]

Now there's a perfect example of British government understatement and euphemism. When that government says it will 'brief to oppose' – look out. What it really means is that it will vilify, demonise and resort to every dirty trick in the book. It means 'crush the INC by any means necessary'.

I can well understand some individuals in Northern Ireland being naturally opposed to the MacBride Principles, and I can respect their opinion. But there was nothing spontaneous about the campaign in the US against the MacBride Principles. Someone in Northern Ireland did not wake up one morning and say to himself/herself: 'There's a hearing on the MacBride Principles in Nebraska or Texas or Washington, DC. I'll get dressed, slip over and give my opinion.'

The anti-MacBride campaign was highly controlled, highly financed, and fiercely fought by the British government, the Dublin government and, sadly, by John Hume. The agencies the British government used to fight the campaign were the Department of Economic Development (DED) and the Fair Employment

Agency (FEA) (now the Fair Employment Commission (FEC) of Northern Ireland). The late Bob Cooper, former head of the FEA and later head of the FEC was dispatched to lobby against the MacBride Principles in California and Pennsylvania. How could Irish Americans, therefore, have had confidence in the FEC? In the United States, the campaign was coordinated by the British Embassy – the largest embassy in Washington. The Embassy hired the top lobbyists, attorneys and Public Relations professionals.

I remember, during the MacBride campaign in Maine, meeting one of the top lobbyists, Severin M. Beliveau. He told us that the British Embassy called and asked to come and see him. He had no idea what it was about. They came to his office, told him they wanted to hire him to block the MacBride Principles from becoming law in Maine, and offered him big money. 'Sorry, gentlemen,' he said, 'but my grandmother from Enniskillen would turn in her grave if I were to work for you.' (As he was telling me this, he had no idea where I came from, until I shouted, 'Up Fermanagh'.)

But not all lobbyists were so principled – even ones with Irish names. In fact, the British Embassy at the beginning always tried to recruit Irish American lobbyists. For example, one very well established law firm in Washington is O'Connor and Hannan, a big Democratic law and lobbying firm. Their home base is in Minnesota. The Embassy hired them to lobby against the MacBride Principles in Minnesota. When they were asked, 'How could you?' O'Connor replied, 'Their money is green, also.' Irish Americans in Washington and Minnesota were disgusted. But the Embassy succeeded in getting an Irish American lobbyist to work for them in Maine: John Doyle of Doyle & Nelson in Augusta.

Another anecdote about a lobbyist hired by the British Embassy is worth recounting. Someone – just for the fun of it – told the lobbyist that other lobbyists were being paid far more than he was and urged him to demand more money. He did, and the Embassy gave it 'without batting an eyelid'.

So clearly, money was no problem when it came to defeating the MacBride Principles. On their own admission, the British government spent millions of dollars to battle the MacBride Principles. A senior official in the Department of Economic Development (DED) said, referring to myself, 'We did not take him very seriously at first but the MacBride Principles have caused serious problems and cost millions to try and counteract'.[3] Isn't it too bad they didn't spend those millions of dollars creating fair employment in Northern Ireland?

I wish everyone in Ireland could have attended a MacBride Hearing. (To get the MacBride Principles passed into law in a particular state or city, the legislature has first to hold a hearing, taking witness from experts or concerned citizens.) The Hearing Room was typically packed with enthusiastic Irish Americans and other supporters. The British Embassy officials were there with one, two, sometimes three or four 'castle-Catholics' whom they had flown from Northern Ireland. Yes, it was nearly always Catholics whom they recruited. I guess they thought it was the clever thing to do.

The first thing those Catholics said when they testified was, 'I'm a Catholic, and the MacBride Principles will only hurt the Catholics of Northern Ireland.'

Legislators – especially African Americans – saw right through that attempted subterfuge. At the MacBride Hearing in Washington, DC, 30 January 1992, it was a delightful sight to watch the Chairman of the Committee, and the author of our MacBride Bill, Councilmember John Ray, systematically shred the arguments of Sean Neeson, a leader of the Alliance Party, and a Catholic from Northern Ireland. Ray told him that he was not surprised (i.e. not fooled) that a Catholic should come before his Committee to argue against MacBride, because he had seen blacks from South Africa come to Washington to argue that US pressure could only hurt blacks in South Africa. Ray might not know all the history of Ireland, but as a proud African American, he understood discrimination. In fact, I have never met a politically aware African American who does not intuitively know that Catholics are oppressed in Northern Ireland. At the DC hearing I knew I had the game won when a friend of mine,

African American Fr Ray East, marched into the Hearing Room with about a dozen determined and formidable black women parishioners. Chairman Ray stopped the hearing and invited them all up to the front. Can you imagine the suppressed groans of Neeson's handlers from the British Embassy?

It had to be a very chastening experience for the British government to see themselves being beaten time after time in the MacBride campaign. (And, I confess, it warmed the cockles of my Kinawley heart. I took huge joy and consolation in it.) The constant defeats created much pressure, which sometimes showed itself. For example, at a hearing on MacBride in Minnesota, after the vote was taken and we had won handsomely, I turned to shake someone's hand in congratulations. As I turned, I saw a woman glare at me with unconcealed venom. I thought to myself, 'My goodness, what's the matter with her?' I immediately asked someone who she was and was told that she was the British Consul from Chicago. On the way out of the Hearing Room, I happened to be walking right behind the same person. She slammed the door right in my face. So much for the British stiff upper lip.

One advantage, from the MacBride point of view, of the British government's practice of bringing out mostly Catholics to testify, was that it did not frame the issue in sectarian terms as it would had the people they brought out been Protestants. Then the press would be reporting that the Protestants and Catholics were clashing at hearings. But since it was, in general, only Catholics who came out, the issue was framed as Irish Americans against the British government.

In the early days of the MacBride Campaign, I had stated publicly in the press that it was very interesting to watch the 'body language' in the MacBride Hearing Room: 'large numbers of enthusiastic Irish Americans looking forward to inflicting another defeat on the ancestral enemy of their homeland. They take over the room . . . And sitting at the back, looking very forlorn, are the few Catholics from Northern Ireland, along with their handlers from the British Embassy. Well, after I had said that, I noticed that at the next hearing the anti-MacBride forces occupied the front-row seats!'

Of course, there was another reason why the British recruited Catholics to testify against the MacBride Principles – they did not want to give Protestants a platform to attack the Anglo-Irish Accord. So for many reasons, the British government was very badly snookered by the MacBride campaign. If they did not oppose the MacBride Principles, they lost by default. But, on the other hand, in opposing the Principles, they alienated a lot of legislators. These legislators got very annoyed when they saw the British government coming into their state and city to oppose their legislation. But, by the same token, the legislators got a kick out of the British opposition. It showed them that their legislation was having an impact – that it was 'tweaking the lion's tail'.

Why was the British government so opposed to the MacBride Principles? Well, the simple answer is that the discriminator always has to oppose a campaign against discrimination – whether it is South Africa, South America, the United States, or Northern Ireland.

But it is important to understand that when it comes to the MacBride Principles, the 'process' is as important as the 'product'. The product is, of course, getting the Principles passed into law, with all their implications, both politically and economically. But consider what is involved in the 'process'.

For a MacBride campaign to begin in a state or city, legislators have to be 'recruited' to introduce the legislation. They have to become familiar with the issue; their colleagues have to be lobbied; supporters have to be activated to make MacBride an issue. And then there has to be a hearing (which often lasts for hours).

When, without the MacBride Principles, would state and city legislators ever have focused on the Northern Ireland issue? The answer is never. And that was a huge reason why the British government feared the MacBride campaign, because it powerfully and non-violently exposed – in a responsible and important setting (the Hearing Room) – the malicious record of British rule in Northern Ireland. Even though the hearing was about discrimination in Northern Ireland, inevitably, and very properly, all the other British government abuses of human rights got an airing – and I made sure they did. And that profoundly embarrassed the British government.

There is another thing that really frustrated the British government: knowing that time, for a change, was on our side. If we failed to get MacBride passed in a particular city or state, we would be back next year or the year after – more determined, better organised, and more experienced. And the harder they fought us, the better we liked it. So the British government was in a no-win situation.

The basic strategy of the British government was to use Catholics (and, of course the Dublin government) for their propaganda in the United States. That, of course, is nothing new. It is as old as British policy in Ireland. Uneducated and politically unaware Catholics can be excused for being used in such a manner. But what can one say about politically sophisticated Catholics? Surely, granting the reality of the anti-MacBride campaign, such Catholics could not argue that they just made statements in a vacuum, not knowing that their statements would be used by the British Government. The two Catholics whose names were most used (apart from the Dublin government) in British government propaganda were John Hume of Derry and the late Bishop Cahal Daly of Belfast, later Cardinal of Armagh.

On 10 December 1982, International Human Rights Day, Seán MacBride spoke at the Caucus Testimonial Dinner in New York. The following day, I travelled with him by car from Manhattan to Huntington, New York. I was asking Seán all sorts of questions about international affairs. I finally asked him if John Hume and Garret FitzGerald had ever consulted him about the problem in the North of Ireland. Seán gave me a very emphatic 'no'. I asked him what he thought the reason was. 'Because they know I'm implacably opposed to Partition' was Seán's equally emphatic answer. Significantly, neither Hume nor FitzGerald attended Seán's funeral in Dublin in 1988.

Hume was in a very strong position as leader of the Social Democratic and Labour Party of Northern Ireland (SDLP) and a member both of the British Parliament (MP) and of the European

Parliament (MEP). He was committed to the Anglo-Irish Agreement of 1985, of which he was a key architect along with Garret FitzGerald.The quid pro quo for that agreement was 'thou shall not criticise the British government'. (In fact, Hume had long since stopped criticising that government.) All problems could and must now be solved within the context of that Agreement. The MacBride Principles were outside the Agreement, and thus beyond the pale for John Hume.

Hume was to be one of the first and potentially most deadly opponents of the MacBride Principles. It is without doubt he blunted the cutting edge of the MacBride campaign. But in the process, he came out the worse − because the campaign was not significantly weakened by him. But he was weakened. His credibility and judgment were put into question. It is probably one of the few times John Hume has been wrong-footed in America.

His opposition to the MacBride Principles did not make sense to Americans − even to many of his own supporters and admirers. The Principles were, after all, what Americans would expect Hume to be for: a modern, progressive, enlightened way to address discrimination in this global economy. We must be responsible investors.

In *The Boston Sunday Globe* of 8 March 1987, Hume had a half-page interview, with photograph, under the headline, 'Ulster Leader Assails American Supporters of MacBride Plan'. And assail he did. 'Those responsible for the campaign just don't know the damage they're doing. Discrimination against Catholics in Ulster had to be attacked on the ground, not in America,' Hume said − missing the whole point of the MacBride Principles.[4]

The huge − and obviously orchestrated − interview was followed up three days later, 11 March 1987, by an editorial. In an appalling example of parroting British government propaganda, the editorial said, 'Unless this long-term economic decline can be reversed, the only way the MacBride Principles could get jobs for the unemployed Catholics is if Protestant workers were fired.'And then it continued with incredible fatuity: 'If new investment arrives, pressure from the Catholic community, and from the

Irish and British governments working together through the Hillsborough Agreement [Anglo-Irish Agreement] will see to it that jobs are fairly apportioned.'[5] Yet everyone knew that the only pressure on the British government on the issue of discrimination was the MacBride campaign.

There is simply no way of avoiding it: Hume allowed himself to be used by the British government in their anti-MacBride campaign. He was, however, smart enough not to get his hands dirty. He never put himself through the indignity of testifying against the MacBride Principles. Hume was not prepared to be on the losing side at a hearing. But the British government used Hume's name as the main weapon in their arsenal, quoting him liberally in their anti-MacBride discrimination material. And when both the previous Governors of the State of California vetoed the MacBride Bill, they quoted John Hume to justify their veto.

The following month *The Boston Globe* ran an interview with Seán MacBride under the headline 'Ex-IRA Leader Fights for Jobs' (even though MacBride had left the IRA in 1936). 'When asked to respond to Hume's statement, "Fairness will prevail but first get companies to invest", MacBride replied, "That's wishful thinking on his part. Ideological baggage. Without pressure there is no reason to believe Catholics would be hired . . ."'

Seán MacBride then proceeded to give his ultimate assessment of John Hume. 'Hume,' he said, 'has become an apologist for British rule in Northern Ireland,' and 'is in a position of defending the existing system in Northern Ireland'.[6]

Hume's anti-MacBride campaign (in conjunction with that of the British and Dublin governments) did ensure that its main target, Senator Teddy Kennedy, would fall into line. Teddy never supported the MacBride Principles. But great credit must be given to former Mayor Ray Flynn of Boston, later Ambassador to the Vatican, for resisting Hume's pressure. Flynn has been a fearless and effective advocate of the MacBride Principles. Credit must also be given to former Congressman Joe Kennedy. He stood firm on his election pledge and supported the MacBride Principles – as did the vast majority of the Massachusetts Congressional Delegation.

Another prominent Catholic from Northern Ireland who was perceived to have joined the British Government anti-MacBride campaign was Bishop Cahal Daly, later Cardinal Daly, Archbishop of Armagh and Primate of Ireland.

In November 1989, as the Bishop of Down and Connor (the diocese that includes Belfast) Cahal Daly came to the United States in what was widely perceived to be, at least in part, an escalation of the British government's campaign against the MacBride Principles. We were in the middle of fighting a very tough battle to get the Principles passed in the state of Pennsylvania. I got calls that one key supporter of the Principles was contacted to see if he would meet Bishop Daly so that the Bishop could show him the error of his ways.

Bishop Daly proceeded to confirm suspicions by an interview he gave to *The Boston Globe*, 25 November 1989, with James L. Franklin, who was a very experienced writer, having been the Religion writer for that newspaper since 1976:

> The Catholic bishop of Belfast yesterday opposed the adoption of the United States of measures to reduce job discrimination against Catholics . . . He was reacting to a recent adoption by Boston and several states of the MacBride Principles. Such legislation is more likely to discourage companies from investing in Northern Ireland, said the bishop.
>
> 'I feel great hesitation about any program that unilaterally insists on fairness without concerning itself at the same time with increased employment opportunities particularly by American investment,' he said.
>
> Instead, he urged support for legislation recently adopted by the British Government.[7]

I was very upset, and issued the following statement: 'It is not the first time in Irish history that the English Government was able to use an Irish bishop'.[8]

This is the same Bishop Daly who, in 1983, had ordered the radio attack on our campaign against Shorts.

From the mid-1940s to the mid-1960s, Cahal Daly taught Moral Philosophy at Queen's University of Belfast – then a bastion of anti-Catholic discrimination. In all these years, he never opened his mouth against discrimination. What if Rev. Martin Luther King, Jr had taught for twenty years in a discriminatory university, and never spoke in protest? Would he have any credibility as a spokesman on justice and peace? The first maxim of non-violent resistance to injustice is that you can only teach it by example. You cannot turn a blind eye to injustice all your life, and then expect people to listen to you lecture them on how to respond to injustice.

When it was known that Cardinal Daly and three leaders of the main Protestant Churches in Northern Ireland were coming to the US in February 1993, some feared that it was another anti-MacBride attempt. I felt it would not be – but only because President Clinton was on record for supporting the Principles. I felt that Irish Church leaders – who are very establishmentarian and somewhat obsessed by 'respectability' – would now 'cut their cloth to suit the fashion of the times', and not publicly denounce the MacBride Principles, which is what happened.

When Cardinal Daly and the other Church leaders were questioned in New York, *The Irish Echo* of 12 February 1993 quoted Daly as saying, 'We are not opposed to the MacBride Principles here or at home'.[9] Quite a backing-off from what he told *The Boston Globe* in 1989.

However, there seems to have been some dissembling in Cardinal Daly's response, as an American bishop would unwittingly expose. In August 1993, Bishop Michael F. McAuliffe STD, Bishop of Jefferson City, Missouri, wrote to John Carr, Secretary of the Department of Social Development and World Peace of the US Catholic Conference: 'the Cardinal indicated there were some others that could very well be added as part of those Principles . . .'[10] Bishop McAuliffe had visited the Cardinal in Ireland during July. It was during that visit, according to Bishop

McAuliffe, that Cardinal Daly had stated that he wanted to see the changes in the MacBride Principles.

Mr Carr's office, as we shall see, had been very much involved in the controversy over a proposal to hold a conference on the MacBride Principles in Washington in the autumn of 1993. He had also been denying any attempt by the Catholic Church leaders either in Ireland or the United States to change the MacBride Principles. And how had Bishop McAuliffe 'unwittingly' exposed Cardinal Daly? Well – again through the grace of God – he had mailed his letter to me instead of to Carr.

I was used to people sending us copies of letters they have written to someone else. So I thought this was a case of a bishop sending me a copy of a letter he had written to the Catholic Conference. I had sent a copy of the letter I had written to John Carr to every bishop in the US. It was only when I had re-read Bishop McAuliffe's letter that I realised it was not a copy, but rather that the Bishop had addressed the letter to John Carr at the address of the Irish National Caucus.

So doesn't providence work in a strange way? Here was a letter he clearly did not want me to see, but yet he had addressed it to my office. So that there would be no further delay with the letter, I very obligingly faxed it on to John Carr and faxed off my own letter to the good Bishop explaining his error.

I had never heard Bishop McAuliffe ever open his mouth about anti-Catholic discrimination in Northern Ireland. Yet he had the bloody nerve to interfere in the MacBride campaign.

A final note on Daly. In 1979, after we had stopped American guns going to the RUC, and when the Caucus group was in Ireland, we met with the late Fr Denis Faul. He had just come from a meeting with Daly, who was still Bishop of Down and Connor. Denis suggested that the Caucus should meet with Daly. I was not too interested, but out of respect for Denis, I agreed and asked him to set it up. Denis got back to me with Daly's response: 'It would not be good for the Church for me to meet with the Irish National Caucus.'

The US Catholic Conference (of Bishops) is in part the

social arm of the Catholic Hierarchy. Its large headquarters in Washington has many departments – one of which is the Office of International Justice and Peace. This is the department, of course, that would deal with the Northern Ireland issue (on the rare occasions it had a mind to). Sadly, it had the same 'establishment-elitist' attitude of all entrenched bureaucracies. On 6 January 1978, I met with that office. Afterwards I said, 'It was just like being at the British Embassy. The Office of Justice and Peace has become the ecclesiastical arm of British propaganda'.[11] As if to prove my point, the then Advisor on European Affairs – Edward Doherty, a layman, and British to his fingertips – wrote in a letter: 'It is the Provos who are mainly responsible for the violence in Northern Ireland and this is recognized by every careful and impartial observer . . . after due consultation with the Irish bishops, and in recognition of the efforts being made by the governments and church bodies directly concerned, we [the US Catholic Conference] had concluded that there is no appropriate basis for public intervention in the problems of Northern Ireland, either by this conference, or any branch of the United States government . . .'[12]

As explained earlier, in August 1979 the Irish National Caucus led a successful campaign to have a ban put on the sale of US weapons to the RUC. Well, later on, in January 1981, Archbishop Hickey of Washington and Bishop Thomas Kelly, Secretary General of the US Catholic Conference, visited the White House to urge President Reagan to continue the ban on military aid to El Salvador.

I wrote to them, begging them also to urge President Reagan to continue the ban on the sale of US weapons to the RUC. Archbishop Hickey responded to me saying, '. . . Bishop Kelly and I will be in touch with our counterparts in Northern Ireland to seek their advice in this vexing question. Our intervention will depend on their response.' And Bishop Kelly replied '. . . We have known of your position [on the RUC] for some time . . . In the case of El Salvador, we have been encouraged to take what action we have taken by the local hierarchy. We have not, at this time, received such encouragement from the Irish hierarchy on the subject you have brought to our attention . . .'[13]

By now you get my drift – dealing with these people was like dealing with the British Embassy. So you can imagine my surprise when I discovered, at the height of the MacBride campaign, a plot from these same folk to muscle in on our work – having never lifted a finger to help. Why would they do that? To enhance MacBride? The very opposite: to sabotage and neutralise it. Here's what happened.

Through a stroke of good fortune in May 1993, a letter from the Presbyterian Moderator, Rev. Dr John Dunlop of Belfast, came into my possession. It made the astonishing revelation: 'I have been advised that the Presbyterian Church USA and the United States Catholic Conference are prepared to convene a conference on fair employment and investment. I believe that such a conference, which would include a discussion about MacBride would be very helpful. Maybe an improved version of the MacBride Principles could command widespread support . . . maybe even the name could be changed or modified to indicate that improvements have been made and at the same time move it from its explicitly partisan association . . .'[14]

And, six days later, Josiah Beeman, Chair of the Northern Ireland Working Group of Presbyterian Church in the United States said in a letter (announcing the Conference) that one purpose of the Conference would be to raise 'support for the MacBride Principles or a modified version of them that would eliminate contentious issues among supporters of fair employment.'[15]

Well, you can imagine I was not going to take this lying down. So I released a blistering press release:

> Is this the latest assault by the English Government against the MacBride Principles? These Church groups have never lifted a finger to support the MacBride Principles; indeed they either passively or actively opposed the Principles. Now they are going to have a conference about the MacBride Principles, with a view to changing the name and contents of the Principles.

Well, with all due respect, I think they have a bloody nerve and a colossal arrogance. Let me make it perfectly clear that no Church leader (Catholic or Protestant) or anybody else in Ireland or the United States has the right or authority to change one syllable – not one jot or tittle – of the MacBride Principles.

If these Church groups have had their conscience pricked by the effective MacBride campaign and at long last want to oppose English Government discrimination in Northern Ireland, then I would welcome that. But surely a little bit of repentance – at least one *mea culpa* – would be in order from these Church people who, either passively or actively opposed the MacBride principles,' McManus argued. 'But instead of a *mea culpa*, they arrogantly call a conference to change the MacBride Principles – the one effective campaign against anti-Catholic discrimination in Northern Ireland.'

I then did one of my massive mailings. The outside envelope carried the eye-catching warning: 'Don't let the English Government use the Catholic Church against the MacBride Principles.' I included a pre-written postcard the recipients could mail to their own Bishops. And I also wrote a very strong letter to each bishop in the US: 'It is beyond doubt that the English Government has often succeeded in using Church leaders in Ireland for its own oppressive purposes. It would be an enormous scandal if that tradition was transported across the Atlantic and that the Catholic Conference would become the latest tool of the English Government'.[16]

Well, it scared the hell out of them, so to speak. You have never seen such scampering in all your life. The bishops became truly alarmed and immediately disassociated themselves from any anti-MacBride implication. All talk of a conference was dropped, even denied it had ever been planned. And in its place, the four main Churches in Ireland and their counterparts in the US issued 'A Call For Fair Employment and Investment in Northern

Ireland'. Not only that, but they were forced to actually endorse the MacBride Principles: 'Many Americans support the MacBride Principles, as amplified, as a good faith, non-violent means to promote fair employment. We urge that any support of these amplified principles, which offer positive values and focus on fair employment, be joined with continued support for strong fair employment measures and an active commitment to investment and job creation . . .'[17]

It was a remarkable turnaround. What started out as a covert and cynical effort to sabotage the MacBride Principles ended up as a ringing endorsement of them, by entities that, to say the least, were never too keen on them.

The Irish Embassy in Washington was one of the very first to oppose the MacBride Principles. The Consul in New York actively lobbied against the MacBride Principles in Albany, New York, in 1986, much to the righteous anger of Paul O'Dwyer, the famed Mayo lawyer in New York.

Taoiseach Garret FitzGerald spelled out his attitude in a speech in Boston on 3 May 1985: 'There is, however, a campaign under way which aims at discouraging American investment in Northern Ireland . . . Those who pursue this campaign should know that they are inflicting injustice on both communities . . . One can only wonder whether some of those who press for disinvestment do so as part of a calculated strategy which has as its goal the further weakening of the already strained Northern Ireland economy so that terrorism may have greater opportunities to flourish.'[18]

I understandably condemned FitzGerald. He knew full well that the very first thing the Irish National Caucus said when it launched the MacBride Principles was that 'they [the Principles] do not call for reverse discrimination, quotas or disinvestment'. This mischievous statement by FitzGerald was used with abandon by the British government in the United States.

But here, again, Kevin McNamara puts a peculiar spin on my reaction to FitzGerald. In his book he writes: 'FitzGerald is reported as saying that "new evidence" had caused him to drop the passage from his speech . . . The Irish Consul-General in New

York specifically informed the Comptroller of the decision to
omit the passage. This did not prevent McManus from declaring it
to be: "The Big Lie. Vintage FitzGerald smear tactics. England has
no better Friend than FitzGerald." It might be argued that these
comments were "vintage" McManus; to attribute to a political
opponent words that he had not used, particularly when the lack
of their use could be portrayed as a victory for McManus's own
campaign.'[19]

McNamara is ridiculous when he says that because
FitzGerald did not use that passage when he spoke, it did not
matter. Nonsense. That passage had been widely disseminated
in the media. Did FitzGerald ever officially withdraw it and
apologise for it? FitzGerald, in effect, accused me (the Irish in
Boston were very familiar with me and would have seen me as
the main leader of the MacBride campaign) of 'inflicting injustice
on both communities . . . so that terrorism may . . . flourish'. And
yet, McNamara reshapes this to make FitzGerald the victim, and
me the culprit. And he does that repeatedly in his book. Each time
I stand up for MacBride, he sides with the governments and the
establishment and tries to make me the villain (as we shall see later
regarding my letter to Taoiseach Charles Haughey).

Finally on this, I remember the late, very just and honourable
Kevin Boland, former TD and Minister, telling me that he was
always shocked by the common tactic of government officials not
saying at actual meetings what their press statements claimed.

However, imagine this delicious irony. Just eleven short years
later, Taoiseach John Bruton in Washington was presented with
a plaque 'commemorating the inclusion of strong support in the
Republican Party platform for the MacBride Fair Employment
Principles'. The presentation was done by presidential candidate
Senator Bob Dole on behalf of the entire GOP (the 'Grand
Old Party', i.e. the Republican Party) leadership. According to a
RNC (Republican National Committee) News Release, 'Prime
Minister Bruton thanked Mr Dole and Republicans in Congress
for . . . the inclusion and endorsement of the MacBride Principles
in their platform'.[20] I was so elated I had to call my brother

Frankie in Ireland, as he would be able to fully appreciate the incredible irony.

I believe the most effective thing Charlie Haughey did regarding Northern Ireland was his reversal of FitzGerald's policy on the MacBride Principles. In an address to the Dáil on 7 April 1986, Haughey said:

> I want to avail of this opportunity to state that I fully endorse the MacBride Principles. I welcome the efforts and initiative of concerned Americans who wish to see something done about the chronic discriminatory patterns in employment in Northern Ireland.
>
> The regrettable position is that fourteen years after the imposition of direct rule in Northern Ireland, the situation in most sectors of employment is as bad as it ever was. The purpose of the MacBride Principles is to ensure that if there is to be American investment, if there are to be American orders, the firms concerned will have to act fairly and in a non-discriminatory fashion in regard to employment.

When Haughey became Taoiseach, his government's position was that there was nothing 'objectionable' to MacBride. However, it took a long time for Haughey's policy to be implemented by the Irish Embassy. On Seán MacBride's last trip to the United States, in April 1987, he spoke at the Eire Society dinner in Boston. He was accompanied by his son, Tiernan. The Irish Ambassador, Pádraic MacKernan, also attended the dinner, quite openly advising people that the MacBride Principles were a bad idea, and that they should follow John Hume's lead. Seán MacBride took the issue up with Haughey, writing to him on 29 April 1987: '. . . there is a general feeling among our leading supporters that our diplomatic and consular staff in the US are using their influence to oppose the adoption of the MacBride Principles'.[21] When Tiernan MacBride returned to Dublin, he complained to Haughey's people. They promised to force MacKernan to comply with Haughey's position, but it took a long time for that to happen.

Indeed, on 11 February 1988, I was forced to write this letter to Mr Haughey – the very first time I ever thought it was worth writing to an Irish Taoiseach. In it, I said:

> Both before and after you were elected Taoiseach, Irish Government officials in the United States have actively campaigned against the MacBride Principles . . . And, I am ashamed to say, there is reason to suspect that this smear campaign was in part orchestrated by the Irish Embassy and Mr John Hume MP SDLP. The first shots in this anti-MacBride campaign were fired by US Senator Daniel Patrick Moynihan (D–NY) – who takes his cue on Irish matters from the Irish Embassy . . . When I challenged Senator Moynihan that he was misrepresenting the MacBride Principles, he retorted: 'You tell your readers that MacBride was the Nobel Peace Prize Winner. Tell them he was, also, the Lenin Peace Prize Winner, and you don't get that for nothing.' It was a shocking and deliberate smear.
>
> The Irish National Caucus is now more than ever dedicated to the MacBride Principles. It is our earnest hope that you will immediately instruct all your officials in the United States to stop opposing the MacBride principles.

Kevin McNamara again chooses to attack me for this letter in his book: 'An intemperate letter from Fr McManus to Haughey, included the old accusation that before and after Haughey's election [to his third term as Taoiseach, 1987 to 1992], "Irish government officials in the United States have actively campaigned against the MacBride Principles".'[22] It was not an 'old accusation' but another example of the Embassy's opposition to MacBride. Then he – very usefully, indeed, and much to the credit of his research – makes public for the first time Ambassador McKernan's response as contained in the DFAMP (Department of Foreign Affairs. MacBride Papers) undated cable: 'Although one can readily dismiss Fr McManus's lurid assertions, at the same time there is a serious and unscrupulous intent behind them . . . This is to try to intimidate Irish officials in the United States . . . it is an attempt to intimidate the government. You have observed the minatory note struck in the letter when Fr McManus says that the Caucus will be monitoring the activities of the Embassy.' McNamara blithely continues: 'The day to day work of the Embassy continued: monitoring the progress of the MacBride campaign . . .'[23] So it was perfectly okay for the Embassy to monitor the MacBride campaign, but it was intimidatory and minatory for me to monitor theirs?

Yet McNamara does not describe the Ambassador's letter as intemperate and he seems merrily oblivious to his own double standard, not to mention the Ambassador's. This is such a pity because Kevin McNamara has had a great record on Ireland and it is truly puzzling that he can't seem to help himself: the 'Brit-speak' holds him captive. For example, when I refer to Seán MacBride's past, I call it heroic and noble – to McNamara it is 'tempestuous'. [24] It is as if he had his computer programmed to automatically enter a negative adjective before MacBride's name and mine.

What should have really upset the Ambassador was Senator Moynihan's attack on Seán MacBride. If Moynihan had accused a former British, Israeli or French foreign minister of being a Soviet agent or mole, their respective embassies would have created uproar. There was not one word of protest from the Irish Embassy. What does that reveal? After the meeting, I confronted him, demanded an apology, and told him that he had slandered a great man. He refused to apologise and walked off in a petulant huff. I refused to have any dealings with Moynihan's office from then on. By the way, this is how Moynihan histrionically ended his speech: 'If the Soviets increase their subsidy to the Provisional IRA, think Lebanon.'

The Irish Embassy's possible role in slandering Seán MacBride – and in their refusal to repudiate it – was similar to their role in blocking the Caucus' campaign to free the Birmingham Six. It was only in 1991, when Dermot Gallagher became Ambassador, that I noticed a change of attitude. Since that time, I have had nothing but respect for the Irish Ambassadors to Washington. I often wonder who really calls the shots in all these events – civil servants or Irish Taoisigh.

I always knew that Teddy Kennedy – with his good heart and right instincts – had to be most uncomfortable with being forced by John Hume and the Dublin government into a position of not supporting the MacBride Principles. And, sure enough, McNamara's book comes up with the evidence.

McNamara – in one of his most important revelations – explains:

> The campaign outside Washington was being carefully watched by those on Capitol Hill, who felt that their position locally might be being undermined by the activities of the INC and the Ad Hoc Congressional Committee. Burke of the Irish Embassy reported a conversation that he had with a senior member of Senator Kennedy's office concerning the possibility of Kennedy introducing a bill into the Senate incorporating the MacBride Principles. The purpose was to pre-empt Representative Biaggi in the House or Senator De Concini in the Senate, both of whom were associated with the INC, and were thinking about introducing similar legislation. Burke cautioned against this course of action . . . it would be perceived as a victory for the Ad Hoc . . . and the INC. Burke's advocacy was successful. The idea of a Kennedy bill was quietly dropped'.[25]

So there you have it: it was all about stopping the Irish National Caucus, and the Irish Embassy would use Kennedy – or any means necessary – to accomplish that.

But I was determined the Irish Embassy would not stop us. And no matter what the British Embassy tried, I was certainly not going to let them beat us, even though they had transferred, as McNamara's book reveals, '[Andrew] Henderson from the British consulate in New York to the embassy in Washington, to operate on a full-time basis to counteract the MacBride campaign'; and even though the Secretary of State for Northern Ireland, Sir Patrick Mayhew, approved that 'Mr Hume should be approached as a potential ally'.[26]

I had earlier exposed that the British Embassy had brought in an MI5 agent to try and defeat us: '[President] Clinton was informed by a White House staffer that Father McManus had discovered . . . a British intelligence MI5 agent used his embassy job to direct a campaign specifically against the MacBride Principles'.[27]

I was not going to allow anyone to stop MacBride from becoming US law – not even Bill Clinton, to whom I felt so deeply grateful for his magnificent work on the Irish peace process.

17

Forcing Clinton to sign MacBride

The time is always right to do the right thing.
Martin Luther King, Jr

Presidential candidate Bill Clinton made his pledge to support the MacBride Principles at the Irish American Presidential Forum in New York City on 5 April 1992: 'I like the Principles very much, I think they are a good thing, and if I were President, I would ask all state governments to take a look at adopting them. There's always that argument [that the Principles discourage investment] with this kind of thing, but I don't buy it. I see the MacBride Principles as a way of helping investment because it would help stabilise the Troubles.'

After Clinton spoke, I remember telling a group of Irish reporters at the Forum that one of the most important effects of Clinton's promise would be to ensure that the new Irish Government did not revert to a position of opposing the MacBride Principles. Charlie Haughey had just ceased being Taoiseach, and I was concerned that his successor would revert to the position of the previous Irish government under Garret FitzGerald.

Because of my direct experience with how FitzGerald had tried to sabotage Jimmy Carter's first pledge to the Irish National Caucus back on 27 October 1976, in Pittsburgh, I was especially concerned at how the new Taoiseach, Albert Reynolds, would react to Clinton's interest in the Irish issue. Reynolds welcomed Clinton's interest. And I knew it was the beginning of a new day. Because had Reynolds rebuffed Clinton, the way FitzGerald had rebuffed Carter, there would not have been an Irish Peace Process.

Surely there would now be plain sailing for MacBride? Well, in Washington, one learns there is no such thing. I had been pushing for a Federal/Congressional Bill on the MacBride Principles for some years now. In 1987 Congressman Fish (R–NY) – whom Irish Ambassador Sean Donlon had so disrespected over the Birmingham Six case – had introduced a Bill in the House (H.R. 725) and Senator Al D'Amato (R–NY) had introduced it in the Senate.[1]

But Congressman Lee Hamilton, Chairman of the House Subcommittee on Europe and the Middle East, would not schedule a hearing. He even told me there was not much interest in the Bill, despite the fact we had signed up almost a hundred co-sponsors.[2]

But it was not just Congressman Hamilton who was opposing us. Let me switch you back here to Kevin McNamara's book on the MacBride Principles. You saw earlier how the Irish Ambassador at that time, Padraic McKernan, had responded to my letter to Taoiseach Haughey. Well, in the same undated cable reply (which was his response to a letter of 11 February 1988, from the Department of Foreign Affairs (DFA) in Dublin) McKernan denied that the Irish Embassy was still conspiring against the MacBride Principles: '. . . Irish government officials have not campaigned and are not campaigning against the MacBride Principles'.[3]

Here again McNamara reveals vital information hitherto unknown. (He had been given 'unfettered access' to the files of the Irish government and Irish Embassy on the MacBride campaign.[4]) He reveals the Fish–D'Amato Bill was, indeed, of concern to the Irish Embassy: 'The Ambassador, Padraic McKernan, wrote a private and confidential letter to Noel Dorr, the Secretary of the DFA, in which he conveyed the alleged concerns expressed by the Friends of Ireland and Tom Foley, the Majority Leader in the House of Representatives, at what they perceived as the shift in policy contained in Haughey's interview. They were concerned that two bills languishing in committee, Fish's in the House and D'Amato's in the senate, might now emerge. Both bills were very divisive.'[5]

So here we go again! Were the Friends of Ireland really concerned or was it Ambassador McKernan? I had been well familiar with that tactic: the Irish Embassy would first wind up Members of Congress and then report to the Irish government that Members of Congress were 'very concerned'.

For years I have been doing my early morning, one-hour walk on the National Mall (the stunning, almost two-mile-long park that stretches from the Capitol Building to the Lincoln Memorial). On the morning of 18 June 1993, I was on the return stretch of my walk, facing the Capitol, plodding along and silently saying my rosary. I heard an unmistakable voice shout hello to someone on the Mall. I turn around, and there comes President Clinton, in shorts and a baseball cap, running at a pretty good clip, with a large retinue behind him, huffing and puffing. Now while my walk on the Mall is sacred time, how often does one get a chance to lobby the President of the United States?

'Bill,' I shouted, 'don't forget your Irish promises.' He turned his head towards me as he kept going and said, 'Don't worry.' I then shouted as he sped away, 'Keep supporting the MacBride Principles.' He put his hand above his head and waved affirmatively. I continued saying the Fourth Joyful Mystery of the Holy Rosary, which the Baptist President had interrupted.

Later that day, Mayor Flynn of Boston telephoned me. 'A good job of lobbying the President on the MacBride Principles, Fr Sean,' he said. 'How did you know that?' I asked. 'The President called me and said, "You know that Irish priest friend of yours? Well, he lobbied me on the Mall about the MacBride Principles."' Clearly, according to Flynn, the President got a real kick out of it.

However, nice as that was, we were still not getting any real Congressional progress on the MacBride Principles. Nor would we, until the Democrats lost the House and Senate and Republicans took over in January 1995. Isn't that an extraordinary thing to say – especially when people in Ireland mostly associate the Irish issue with Catholic Democrats?

For me, the Republican takeover meant one thing: the great Ben Gilman would be Chairman of the Foreign Affairs Committee (which would then be called the International Relations Committee). And, not just a Subcommittee but the full Committee. It was a perfect – although ironic – confluence of events. Bill Clinton in the White House, and Ben Gilman in the Chair of the House International Relations Committee.

With Ben as Chairman, I was now able to do in two minutes what I had not been able to do in twenty years. Immediately Ben told me I would get two hearings: one on the MacBride Principles and one on acceptable policing in Northern Ireland. My two top issues, just like that.

While two Irish Catholic Speakers – Tip O'Neill and Tom Foley – were in power, human rights hearings on Northern Ireland were banned. Yet when Newt Gingrich became Speaker, hearings were allowed. It took a Protestant Speaker and a Jewish Chairman to end the Congressional cover-up of British oppression of Catholics in Northern Ireland. For all time, that has to be a powerful ecumenical message for Irish American Catholics. Their Church was silent, famous Irish Catholics were silent, even complicit. A Protestant and a Jew stood up to the British – broke the ban – and had hearings.

With Ben Gilman becoming Chairman, Congressman Chris Smith of New Jersey, became Chairman of the Human Rights Subcommittee. He would go on to hold eleven hearings on the Pat Finucane case and other human rights issues. Chris is the quintessential good guy – dedicated, courageous, and committed to human rights everywhere.

Ben told me to get him a list of witnesses for a MacBride Hearing, and told me to gird for battle because, although he could schedule a hearing, I had get the Committee members to vote for the MacBride Principles.

But first we had to have a Congressional Reception to celebrate Ben becoming Chairman. On 26 January 1995, the Irish National Caucus hosted an evening reception in Ben's new fiefdom – the huge and impressive House International Relations Committee Hearing Room. Forty Members of Congress and about two hundred local Irish Americans attended. And in a sign of how completely things had changed for both Ben and me, the new Chairman of the Friends of Ireland, Congressman Jimmy Walsh, attended and expressed total solidarity with the Irish National Caucus and the Ad Hoc Congressional Committee for Irish Affairs. Chairman Gilman lavishly praised my work, which he said had been unfairly condemned by both the Irish and British governments, and by some big names in Congress 'who should have known better'. Then he officially announced that he was going to give 'Fr McManus his long-sought prize: a hearing on the MacBride Principles'.[6] And so it came to pass. On 15 March 1995, I had my long-sought-for hearing. This despite the fact that the US Ambassador to Ireland, Jean Kennedy Smith, had telephoned from Dublin to urgently beseech Chairman Gilman to call off the hearing.

The hearing would consider linking the MacBride Principles to the International Fund for Ireland (IFI).

Congressman Payne, the first speaker after Chairman Gilman's introduction, quickly set the scene: 'As an African American, I and eight other Members of the Congressional Black Caucus who are Congressional Friends of the Irish National Caucus can easily identify with the Catholic minority [in Northern Ireland] . . . The MacBride Principles were modelled after the Sullivan Principles . . . In the campaign for a free South Africa, we received a lot of help from Irish Americans. For example, Fr Sean McManus, president of the Irish National Caucus, was the first white Catholic priest to go to jail overnight for protesting outside the South African Embassy'.[7]

After that opening salvo, it was almost all downhill for the British government. The Clinton Administration attempted to bail them out. Assistant Secretary of State for European and

Canadian Affairs, Richard Holbroke, speaking on behalf of President Clinton and responding to questions later submitted by Committee members, said: 'While we support the MacBride Principles, the Administration sees no reason to promote additional legislation in the Congress. Federal enactment of the MacBride Principles would add reporting requirements on US companies investing and operating in Northern Ireland. To put the Principles into specific legislation could have an inhibiting effect on the investment goals we seek.'

Assistant Secretary of State for Legislative Affairs, Wendy R. Sherman, testified on behalf of the Clinton Administration at another hearing on 15 May 1995:

> We support and strongly prefer Mr Hamilton's version of this. We believe that the amendment that Mr Hamilton is offering [i.e. to delete mandatory linking of the MacBride Principles to the IFI] offers a constructive way forward to advance objectives that we all share. As Mr Hamilton has appropriately pointed out, *senior levels of the Irish government have told Administration officials that linkage of the basic MacBride Principles to IFI funding will be controversial and could disrupt the White House Conference* [emphasis added], which is aimed at increasing economic activity toward the disadvantaged and discriminated in Ireland.
>
> As was mentioned, all the parties, Ambassador Jean Kennedy Smith and Ambassador Crowe both do not support the mandatory linkage through the IFI. We think it is quite important to advance the objectives and goals, but do not think it should be mandatory.
>
> Certainly, the President absolutely, positively embraces the MacBride Principles completely, as does Mr Hamilton's amendment. The only difference is whether it should or shall be mandatory. And I don't think anyone for a minute would think Ambassador Jean Kennedy Smith does not endorse and completely embrace the MacBride Principles or Ambassador Crowe or this Administration.

Chairman Gilman dismissed all that mallarkey with: 'Saying one supports the MacBride Principles without implementing them is like saying one supports the Ten Commandments as long as I don't have to implement them'. He also dispensed with that old canard, beloved by the establishment and administrations, that although the idea was good, 'the time was not right'. Quoting Martin Luther King, Jr he told the Clinton Administration, 'It is always the right time to do the right thing.'

Throughout the hearing – whenever possible – I was grabbing every Member of the Committee urging them to vote for MacBride.

Remember, just six months previously, Congressman Hamilton was the all-powerful Chairman who had been resisting me for years, trying to tell me there was no support for the MacBride Principles in the Committee. However, later that day when the Committee voted on the Hamilton Amendment, we beat him by thirty-two votes to eight. It was a sweet victory. All the members of the Democratic Minority panel in deference to Hamilton, now Ranking Member, prefaced their remarks with something like, 'As much as I respect Mr Hamilton, etc . . . I cannot support his Amendment'. When it came his turn, the usually unflappable Hamilton was visibly annoyed: 'I could do with less respect and more support,' he huffed at the Democrats. 'I know what has happened here. The Irish National Caucus did its work on this Committee.'

Later during the hearing, I went up to Chairman Gilman (while Hamilton still sat on his left). 'You have just been handed your diploma in lobbying,' said Gilman – referring to Hamilton's bellyaching.

On 28 February 1996, Ms Sherman wrote as follows to Members of the House and Senate Conference, giving the 'Administration's Position on Provisions in HR 1561': 'The Administration opposes this provision . . . Requiring compliance with the "principles of economic justice", as defined in this provision would place an undue burden on small business and community development organizations . . . We propose that all reference to the "principles of economic justice" be deleted.'

On 11 April 1996, Tony Lake, Assistant to the President for National Security Affairs, wrote to me. 'Thank you for your letter about the legislation linking the MacBride Principles of fair employment to the funding for the International Fund for Ireland . . . The President does not believe it would be useful to place conditions on the funding we provide to the International Fund for Ireland . . .'

On 12 April 1996, President Clinton vetoed HR 1561.

I got eleven major Irish American groups to co-sign a letter that I sent to President Clinton on 19 April 1996: 'Because of our great gratitude for your crucial support of the Irish peace process, we've been reluctant to say anything up to now. But you cannot expect us to be silent as you continue to oppose one of our very top legislative issues. It is ironic that Senator Dole, the entire Republican leadership and the Republican National Committee are all supporting Congressional legislation on the MacBride Principles and you are opposing it. The peace process in Ireland cannot be separated from non-discrimination . . . We are totally committed to both.'

The letter was signed by the following organisations (in alphabetical order):

– John Finucane, President, American Ireland Education Fund

– Kathleen Holmes, Chairwoman, American Irish Congress

– Edward J. Wallace, National President, Ancient Order of Hibernians

– Larry Downes, Chairman, Brehon Law Society

– Mike Moroney, Secretary, Clan na Gael

– John D. Worral, President, Federation of Irish American Societies of the Delaware Valley

– James V. Mullin, Coordinator, Irish-Action Coalition

– Fr Sean McManus, President, Irish National Caucus

– Paul Doris, Chairman, Irish Northern Aid Committee

– Edmund Lynch, Chairman, Lawyers Alliance for Justice in Ireland

– Jean Forest, US Coordinator, Voice of the Innocent

(Of the principal activist groups on the North, the Irish American Unity Conference was the only organisation that refused to sign on.)

The letter from the Irish American leaders caused considerable attention, and put considerable pressure on President Clinton in the middle of an election.

Because of my deep gratitude for President Clinton's role in the Irish peace process, initiating that letter was one of the most difficult decisions I have ever made. I did not want to do it, yet I knew it would be a dereliction of duty not to. Behind the scenes, I had privately talked to White House officials and other key players in an effort to get the Administration to stop opposing the MacBride legislation. But I met with no success, and so I was reluctantly forced to go public. Some Irish Americans condemned me for criticising President Clinton. Maybe they did so because they lacked political self-confidence, or maybe it was because they did not have the experience of sitting for hours at hearings and listening to Clinton Administration officials opposing the MacBride legislation. Journalist Jimmy Breslin called to curse me out. In a tirade loaded with the F-word he berated me. 'Clinton is the only president who has ever done so much for Ireland,' he screamed. 'Don't you think I know that, Jimmy,' I replied. 'Didn't I stress that in our statement.' Uttering a few more expletives, he hung up on me.

But because I had stood up to President Clinton on principle (pun intended), I was later able to stand up for him with credibility. During his impeachment difficulty I wrote to every member of the House and Senate, telling them 'Let those without sin, cast the first stone'. Jimmy Breslin went on to write the most outrageous stuff against Clinton.

But whatever their reasons for opposing my standing up to Clinton, those Irish Americans were ignoring a fundamental principle in political campaigning: when a political leader does the right thing on your issue, you praise him; when he does the wrong thing on your issue, you call him on it.

Just look at what the President's two most loyal constituencies – African Americans and the Labor Movement – do. When the President goes against them on basic issues they do not hesitate to criticise him publicly.

Indeed, when one very prominent Labor leader chastised me on the phone for criticising President Clinton, I pointed to how Labor criticised him over NAFTA. He objected by saying, 'But that was about jobs for our people.' I replied, 'And what do you think the MacBride Principles are about, but jobs for our people?' He had no answer to that.

There is another hard political reality in all of this. How could I go back to Members of Congress and campaign again for the MacBride Principles if I let the President roll us over without a murmur of protest? How could I expect Members of Congress – both Republican and Democrat – to fight for the MacBride Principles if I was not prepared to fight for them? By my silence I would be taking a dive and jeopardising the integrity of the MacBride campaign.

Here again, Kevin McNamara 's book on the MacBride Principles shows an inability to appreciate the dynamics of American politics. He asserts that my standing up to President Clinton'... was probably the most significant political error that he [McManus] had made ... he shot himself in the foot'. McNamara was clearly misled, again, by Pat Doherty, whom he quotes as saying that I should not have stood up to Clinton, 'despite this one difference' (i.e. Clinton's opposition to the MacBride Principles becoming US law). However, 'this one difference' would have in principle invalidated the entire MacBride campaign. If one accepted Clinton's argument against the Federal MacBride Bill, then one would have to accept the same argument against all state and city bills. Pat had absolutely no role in lobbying Congress on the Federal MacBride Bill. Indeed, his position – in effect, that I should have rolled over and sold out the Federal MacBride Bill – shows that he was not committed to Federal legislation – just as he was not at first committed to state and city legislation.

Despite his claim that I had shot myself in the foot, McNamara proceeds to prove that my strategy was very effective and successful. He writes: 'The administration was caught unawares by the size of the storm . . . There was no one better to orchestrate such an uproar than McManus . . . The strength of McManus's attack . . . forced the administration to consider making a gesture to placate the pro–MacBride Democrats . . . The truth of the matter is that the President did not wish to go to Chicago . . . without attempting to achieve a reconciliation with the MacBride campaign . . . In an attempt to quell the controversy . . . James Lyons (the US observer to the IFI) wrote [to *The Irish Echo*, 22 May 1997] ". . . whether or not Congress sees fit to incorporate the principles . . . in legislation, the Clinton administration and I . . . will continue to see that these principles remain fully implemented in the International Fund for Ireland . . . "'

Then McNamara adds the clincher of all clinchers, delighting this Kinawleyman's heart: 'Officials in the DED privately acknowledged that the UK government had lost the battle on MacBride. The UK Embassy in Washington immediately recognized that the Lyons letter was likely to encourage McManus to press for legislation'.[8]

In further evidence that our strategy was right, on 24 August 1996, President Clinton – in a move widely regarded as an attempt to defuse the MacBride controversy – issued a directive to the United States representative for the International Fund for Ireland, James Lyons:

> In the 1996 Foreign Affairs Authorization Act (HR 1561) as passed by Congress, Section 1615 stated that U.S. contributions to the Fund 'should be used in a manner that effectively increases employment opportunities in communities with rates of unemployment higher than the local or urban average of unemployment in Northern Ireland. In addition, such contributions should be used to benefit individuals or entities which employ practices consistent with the principles of economic justice' as defined by the Act.

I vetoed HR 1561 for reasons entirely unrelated to the language in Section 1615. I am committed to equal opportunity and fair employment as necessary foundations for a just, peaceful, and prosperous future for all the people of both jurisdictions in Ireland. I therefore ask you, in discharging your duties under the Anglo-Irish Agreement Support Act of 1986, to ensure that the intent of Section 1651 of HR 1561 is carried out to the greatest extent possible.'[9]

Ray O'Hanlon of *The Irish Echo* – the most professionally objective journalist I've ever known – summed it up this way, 'Against the backdrop of the Democratic National Convention in Chicago, President Clinton has moved to mend damaged fences with Irish American backers of the MacBride Principles.' The Irish National Caucus put out a press release: 'Caucus Welcomes President Back to MacBride Fold'.[10] Remember, all this was happening in August 1996, with the Presidential elections scheduled for 5 November, between President Clinton and Senator Bob Dole (R-KS).

On 9 August, the Republican Party at their National Convention included support for the MacBride Principles in their party platform language. And on 27 August, the Democratic National Convention also included the MacBride Principles in their platform. *The Irish Times* observed: The reference to the MacBride Principes could be seen as a mild criticism of British rule in Northern Ireland but it is also intended to mollify . . . the Irish National Caucus.'[11]

As I told Kevin McNamara in my review of his book, 'For results like that, I would have shot myself in both feet'.[12]

Let's take a moment to reflect on what had been achieved to date.

We had routed the Philistines on the MacBride Principles. Against all odds – the British government, the Irish government, John Hume, Tip O'Neill, Teddy Kennedy, etc., – we had taken the MacBride Principles from a simple press release on 5 November 1984, all across the United States, into the White House, to being endorsed by both the Democratic and Republican parties.

By any criterion, it was a stunning achievement. And it was done by the so-called 'little people', the ordinary decent Irish Americans, without big power or big money. Now, surely, we would get the Federal MacBride Bill passed into law?

But things were not as rosy as they appeared. Because, after the 1996 election, the Clinton Administration would again unbelievably oppose the MacBride Principles being attached to the International Fund for Ireland.

In 1997, Congressman Ben Gilman (R-NY) again attached the same MacBride language to the Foreign Policy Reform Act (HR 1486). On Wednesday 30 April 1997, HR 1486 was in Markup (when Committee Members can make amendments). I spoke with Rep. Lee Hamilton, former House International Relations Committee (HIRC) Chairman, at his seat in the Committee Room and asked him if he was still opposed to the MacBride legislation. He emphatically said he was. I asked him what form his opposition would take. He said he wasn't sure yet. He then asked me if the language was the same as last year. I told him it was. Then he said, 'You know that it will never become law.' I asked why. 'Because the President is opposed to it,' he replied, with great emphasis.

I then lobbied the other Democrats on the Committee and expressed concern that Hamilton was still opposing the MacBride legislation. Next I spoke to Barbara Larkin, Assistant Secretary of State for Legislative Affairs, in the Committee Room. She confirmed the Administration's continued opposition to linking the MacBride Principles to the IFI in the legislation. Later that day, I called Steve Kashkett, at the Irish desk of the State Department. He said the President's letter to Lyons did not represent a softening of the President's opposition to legislation linking the MacBride Principles to the IFI. I told him that Mary Ann Peterson, Director for European Affairs at the White House, was supposed to have said that President Clinton was no longer opposed to linking MacBride to the IFI. He expressed surprise and disbelief at that, and told me he would check it out and call me back.

On Thursday 1 May 1997, the Markup continued. I spoke to Barbara Larkin in the Committee Room. She said, 'This is the man who knows all about Ireland,' and introduced me to Michael Klosson, her assistant for legislative affairs. He told me that the Administration was opposed to legislation linking MacBride to the IFI for a two-fold reason: because the British Fair Employment laws made MacBride unnecessary; and because MacBride would place onerous burdens on recipients of the Fund.

On Friday 2 May 1997, at 4.40 p.m., Steve Kashkett called me back and told me he could find no indication that the President had changed his position, or that Mary Anne Peterson had ever said the President was no longer opposed to Congressional legislation linking the MacBride Principles to the IFI. The President, he said, was opposed to Congressional legislation linking MacBride to the IFI for the reasons stated last year. Those reasons still stand, and that is the position of President Clinton, Kashkett emphasised. However, despite Clinton's opposition, the House passed HR 1486 on 27 March 1998.

Because the MacBride language was not contained in the Senate version of the Bill, the House and Senate Conference had to reconcile the two versions, (and not, of course, only on MacBride).

The reconciled Bill – now called the Omnibus Appropriations and Authorization Bill – was passed by the House on Tuesday evening, 20 October 1998, and by the Senate on Wednesday morning, 21 October 1998. Because the Omnibus Appropriations and Authorization Bill had bi-partisan support – and because the Administration wanted it – President Clinton signed it into law. He did not have the option of removing the MacBride section. It was either accept the whole Bill, or veto the whole Bill.

Although the Administration was adamantly opposed to the MacBride Principles being linked to the International Fund for Ireland, the Administration was forced to accept that link.

Thus, because of the determined leadership of Congressman Ben Gilman, Chairman of the House International Relations Committee, and the Irish National Caucus, the MacBride

Principles became US law.

There is no other victory to match it in the history of Irish American nationalism. John Devoy (1842–1928) would have been proud of us, and I dedicated this victory to him. His grave lies close to Seán MacBride's grave in Glasnevin Cemetery, Dublin. Each year I kneel and say an 'Ave' there at the graves of my two Irish heroes.

18

'A Protestant Boy' on Capitol Hill

May the Lord in His mercy be kind to Belfast
Maurice Craig

I arrived in America on 2 October 1972. And in one year and one week I had arranged my first Congressional Hearing on 9 October 1973 – at which my brother Frank and Ruairí Ó Brádaigh, President of Sinn Féin testified. Who would have thought that my latest (though maybe not my last) hearing would be for a hardy 'Protestant boy' from Belfast?

In Northern Ireland parlance, 'a Protestant boy' refers not to a child but to an adult, a hardy defender of the Unionist/Protestant cause.

The folk-song 'The Protestant Boys', gives the flavour:

> The Protestant Boys are loyal and true
> Stout hearted in battle and stout handed too
> The Protestant Boys are true to the last
> And faithful and peaceful when danger has passed
> And Oh! they bear
> And proudly wear
> The colours that floated o'er many a fray

Where cannons were flashing
And sabres were clashing
The Protestant Boys still carried the day ...

On 22 October 2009, before the same House Human Rights Subcommittee, I facilitated a hearing for Raymond McCord, Sr – a staunch Unionist/Protestant, though never a paramilitary. I had been deeply touched by the compelling narrative of his heroic struggle to get justice for his son, Raymond Jr, murdered in 1997 near Belfast.

Because young Raymond's killers were part of a Protestant paramilitary group – and because some were police informers and British agents – the killers were protected, and their crime covered up by the Northern Ireland police and the British government.

Raymond Sr embarked on a long quest for justice. His persistence persuaded Police Ombudsman Nuala O'Loan to launch an investigation that essentially vindicated his charges. Her report, 'Operation Ballast', was published in 2007.[1] Still, despite that, nobody was arrested for the murder. Raymond then felt his only hope lay in the US Congress.

I brought Raymond to Capitol Hill from 3 to 15 May 2009. We did a political blitz of Capitol Hill or, as one observer put it, 'the priest and the Protestant took the Halls of Congress by storm'. I introduced Raymond to many Members, especially Congressman Don Payne (D-NJ), Congressman Joe Crowley (D-NY), one of the co-chairmen of the Ad Hoc Congressional Committee for Irish Affairs, and Congressman Ritchie Neal, Chairman of the Friends of Ireland – all of whom treated Raymond with great respect and kindness. Then I brought him along to meet the Chairman of the Human Rights Subcommittee, Congressman Bill Delahunt (D-MA).

I began by saying: 'Bill, for over thirty years I have been telling the Congress about how the British government covered up the murder of Catholics in Northern Ireland. But today I bring you a staunch Protestant from Belfast to tell you how the British government has covered up the murder of his son.'

I then sat back and let Raymond do the talking. Within fifteen minutes, Congressman Delahunt promised a hearing.

Raymond could not believe it. That hardy boy – considered to have been one of the toughest street fighters in Belfast for the past forty years – was deeply moved by Delahunt's compassion and solidarity.

We took time out to meet with the Northern Ireland Bureau, which treated Raymond very nicely. But because justice and policing had not been devolved back to Northern Ireland, the Bureau could not deal with Raymond's case. They did, however, arrange for him to meet with the duly accredited spokesman at the British Embassy, Nic Hailey. Because of my own particular history with that Embassy, I excused myself from the meeting. However, I did drop Raymond off outside the Embassy.

I sat and watched him walk towards the massive building (the biggest Embassy in Washington, with over 600 employees) all by himself. A small man, with a slight limp that day – his knee was acting up. I watched as others passed him on the footpath, thinking how they would not have any idea of who he was . . . and the huge mistake any young hood would have made trying to mug this hardy Protestant boy. I felt an overpowering sense of sadness as I watched Raymond enter the Embassy. I reflected on my own two past visits to the Embassy, on the arrests, and the nights in prison and thought how different it was for Raymond . . . I was an Irish Catholic rebel, he a staunch Protestant Unionist.

For me, the British Embassy was the symbol of institutionalised violence, injustice and bigotry in Northern Ireland. But for Raymond, entering the British Embassy had to be a vastly different experience. It was his Embassy; his flag, the Union Jack, flew outside it; and his government operated it. Yet there he was, going in alone, to charge his Embassy with participating in the cover-up of the murder of his beloved Protestant and Unionist son.

I drove off, ruefully pondering how the British government had used and abused the Protestants and Catholics of Northern Ireland. And yet I waited with optimism for Raymond's report when he came back. Because he had not just walked in from the street, but had his visit arranged by the Northern Ireland Bureau, and because we were so well into the peace process, I was expecting the British Embassy to give Raymond some sort of satisfaction and comfort (the word 'closure' is over-used and besides, for the bereaved, there is no such thing). 'Well, how did it go?' I asked Raymond the moment he walked back into the Caucus office. 'Useless, a waste of time,' was his answer. I was really disappointed and said so. 'That's because you don't know the British government as well as I do, Sean,' said Raymond.

What is wrong with that picture? I, a Kinawleyman, disappointed that the British were not more generous, and Raymond, a staunch Ulster Protestant telling me I was naive. Raymond then issued a statement:

> I was low-keyed and respectful but Mr Hailey never answered one question. He never even tried, maintaining almost virtual silence throughout the hour meeting. And when he did speak, it was to ask: Whom are you meeting on Capitol Hill? Do you think you are having any impact, and when are you going home? See here, I am an Ulsterman, a British citizen. The British Government and the Northern Ireland police colluded in the brutal murder of my son, Raymond Jr. I am given a fantastic reception on Capitol Hill. Then I go to my own Embassy in Washington, and I get nothing, absolutely nothing. Hailey's treatment of me is exactly what I get from his colleagues in the Northern Ireland Office in Belfast . . . My treatment at the British Embassy illustrates and vindicates the need for my visit to Capitol Hill. It confirms my conviction that Congressional pressure in my son's case is my only hope . . .'[2]

But Raymond would have the last word. On 22 October 2009, he had his Congressional hearing before the House Human Rights Subcommittee – and he gave the fight of his life. There was a stunned, sombre atmosphere as he recounted his son's murder, the collusion and the cover-up. And I knew that from then on, I would never have any difficulty convincing the Congress that the British can do bad things in Ireland.

But I was also deeply sad at how difficult it had to be for Mrs McCord, young Raymond's mother, who had to listen to the retelling of the slaughter of her son. Raymond Sr somehow got through it all, with his voice breaking only once. Indeed, not only did he get through it – but also, very importantly, he kept to his allotted time. At hearings, the oral testimony is five minutes (to allow for other speakers and for question-and-answer time) with the written testimony – submitted for the record – being much longer. It is generally acceptable that the oral testimony can actually go a bit over five minutes, but witnesses abuse the privilege and courtesy of the Congress if they go over seven minutes. Raymond – a rough and ready working-class man – spoke for six and a half minutes – further earning the respect of the Subcommittee.

As I said, that may not be the last Congressional hearing I arrange, but I think it is fitting to bookend this story of my American struggle for Irish justice with the hearing at which my brother Frank testified on 9 October 1973 and the McCord Hearing, 22 October 2009. It gives new meaning to the famous phrase, 'Observe the Sons of Ulster'.[3] And maybe it beckons a new dawn.

Epilogue

Rem tene, verba sequentur (Hold to the cause, the words will follow)

Cato the Elder[1]

Writing this book has been quite an experience: joyful, sorrowful, exciting, frustrating. But above all, it has been liberating to get all that stuff out of my head and onto paper. I knew I would not be content until I did so.

Furthermore, I was very aware if I did not write this book, nobody would – indeed, nobody could. Nobody – and certainly no Catholic priest – ever lobbied the US Congress full-time and for as long as I have, with one mission: to maximise American pressure on the British government to end injustice in Northern Ireland.

Of course, one disadvantage of going through almost forty years of files is that it raises a lot of ghosts, and inevitably rakes up old issues one has put to rest. In retelling the story, and revisiting the evidence in cold print, I could feel the old righteous Kinawley anger bubbling up again.

I should point out one thing here. For much of this book, I have referred to the 'Dublin' government. However, because of my respect for the way Taoiseach Albert Reynolds bravely supported the peace process – and in deference to the person and office of President Mary McAleese – I no longer use that terminology. Instead, I use the term, Irish Government. As a Northerner, I was deeply encouraged when Mary McAleese became the Irish President. I saw it as a critical and integral part of the peace process. I have been proud of the way she has reached out to Northerners, especially the Protestants.

And, now, since the Irish Embassy and Consulates have ceased their campaigns to vilify and demonise me, I have no longer reason to be angry at them. Indeed, I am now able to appreciate the important work they do in support of the peace process. I am grateful that there are no more Sean Donlons and Carmel Heaneys trying to destroy me.

I had considered editing out 'the old anger' but decided that would be unrealistic and unhistorical. Anger at injustice was an integral part, an ever-present dynamic of the Troubles – at least for those who were troubled by injustice. Furthermore, one cannot understand the Troubles if one does not understand the anger of Catholics at how they were treated by the British government, and how they were abandoned by the Dublin government, with all the resulting feeling of powerlessness that entailed.

Now, of course, anger can lead to very bad things – spite, revenge and murder. That is why I use the term 'righteous anger'. My online dictionary says: 'Righteous is similar in meaning to virtuous but also implies freedom from guilt or blame (i.e. righteous anger)'. St Thomas Aquinas tells us that anger used for revenge is bad, but good when used to 'maintain justice'.[2] The Black Freedom Struggle in the United States would never have succeeded had Martin Luther King, Jr not blazed with righteous anger at injustice. But when did Irish bishops show sustained righteous anger at British injustice?

I, long ago, came to the conviction that my righteous anger could only be channelled through non-violence. But (and this is something apparently often forgotten) 'non-violence' is only short for 'non-violent resistance'. Many of the reports on the death of the late Cardinal Daly mentioned he was 'committed to non-violence'. Well, whatever the cardinal was committed to, it certainly was not non-violence. Unless you resist, you are not practising non-violence. If you close your eyes to injustice and violence – as so many Churchmen do – you are not being non-violent: you are being cowardly, lazy and indifferent to human suffering. Instead of 'staying out of politics' you are being complicit in the worst politics of all – political collaboration in oppression and injustice.

I have told my story. It is not the full story and it is certainly not the only story: many dedicated people in America were doing a lot of work of which I was not even aware, but they must give their own account. I feel it is a blessing from the Lord to have been able to do what I've done. Others could have done it better, but they did not, so I had to do it the best I could. In my haste to get the job done, I may have rubbed some people the wrong way, and for that I am sorry. But I always tried to treat people with kindness and respect.

Since I started writing this book, my large family has again been visited by death – but equally by the sure hope of eternal life. My lovely sister Celia in Enniskillen died from cancer on 24 November 2008, at the age of seventy-seven, and my indomitable brother Thomas, in Cornwall on the Hudson, New York, died on 16 May 2009, at the age of seventy-six, after a long battle with Alzheimer's.

I am hopeful for the future of Ireland – the whole island of Ireland. Even though, I think, we have still a long way to go. I believe 'the Union' will die on the vine. The only way it can be saved is if the IRA came back into business. One of the great Irish ironies! But it is an irony I hope that patriotic young Irish men and women take heed of: no Irish person need be killed – or kill – for full Irish freedom.

There is one thing, however, that really concerns me about the present process: the digging-in of MI5. Instead of disengaging, they are building a massive infrastructure in Northern Ireland. Their withdrawal would be far more important than that of the British Army (which, of course, is still there). The British Army has always been just the crude symbol of British rule in Ireland. How often were there pitched battles between the British Army and the IRA in the past forty years?

British control of Ireland has always essentially been a

policing and intelligence operation. I believe acceptable policing will eventually be achieved. But even with the best of good faith, the police will have absolutely no control over MI5. And that shadowy organisation can so easily manipulate the still deeply entrenched anti-Catholic sectarianism in the North.

However, I want to finish this book on an appreciative note. I am deeply grateful to former British Prime Minister, Tony Blair. He is the only British Prime Minister of whom I could ever think kindly. And God rest Mo Mowlam. She, more than anyone else, symbolised the sea change that was going to take place in Britain's attitude toward Ireland. When she saw me at an event in Washington, she came right over and said, 'You're the MacBride Principles priest,' and hugged me. Being hugged by a British Minister was definitely a new experience for me. And, of course, like all Irish Americans, I will always be grateful to Bill and Hillary Clinton. Without them, there would not have been an Irish peace process.

From the bottom of my heart, I am grateful to all those dedicated and generous Irish Americans who made my work possible. I could not have done a thing without them. They are the salt of the earth. Nor could I have done anything without some magnificent Members of Congress. I was always particularly moved by help from Members who were not Irish or Catholic. The entire Jewish American congressional delegation over the past forty years has been superb. There are too many Members to mention by name, but here are some of them: Lester Wolff (D-NY) 1965-1973; the already mentioned Dick Ottinger; Nita Lowey (D-NY); Elliott Engel (D-NY); Gary Ackerman (D-NY) former vice-chairman of the House Foreign Affairs Committee; Senator Chuck Schumer (D-NY); and, of course, the great Ben Gilman.

Don Payne (D-NJ), as I keep telling him, has been to Northern Ireland more often than I have! This African American Baptist lends the moral authority – and the insight – of Martin Luther King, Jr to the Irish cause.

It gives me great ecumenical joy when Protestant Irish American Members of Congress stand up for justice and peace in Ireland. Carolyn Maloney (D-NY) is a Presbyterian and a fervent Irish woman. As a member of New York City Council, she strongly backed the MacBride Principles, and takes great pride in having played a key role in naming a street after Joe Doherty when he was imprisoned in New York.

I expect great things from Congressman Russ Carnahan (D-MO) a Methodist, and an ardent Irishman, who is former Chairman of the Subcommittee on Human Rights.

The other ethnic group that has featured very significantly in my work are the Italian Americans. I have already mentioned Mario Biaggi who, despite massive opposition, stayed the course and backed me all the way. Former Speaker Nancy Pelosi is also Italian American. When she became Speaker, she did not follow Democrat Tip O'Neill's disgraceful ban on human rights hearings on Northern Ireland. Speaker Pelosi always invited me to her St Patrick's Day Lunch – as, indeed, did Speaker Newt Gingrich (R-GA) and Speaker Denny Hastert (R-IL).

And in speaking of Nancy Pelosi, I have to mention another great lady – not a Member of Congress but my valued and trusted colleague in the Irish National Caucus – Barbara Flaherty. Barbara was first introduced to the Irish community in 1968 by her late husband, Martin, who was born and reared in Galway. He was a committed Irish patriot. After his death, Barbara wanted, in his honour, to devote more time to the Irish cause. Since then, she has played a key role in the Irish National Caucus – and in the production of this book. I can never adequately thank her for her help and counsel, and the friendship for her wonderful family.

Finally, let me conclude with a profession of faith, so to speak. After all these years, I still believe that God is the mystery at the centre of all reality; that Jesus Christ is the Person at the centre of all human history; that the Holy Spirit gathers us all into the Body of Christ – the Church, which is the Sacrament of Christ on earth. Throughout my long struggle, I have – despite by faults and failures – been sustained by faith and prayer and nourished by the Word of God and the Eucharist – the Bread of Life and the Cup of Eternal Salvation.

God bless America and God save Ireland.

References

Introduction

1. The four letters – CSsR – that follow a Redemptorist's name represent the Congregation's official Latin name: *Congregatio Sanctissimi Redemptoris* ('The Congregation of the Most Holy Redeemer). They are more popularly known as the Redemptorists: 'A society of missionary priests [and Brothers] founded by St Alphonsus Maria Liguori, 9 Nov., 1732, at Scala, near Amalfi, Italy, for the purpose of labouring among the neglected country people in the neighborhood of Naples. The Redemptorists are essentially and by their specific vocation a missionary society'. (Catholic Encyclopedia, www.newadvent.org/cathen/12683a. htm). JMJA stand for Jesus, Mary, Joseph and Alphonsus. Fr Shepherd was the Provincial, the superior, with total power, of the London Province of Redemptorists, which was then comprised of England, Scotland, Wales, and a Vice-Province of South Africa. Since that time South Africa has become its own independent Province.

2. The full poem can be read on www.irishnationalcaucus.org.

3. 'With malice toward none, with charity for all, with firmness in the right as God gives us to see the right, let us strive on to finish the work we are in; to bind up the nation's wounds; to care for him who shall have borne the battle, and for his widow and his orphan – to do all which may achieve and cherish a just and lasting peace, among ourselves, and with all nations.' Abraham Lincoln's Second Inaugural Address, 4 March 1865.

4. 'Action on behalf of justice and participation in the transformation of the world fully appear to us as a constitutive dimension of the preaching of the Gospel, or in other words, of the church's mission for the redemption of the human race and its liberation from every oppressive

situation.' Justice in the World. Number 6. Synod of Bishops. Rome, 30 November 1971. www.osjspm.org/majordoc_ justicia_in_mundo_ offical_test.aspx

5. There was one splendid exception, one American Bishop who was not scared to take a stand against Britain's oppression in Ireland: my good friend, the late Bishop Thomas Drury of Corpus Christi, Texas. The late Bishop Mark Hurley of Santa Rosa and the late Cardinal O' Connor of New York were fairly outspoken but were not in the same league as Bishop Drury, a native of Gurteen, County Sligo.

6. Social Gospel: 'Christian faith practised as a call not just to personal conversion but to social reform.' *New Oxford American Dictionary*

Chapter 1: Bonny Banks of Lough Erne

1. St Naile was a contemporary of St Columcille (AD 521–597). He became the second abbot on Devenish Island on Lower Lough Erne, just north of Enniskillen. Devenish is one of the finest monastic sites in Ireland, first established in the sixth century. The site is dominated by a round tower thought to date from the twelfth century (see www. kinawleyparish.com).

2. The Big Snow of '47 (www.irishidentity.com/extras/weather/stories/ snow.htm).

3. Kinawley Parish Bulletin, 29 July 1984.

4. Nicholas Christopher Michael Ring (12 October 1920 – 2 March 1979), better known as Christy Ring, was a famous Cork hurler. He is generally regarded as one of the greatest hurlers in the history of the game.

5. Frank McCourt, *Angela's Ashes* (Scribner, New York, 1996), p. 1. When I told Frank that an elderly lady in Kinawley had read *Angela's Ashes* five times he was so touched he wrote her a lovely letter. Later when I was coming out of Kinawley chapel after saying Mass, there was that wonderful lady, since deceased, waiting to thank me for putting Frank McCourt in touch with her. I asked her if she had told the *Fermanagh Herald* about the letter but she responded with great dignity: 'No, that's between Frank McCourt and me'. And then added with obvious pride, 'But I will leave it in my will.'

Chapter 2: The Day Celia Was Married and Patrick Was Killed.

1. J. Bowyer Bell, *The Secret Army: the IRA, 1916–1970* (John Day Company, New York, 1970), p. 309, footnote 14.

2. In 1953, Rocky Marciano defended his world heavyweight title against

Jersey Joe Walcott, knocking him out in the first round with his deadly uppercut. The previous year, Marciano had taken the title from Jersey Joe.

Chapter 3: The Call

1. Bayard Rustin (17 March 1912 – 24 August 1987) was an American civil rights activist and principal organiser of the 1963 March on Washington for Jobs and Freedom. He counselled Martin Luther King, Jr on the techniques of non-violent resistance.

Chapter 4: Kinnoull and Hawkstone Years

1. Karl Barth (10 May 1886 – 10 December 1968) (pronounced 'Bart') was an eminent Swiss Reformed theologian, one of the most important Christian thinkers of the twentieth century. Even Pope Pius XII described him as the most important theologian since Thomas Aquinas.
2. Hawkstone Hall is an early eighteenth-century Georgian mansion set in extensive parkland in Shropshire, England. It now serves the Church as an international centre for spiritual renewal.
3. Richard P. McBrien (ed.), *Encyclopedia of Catholicism* (HarperCollins, New York, 1995), p. 1,254.
4. Thomas F. O' Meara, O.P., *A Theologian's Journey*, (Paulist Press, New York, 2002), p. 25.
5. McBrien, *ibid.*, pp. 1,254–1,255.
6. Fergus Kerr, *Twentieth-Century Catholic Theologians* (Blackwell Publishing, Malden, MA., 2007) pp. 4–5.
7. 'This decree of condemnation may be found in *Acta Sanctae Sedis* (5th ed., Rome, 1872–1911), V (1911), 389'. Fr William D'Arcy, O.F.M. Conv., *The Fenian Movement in the United States: 1858–1886.* (The Catholic University of America Press, Washington, D.C., 1947), p. 329.
8. From 'Flower of Scotland' (1974) by the Scottish folk group, The Corries. It celebrates the victory of the Scots, led by King Robert the Bruce over the King of England, Edward II, at the Battle of Bannockburn, 1314. It has become the unofficial Scottish Anthem for rugby and soccer events.

> 'O flower of Scotland
> When will we see your like again
> That fought and died for
> Your wee bit hill and glen
> And stood against him
> Proud Edward's army
> And sent him homeward
> Tae think again

9. Seán Mac Stíofáin, *Memoirs of a Revolutionary* (R. & R. Clark Ltd, Edinburgh, 1975), p. 4.

Chapter 5: The Troubles Come Back to Haunt

1 'But just when I thought I was out, they pull me back in'. Michael Corleone in *Godfather III* (Marion Puzo and Francis Ford Coppola, 1990).
2. Michael Farrell, *Arming the Protestants: The Formation of the Ulster Special Constabulary and the Royal Ulster Constabulary, 1929–27* (Brandon Books, Kerry, 1983).
3. 'Enniskillen Anti-Internment Meeting', Letters to the Editor, *Fermanagh Herald*, Saturday 21 August 1971.
4. J. M. Synge, *Playboy of the Western World* (J. W. Luce, Boston, 1911).
5. Henry David Thoreau's essay 'On the Duty of Civil Disobedience', 1849.
6. 'The Devlin made me do it', *The Big Issue*.
7. Letter from Birmingham Jail, 16 April 1963. Penn University, African Studies Center (www.upenn.edu).

Chapter 6: Bound for America

1. Bernard Haring, *Priesthood Imperiled* (Triumph Books, Chicago, 1989), pp. 146–147.
2. Thomas Merton, *Passivity and Abuse of Authority* (The McCall Publishing Company, New York, 1968), pp. 128–133.
3. Raymond Arsenault, *Freedom Riders* (Oxford University Press, Oxford, 2006), p. 419.

Chapter 7: Formation of Irish National Caucus

1. Joseph E. Thompson, *American Policy and Northern Ireland: A Saga of Peacebuilding* (Praeger, Wesport, Connecticut, 2001), p. 38.
2. Frank McManus statement, 6 June 2008.
3. Jack Holland, *The American Connection*. (Viking Penguin, New York, 1987), p. 117. Two later books repeat Holland's error: Andrew J. Wilson, *Irish America and the Ulster Conflict 1968–1995* (The Catholic University of America, Washington, DC, 1995), p. 99 and Joseph E. Thompson, *American Policy and Northern Ireland: A Saga of Peacebuilding* (Praeger, Wesport, Connecticut, 2001), p. 51. This latter book seems to confuse the formation of the Irish National Caucus with its later endorsement by many different Irish American organisations.
4. Statement issued by Jack Keane to the author in a telephone interview on Friday 30 May 2008, 7.30 p.m.

Chapter 8: Caucus Baptised in Blood at British Embassy

1. 'Stickies' and 'Pinheads': after the 1969–70 IRA split, which led to the emergence of the Provisional IRA, the Official IRA used a type of Easter Lily with a self-adhesive backing. This led to them being branded as the 'Stickies'. The Provisionals retained the traditional paper-and-pin Easter lily and thus became known as the 'Pinheads', a nickname which has not lasted.

2. 'Embassy Protest Held By An Unlikely Band'. Carl Schoettler, *Baltimore Sun,* Saturday 27 April 1974.

Chapter 9: All the News That's Fit to Print – Or Not

1. 'Papacy at the crossroads'. John Organ, *Sunday Telegraph,* 4 January 1976.

2. 'Irish-American Group Aired Issue In Vatican'. Carl Schoettler. *Baltimore Evening Sun*, Friday 26 December 1975; 'Irish Caucus Delegation Well Received', *The National Hibernian Digest*, January–February 1976; 'Jackson's bid to scoop the Irish', *Irish Post* (London), 24 January 1976.

Chapter 10: The Caucus and Jimmy Carter

1. Joseph E. Thompson, *American Policy and Northern Ireland: A Saga of Peacebuilding* (Praeger, Wesport, Connecticut, 2001), p. 38.

2. 'Boston, Where it Began, Salutes the English Queen', *The New York Times*, 12 July 1976.

3. Telegram from Al Stern, 8 September 1976. INC files.

4. 'The peanut and the shamrock', the *Guardian,* Friday 29 October 1976.

5. *Boston Globe*, Monday 18 April 1977.

6. Tim Pat Coogan, *A Memoir,* (Weidenfeld & Nicolson, London, 2008), p. 198.

7. 'Irish priest denies forcing Carter remark in talk here'. National Catholic News Service, week of 17 November 1976.

8. 'The one about Jimmy & the Irish', Jack Anderson with Les Whitten, *Daily News*, Tuesday 16 November 1976.

9. Paul O'Dwyer's letter to Jimmy Carter. INC files.

10. 'President's hearty welcome in Massachusetts shows strength of popular support'. *The Times*, 18 March 1977.

11. White House mailgram from Stephen Aiello, special assistant to the President for Ethnic Affairs, 2 April 1980. INC files

12. 'Fr McManus Meets Carter in White House', *Fermanagh Herald*, 14 June 1980.

13. Professor Paul Power, 'The United States and Northern Ireland: the Carter Initiative and its Aftermath', (paper presented at annual meeting of American Committee for Irish Studies, University of Delaware, 24–26 April 1980).

14. Joseph E. Thompson, *American Policy and Northern Ireland: A Saga of Peacebuilding* (Praeger, Wesport, Connecticut, 2001), p. 38.
15. 'President Carter States Policy on Northern Ireland' (Department of State Bulletin, 77, 26 September 1977).
16. 'The Carter Initiative: How the Caucus got their Man', John Kelly, *The Sunday Press* (Dublin), 4 September 1977.
17. 'Irish Caucus cued Carter: McManus'. *The Irish Times*, 31 August 1977.

Chapter 11: The Long Knives of the Irish Government

1. Letter from INC member, INC files.
2. *The New York Times,* Sunday 20 March 1977.
3. 'Dublin players get warning on US tour', *The Irish Press,* Thursday 21 April 1997.
4. 'GAA tour of United States is on', Paddy Downey, *The Irish Times,* Saturday 23 April 1977.
5. 'Hub priest denies he backs IRA', David Nyhan, *Boston Globe,* 18 April 1977.
6. '"Ireland putting heat on me", says priest', David Nyhan, *Boston Globe*, 19 May 1977.
7. 'Hub priest charges Irish consul with "dirty trick"', *Boston Herald American*, Friday 20 May 1977.
8. 'Consul accused of "dirty tricks"', *Irish Post*, Saturday 11 June 1977.
9. *The Evangelist,* Diocese of Albany, NY, Thursday 9 June 1977.
10. Letter of Charles H. Gibbons, Jr to editor of *Boston Globe*, 3 June 1977. INC files.
11. 'Priest hits at bishops over silence on North', *The Irish Press,* 30 December 1976.
12. 'Court Tells Writer to Name Informant', *The New York Times,* Sunday 29 April 1979.
13. 'Reveal the Name or go to Jail', Russell Warren Howe, *Washington Journalism Review,* January/February 1991.
14. 'Lobby ... gaining support in Congress', *The New York Times*, 21 September 1979.
15. 'Formation of Ad Hoc Committee for Irish Affairs', INC press release, 27 September 1977. See also 'Kinawley-born Rev. Sean McManus Chairs Press Conference in Washington', *Fermanagh Herald*, 19 November 1977; 'Irish Get Ear of Congress', *Irish News* (Belfast), Thursday 29 September 1977; 'US Committee to Consider Injustice', *The Irish Times*, Thursday 29 September 1977.
16. 'Irish Priest Blasts US Hierarchy', Religious News Service, 28 September 1977.

17. *The Irish Times*, 29 June 1978.
18. 'Northern Ireland: A Role for the United States?', report by two members of the Committee on the Judiciary (Ninety-Fifth Congress, US Government Printing Press), p. vii.
19. *Ibid.*, p. 219.
20. 'Provisionals Disown US Caucus Man', *The Irish Press*, 27 September 1978.
21. INC press release, 18 October 1977; 'Caucus to Boycott Provisionals', *The Irish Times*, 19 October 1978.

Chapter 12: Move to Washington

1. Joseph E. Thompson, *American Policy and Northern Ireland: A Saga of Peacebuilding* (Praeger, Wesport, Connecticut, 2001), p. 38.
2. 'Blaney elated at FF choice', Sean Cronin, *The Irish Times*, Saturday 8 December 1979.
3. 'Irish Caucus in the Corridors of Power', *The Irish Times*, 4 September 1979.
4. 'The American Connection ... the men behind the mounting anti-British chorus in Congress', *Belfast Telegraph*, 16 May 1979.
5. 'A Shift on Ulster', Ken Hartnett, *Boston Globe*, 17 March 1979.
6. Garret FitzGerald, *All in a Life: An Autobiography*, (Macmillan, London 1991), p. 348.
7. Fr William D'Arcy, OFM Conv., *The Fenian Movement in the United States: 1858–1886* (The Catholic University of America Press, Washington, D.C., 1947), p. 364.
8. Sean Donlon's letter to Congressman Fish, 6 November 1979, copy in INC files.
9. 'Irish Drop Plans to Replace Envoy', Leonard Downie, Jr, *The Washington Post*, 9 July 1980.
10. 'Birmingham Six Case "discredited"', *The Irish Press*, Monday 4 November 1985.
11. 'FitzGerald Calls on Haughey to Reject IRA "Front" Groups', Geraldine Kennedy, *The Irish Times*, 21 July 1980.
12. 'FitzGerald Asked for Condemnation', *The Irish Times*, 28 July 1980.
13. FitzGerald, *ibid.*, p. 350.
14. 'Report from Capitol Hill: As if Congress Were Not Already Splintered', *US News and World Report*, 4 February 1980.
15. 'What's a Boycott Between Friends?', *The New York Times*, 28 May 1980.
16. 'The Donlon Affair: Irish May Replace Envoy to U.S. in Policy Shift on Northern Ireland', Leonard Downie, Jr and Virginia Hamill, *The Washington Post*, 8 July 1980.
17. 'US is reviewing RUC arms sales', *The Irish Press*, 3 August 1979.

18. Letter of State Department Counselor Matthew Nimetz to Mario Biaggi and twenty-eight other members, 15 June 1979.
19. 'No Guns for Violating Irish Rights: Letter on Arms Sale to Britain', Mario Biaggi, *The New York Times*, Saturday 7 June 1980.
20. 'Paisley's Visa is Revoked by US', *Boston Globe*, Tuesday 22 December 1981.
21. 'Kennedy, O'Neill ask US to bar Paisley', *Boston Globe*, Wednesday 9 December 1981.
22. 'Taking the Bob Out of Bob Jones U[niversity] – Christian Institution Readies For the Next Generation', Peter Carlson, *The Washington Post*, Thursday 5 May 2005.
23. Statement, 30 May 1981, INC files.

Chapter 13: The Old Sow that Eats Its Own Farrow

1. Horace, Roman poet, 65 BC – 8 BC.
2. James Joyce, *Portrait of the Artist as a Young Man* (Modern Library, New York, 1928), p. 238.
3. 'Provos Fall Out with Caucus Priest', *Sunday World*, 21 March 1982.
4. Interview with Gerry Adams, *Hibernia Review*, October 1979.
5. David Lynch, *Radical Politics in Modern Ireland: the Irish Socialist Republican Party, 1896–1904* (Irish Academic Press, Dublin, 2005), p. 2.
6. 'Washington Caucus', editorial, the *Irish People*, 18 October 1980.
7. 'Banished Priest Who Has Ear of All America's Top Politicians', John Cassidy, *Sunday World*, 18 March 2007.
8. Telephone conversation on Sunday 24 January 2010.
9. Joseph E. Thompson, *American Policy and Northern Ireland: A Saga of Peacebuilding* (Praeger, Wesport, Connecticut, 2001), p. 55.
10. 'Ford Admits Plot to Rewrite MacBride Principles.' INC press release, 29 August 1990.
11. 'MacBride Campaign Takes Harrisburg by Storm.' INC press release, 20 September 1989.
12. 'Caucus Leader Grand Marshall in Harrisburg.' INC press release, 12 March 1990.
13. Letter of Mary Pat Clarke, President, Baltimore City Council, 9 August 1993, INC files.
14. 'Funeral Guns Mute Ministerial Offensive,' David Blundy, *The Sunday Times*, 12 July 1981.

Chapter 14: Capitol Hill Struggle

1. Frederick Douglass, American Abolitionist, lecturer, author and slave,

1817–1895. The quote is from a 'West India Emancipation' speech he gave on 3 August 1857 at Canandaigua, New York, on the twenty-third anniversary of the event.

2. 'Growing Interest in NI', Vincent Browne, *Evening Herald*, 3 August 1979.

3. Joseph E. Thompson, *American Policy and Northern Ireland: A Saga of Peacebuilding* (Praeger, Wesport, Connecticut, 2001), p. 80.

4. *Ibid.*, p. 80.

5. *Ibid.*, p. 84.

6. *Ibid.*, p. 229.

7. Kevin McNamara, *The MacBride Principles: Irish America Strikes Back* (Liverpool University Press, 2009), p. 15.

8. *Ibid.*, p. 15.

9. 'Kennedy, Donnelly Unveil Visa Proposal: Sen. Edward M. Kennedy and Rep. Brian J. Donnelly yesterday introduced legislation to increase annually by 50,000 the number of visas available to people from Ireland, Italy, some other Western European countries and Canada who wish to immigrate to the United States. Charging that the present system discriminates against countries . . .' *Boston Globe*, 7 August 1987.

10. The Sunningdale Agreement, signed on 9 December 1973, led to the establishment of a cross-community, power-sharing Executive to govern Northern Ireland. The Agreement collapsed six months later because of strenuous opposition from Unionists and Loyalists.

11. 'The Status of the North: It's not F.F. Policy', Vincent Browne, *Sunday Independent*, 29 January 1978.

12. 'Departure of Two Top O'Neill Aides Marks Loss Of Key Participants in Shaping House Agenda', Al Hunt, *The Wall Street Journal*, 9 December 1985.

13. 'Irish Politics', Jack Anderson and Les Whitten, *New York Daily News*, 21 October 1977.

14. 'White House Policy', Jack Anderson, *The Washington Post*, 17 June 1978.

15. 'Carter Pressured on Northern Ireland', Jack Anderson, *Detroit Free Press*, 29 October 1978.

16. Joseph E. Thompson, *American Policy and Northern Ireland: A Saga of Peacebuilding* (Praeger, Wesport, Connecticut, 2001), p. 57.

17. 'Tip O'Neill', *Irish America*, October 1986.

18. 'The Anglo-Irish Agreement Support Act of September 19, 1986 (P.L. 99–415) authorized U.S. contributions to an international fund for economic development projects in Northern Ireland and the Republic of Ireland . . . This is the first time the U.S. Government has ever given economic aid to this region', CRS Issue Brief, Northern Ireland and the Republic of Ireland: U.S. Foreign Assistance Facts, 6 October 1989.

19. T. S. Elliot. *Murder in the Cathedral*, (Harcourt Brace and Company, Florida, 1935).
20. 'Irish-American Leader Seeks Roadblocks in Aid to Ireland', *New Hampshire Sunday News* (the Sunday edition of the *Union Leader*), 9 March 1986. Of course, I wanted conditions, not 'roadblocks' – but Tom Gorey did not write the headline.
21. 'The most helpful ally Ireland has ever had in Washington', Garret FitzGerald, *The Irish Times*, 8 January 1994.
22. 'The Government Strikes Back', Kate O'Callaghan, *Irish Voice*, 6 May 1989.
23. *Ibid*.
24. 'Angry Words at Ireland Fund Hearing', Sean Cronin, *The Irish Times,* 26 April 1989.
25. 'This Week They Said', *The Irish Times*, 20 May 1989.
26. INC press release, 5 August 1985. Biden's quote from stenographic transcript of hearing on 5 August 1985 before Senate Committee on Foreign Affairs, p. 34.
27. 'Britain and Irish in Battle on Capitol Hill', Simon Hoggart, *Observer*, 15 September 1985.
28. 'When Irish Eyes Are Frowning', *The Washington Post* National Weekly Edition, 7 October 1985.
29. 'Attacking an IRA Refuge', Christopher Hitchens, *Spectator*, 5 October 1985.
30. 'Battling Extradition Treaty', David Blundy, *The Sunday Times*, 11 August 1985.
31. 'Treaty Stalled', John Robinson, *Boston Globe*, 23 October 1985.
32. 'Caucus Blocks Anti-IRA Move', Niall O'Dowd, *The Sunday Press*, 21 July 1985.
33. 'Delay in Extradition Law Irks Thatcher', Fergus Pyle, *The Irish Times*, 28 April 1986.
34. Senator Hatch correspondence, INC files.

Chapter 15: The MacBride Principles: Genesis and History

1. 'An Army of Principles Will Penetrate Where an Army of Soldiers Cannot', Thomas Paine, *Agrarian Justice*. Pamphlet was written in 1775, published in 1797.
2. The Sullivan Principles are a corporate code of conduct developed by the African American preacher Rev. Leon Sullivan in 1977 for US companies doing business in South Africa to protest against apartheid.
3. 'Caucus in Jobs Blacklist Move: Americans Probe Workers' Religions', *Sunday News*, 29 July 1979.

4. 'Irish Caucus Investigates American Firms', *The Irish Times*, 30 July 1979.
5. 'Investigating Behaviour of American Firms', *The Irish Press*, 28 July 1978.
6. 'Investigating Alleged Discrimination', *Belfast Telegraph*, 28 July 1979.
7. 'MacBride to head new Irish Caucus group', *The Irish Times*, 4 August 1979.
8. 'Sean MacBride Heads Caucus Liaison Group', *Irish World*, 15 September 1979.
9. INC press release, 4 November 1983, INC files.
10. 'Irish Embassy Move Angers US Groups', *The Irish Press*, 4 November 1983.
11. 'Americans in Ulster Maelstrom', *Daily Telegraph*, 18 August 1983.
12. 'Anti-British to the hilt', *News Letter* (Belfast), 18 August 1983.
13. 'Rancid Bigot', *Daily Express* (UK), 18 August 1983.
14. Cardinal Ó Fiaich's mailgram, 22 April 1987, INC files.
15. 'Eccles Not Paid', *Sunday News*, 2 April 1989.
16. Kevin McNamara, *The MacBride Principles: Irish America Strikes Back* (Liverpool University Press, 2009), pp. 103–104.
17. 'FEA man's Firm Lashed Over Bias', *Sunday World* (Dublin), 3 June 1990.
18. 'Aer Lingus Covers up for Shorts', INC press release, 30 June 1983.
19. Congressman Shannon's letter, 2 September 1983, INC files.
20. 'MacBride Principles Spell Kiss of Death', Paddy Devlin, *Sunday World*, 11 May 1986.
21. 'The MacBride Principles a Sham', Paddy Devlin, *Sunday World*, 7 June 1987.
22. 'Caucus Proposes New Initiative to Stop Discrimination in Northern Ireland', *Irish Echo* (New York), 10 November 1984.
23. 'New US Company code endangers NI investment', Michael Farrell, *Sunday Tribune*, 4 November 1984. Of course, Farrell did not write the headline, and he was one of the first journalists in Ireland to immediately realise the importance of our initiative.
24. 'Albanese urges bias bill on U.S. firms in Ulster', *New York Daily News*, 2 January 1985.
25. 'Fr McManus Press Conference', *Irish Echo*, 2 January 1985.
26. 'Investment Pressure for NI Catholic Rights', *Chief Leader*, 11 January 1985.
27. 'Pension Fund Proposal', Tricia Gallagher, *Catholic New York*, 7 February 1985.
28. 'New York Threat of Ulster Shares Boycott', Will Ellsworth-Jones, *The Times*, 6 January 1985.
29. 'US bill on North Bias by Companies', Niall O'Dowd, *The Irish Press*, 4 January 1985.

30. 'Koch & Goldin Oppose Ulster Investment Ban', *New York Daily News*, 4 January 1985.

31. 'Of pension fund investments', from Patrick Campbell's column, 'Campbell's Scoop', in *The Irish Echo*, 19 January 1985.

32. 'Investment in Ulster Opposed', Jesus Rangel, *The New York Times*, 4 January 1985.

33. 'Goldin visit to NI', *New York Daily News*, 25 June 1985.

34. 'Goldin's Irish Tenor is Way Off Key', *New York Daily News*, 19 July 1985.

35. 'Unfair to Ulster', *The New York Times*, 5 July 1985.

36. 'Goldin and Northern Ireland', *New York Post*, 27 June 1985.

37. 'Economic Influence Suggested for Ulster', *The Sunday Republican*, 3 February 1985.

38. State Representative Tom Gallagher's letter to the author, 1 October 1985, INC files.

39. Tiernan MacBride's letter to the author, 25 January 1988, INC files.

40. Caitriona Lawlor's letter to Ken Bertsch, 28 June 1993, INC files.

41. Kevin McNamara, *The MacBride Principles: Irish America Strikes Back* (Liverpool University Press, 2009), p. 27.

42. *Ibid.*, p. 24.

43. 'Agonizing over a few principles.' Mary Holland, *The Irish Times*, Wednesday 7 October 1987.

44. Mary Holland's letter, 15 November 1987, INC files.

45. 'Doherty's Way. NYC Aims to Keep Investments Ethical', Peter McDermott, *Irish Echo*, 12 November 2008.

46. Ray MacManais, *The Road From Ardoyne: The Making of a President* (Brandon Press, Dingle, 2004), p. 153.

Chapter 16: Anti-MacBride Campaign

1. N. E. Sheinwald's letter to Tom Donahue, Secretary-Treasurer, AFL-CIO, 1 March 1985.

2. Kevin McNamara, *The MacBride Principles: Irish America Strikes Back* (Liverpool University Press, 2009), p. 89.

3. *Sunday Life* (Belfast), 22 March 1992.

4. 'Ulster Leader Assails American Supporters of MacBride Plan', *The Boston Sunday Globe,* 8 March 1987.

5. 'Principles that Burden', *Boston Globe* editorial, 11 March 1987.

6. 'Ex-IRA Leader Fights for Jobs,' *Boston Globe*, 25 April 1987.

7. 'Bishop Opposes Jobs Measures', *Boston Globe*, 25 November 1989.

8. 'Bishop Daly Questioned on MacBride', *Irish Voice*, 9 December 1989.

9. 'Daly Denies He's Opposed to MacBride, *Irish Echo*, 12–23 February 1993.

10. Bishop McAuliffe's letter to John Carr, 3 August 1993, INC files.

11. 'INC and Office of Justice and Peace Meeting', INC press release, 6 January 1978, INC files.
12. Letter to Caucus member, dated 17 October 1979. Edward Doherty writing on the official stationery of the United States Catholic Conference, INC files.
13. Archbishop Hickey's letter to the author, 6 February 1981; Bishop Kelly's letter to the author, 29 January 1981, INC files.
14. Moderator Dunlop's letter to Sister Regina, 14 May 1993; letter of Josiah Beeman, Chair of the Northern Ireland Working Group of Presbyterian Church in the United States, to Sister Regina, INC files.
15. 'Proposed Church Conference on MacBride Principles Provokes Questions, Suspicions', INC press release, 26 May 1993, INC files.
16. Author's letter to all US Catholic Bishops, 26 May 1993, INC files.
17. 'A Call For Fair Employment and Investment in Northern Ireland', statement issued by the four main Churches, 14 January 1993.
18. 'The Path to Peace', remarks by An Taoiseach, Dr Garret FitzGerald, Kennedy Library, Boston, 3 May 1985.
19. Ibid., p. 131.
20. 'Dole, GOP Congressional Leaders Meet With Irish Prime Minister', RNC News Release, 11 September 1996.
21. Ibid., p. 150.
22. Ibid., p. 131.
23. Ibid., p. 159.
24. Ibid., p. 160.
25. Ibid., p. 23.
26. Ibid., p. 141.
27. Ibid., pp. 124–125.

Chapter 17: Forcing Clinton to Sign MacBride

1. 'Andrews Backs MacBride Principles', 30 September – 6 October 1992, *Irish Echo*
2. H.R. 725: 'To provide for adherence with the MacBride Principles by United States persons doing business in Northern Ireland. Sponsor: Rep Fish, Hamilton, Jr. [NY-21] (introduced 1/31/1989). Cosponsors (97). Latest Major Action: 5/5/1989. Referred to House subcommittee. Status: Referred to the Subcommittee on Rules of the House.

SUMMARY AS OF: 1/31/1989 – Introduced.

Northern Ireland Fair Employment Practices Act – Prohibits an article from being imported into the United States from Northern Ireland unless documentation is presented at the time of entry indicating that the enterprise which manufactured or assembled such article complied at the time of manufacture with certain fair employment principles (such as freedom from religious discrimination). Bases such principles on the MacBride Principles, a nine-point set of guidelines for fair employment in Northern Ireland.

Requires any US person who has a branch or office in Northern Ireland or who controls an enterprise in Northern Ireland in which more than 20 people are employed to insure implementation of such employment principles and compliance with this Act . . .'

3. Congressman Lee Hamilton's letter to the author, 14 August 1987, INC files.
4. Kevin McNamara, *The MacBride Principles: Irish America Strikes Back* (Liverpool University Press, 2009), p. 159.
5. *Ibid.*, p. viii.
6. 'Capitol Hill Reception Huge Success: Gilman Announces MacBride Hearing', INC press release, 27 January 1995, INC files.
7. Hearing before House International Relations Committee, 15 March 1995. (US Government Printing Office, Washington, 1995), p. 2.
8. *Ibid.*, pp. 74–79.
9. 'Clinton Bids to Quell Storm Over MacBride', Ray O'Hanlon, *Irish Echo*, 28 August – 3 September 1996.
10. 'Caucus Welcomes Clinton Back to MacBride Fold', INC press release, 28 August 1996, INC files.
11. 'Democratic platform renews support for NI peace moves', Joe Carroll, *The Irish Times*, 27 August 1996.
12. Author's reviews of Kevin McNamara's book: *The MacBride Principles: Irish America Fights Back*, INC website (www.irishnationalcaucus.org).

Chapter 18: 'A Protestant Boy' on Capitol Hill

1. 'Operation Ballast, A Report on the Police Ombudsman's investigation into matters surrounding the death of Raymond McCord Jr' by Nuala O'Loan, 2007.
2. 'McCord at British Embassy: Deep Disappointment, Thursday 14 May 2009, INC press release, INC files.
3. *Observe the Sons of Ulster Marching Towards the Somme* is, perhaps, one of Frank McGuinness' most respected plays.

Epilogue

1. Cato, Marcus Porcius (234–149 BC), Roman statesman, orator and writer; known as Cato the Elder.
2. St Thomas Aquinas, *Summa Theologica*, 11-11, 158, 1 and 3.

Index